EVERYMAN, I will go with thee, and be thy guide,
In thy most need to go by thy side

SNORRI STURLUSON, historian, poet and politician, was born at Hvamm in western Iceland in 1179. He belonged to an aristocratic family, the Sturlungar, who gave their name to the period of violence and turmoil in the early thirteenth century which led to the loss of Icelandic independence to the king of Norway in 1262–4. Snorri acquired great wealth and power and was twice lawspeaker at the Icelandic parliament (Althingi), and twice visited Norway where he became embroiled in the politics of King Hakon Hakonarson and the king's father-in-law, Earl Skuli. The latter rebelled against the king and was killed in 1240, and Snorri also became subject to the king's displeasure and in 1241 was killed in his own cellar at Skalholt.

As he is depicted in contemporary records, Snorri was not an attractive character, but he is acknowledged to be one of Iceland's greatest writers, and appears in his books as urbane, intelligent and sensitive. His *Heimskringla* is the best account of medieval Scandinavian history, and his *Edda* is a masterpiece of organization, wit and irony. He may also be the author of one of the finest of the Sagas of Icelanders, *Egils saga*. He was a man of great learning, and in spite of belonging to a society that had been fully Christian for two centuries, was deeply immersed in the traditions of his pagan Viking ancestors.

ANTHONY FAULKES is Reader in Old Icelandic at Birmingham University. He studied Old Icelandic and Medieval English at Balliol College, Oxford, and was lecturer for ten years at Birkbeck College, University of London. He has travelled widely in Iceland, and took his doctorate at the University in Reykjavík in 1981. He has carried out extensive research on Icelandic manuscripts and has edited a number of Icelandic texts, including various versions of Snorri Sturluson's *Edda*. He is at present President of the Viking Society for Northern Research and joint editor of the Society's *Saga-Book* and Text Series.

EVERYMAN CLASSICS

SNORRI STURLUSON

Edda

Translated from the Icelandic and introduced by
Anthony Faulkes
Reader in Old Icelandic, University of Birmingham

Dent: London and Melbourne
EVERYMAN'S LIBRARY

© J.M. Dent & Sons Ltd, 1987
All rights reserved

Made in Great Britain by
The Guernsey Press Co. Ltd., Guernsey, C.I. for
J.M. Dent & Sons Ltd
Aldine House, 33 Welbeck Street, London W1M 8LX

First published as an Everyman Classic, 1987

British Library Cataloguing in Publication Data

Snorri Sturluson
[Edda. *English*]. Edda.
I. [Edda. *English*] II. Title
839'.68   PT7335

No. 499 Paperback ISBN 0 460 01499 4

Contents

This book is called *Edda*. It was compiled by Snorri Sturluson in the manner in which it is arranged here. There is told first about the Æsir and Ymir, then *Skaldskaparmal* [the language of poetry] and terms for many things, finally *Hattatal* [list of verse-forms] which Snorri has composed about King Hakon and Duke Skuli.

(Uppsala manuscript)

Introduction

Snorri Sturluson's *Edda* contains some of the best known and most effective of Norse mythological stories. Many of these have their origin in primitive pagan times, though they are retold by a learned and Christian author. They come chiefly in the first part of the work, *Gylfaginning* (the tricking of Gylfi), where we hear about the creation and end of the world, and many of the adventures of the Norse gods, especially those of the blustering, half-comic Thor, and the tragic account of the death of Baldr. These stories were based on traditional poems (some of which survive elsewhere) or in some cases perhaps oral prose stories, though they are probably much changed from the form in which they would have been told in heathen times. In the second part of the work, *Skaldskaparmal* (the language of poetry), there are also some stories about human heroes, again mainly based on early poems. Altogether the work contains the most comprehensive and systematic account of Norse mythology and legend found anywhere in the Middle Ages. It can be supplemented principally from the poems of the *Elder Edda*, *Ynglinga saga* (the first part of Snorri Sturluson's *Heimskringla*), and the *History of the Danes* of Saxo Grammaticus, though some mythological and many heroic stories are also told in the mythical-heroic sagas of medieval Iceland and Norway, such as the *Saga of the Volsungs*. Snorri Sturluson's *Edda* also contains a large body of early poetry of various kinds, some of it mythological, some of it court poetry in praise of Norse kings, much of it from the Viking Age. This is mostly included in the form of quotation of short extracts in *Gylfaginning* and *Skaldskaparmal*, and a good deal of it is not preserved elsewhere.

The *Prose* or *Younger Edda* (so called to distinguish it from the collection of traditional mythological and heroic poems known as the *Elder* or *Poetic Edda*), was, according to the oldest manuscript that contains it, which was written about 1300, compiled by Snorri Sturluson (1179–1241). Snorri belonged to an aristocratic Icelandic family – unlike many earlier writers in Iceland, he was not a cleric – and during his turbulent life became involved not only with Icelandic politics and feuding, but also – and this led to his violent death – in Norwegian politics. He became a rich man and was lawspeaker (president of the Icelandic parliament or Althingi) for two terms (1215–18 and 1222–31). He visited Norway twice (1218–20 and 1237–9) and became acquainted with both King Hakon Hakonarson (ruled 1217–63) and the king's father-in-law Earl Skuli (died 1240), who acted as regent during the early years of the king's reign and was for a while the most powerful man in Norway. The last part of Snorri's *Edda* contains an elaborate poem of 102 verses which he wrote as a formal compliment to these two rulers, probably soon after the first of his visits.

The thirteenth century was a time of great political, economic and cultural change in Iceland. The church had become a powerful institution and was attacking the traditional power of secular chieftains, who were also finding that economic developments were enabling other elements in society to rival their wealth and influence. The heroic world of independent Viking colonists was giving way to the medieval world of feudalism and trade. In 1262–4 Iceland accepted Norwegian rule and its political independence came to an end. During this time one significant development was that oral poetry, which from Viking times and perhaps earlier had been Scandinavian culture's principal means of expression and preservation, was being rapidly supplanted in this function by written prose. Poetry was no longer, as it had been from the time of Tacitus (second century AD), the only form of recorded history for the peoples of northern Europe. Sagas were now being written, and at the court of Norway were replacing poetry as entertainment for the court and as the official record of the king's achievements.

From early in the Viking Age (which may notionally be said to run from about 800 to 1050 AD), poets or skalds had attached themselves to Scandinavian courts and had composed and recited poems in honour of kings and earls. By the eleventh century it seems that it was principally Icelanders who performed this function in Norway. Later on, when Norwegian kings wished to have sagas written about themselves, they often continued to employ Icelanders, who were already coming to be seen as a particularly literary nation. One of the earliest of such royal biographies was that of King Sverrir (1177–1202), which was probably mainly written by Karl Jonsson, abbot of the monastery at Thingeyrar in northern Iceland, and Styrmir Karason, prior of the monastery on Videy near Reykjavik and a friend of Snorri Sturluson, and like him serving two terms of office as lawspeaker. Other biographies followed, both of contemporary and earlier kings, and King Hakon Hakonarson himself had his saga written by a nephew of Snorri, Sturla Thordarson (died 1284).

Sagas and poetry on native subjects were not the only sorts of writing cultivated in Iceland. Literature of other kinds was penetrating the north from southern Europe. From early in the twelfth century at least, saints' lives and other Latin works had been known and soon translated in Iceland. Stories of love and chivalry, like that of Tristram and Yseult, and ballads, were becoming known and popular in Scandinavia. It is likely that Snorri Sturluson, traditional aristocrat that he was, would have foreseen and regretted that the traditional poetry of the skalds was to be superseded on the one hand by the writing of prose sagas (an activity in which he himself engaged, ironically with greater success than in his poetical compositions), and on the other by new kinds of poetry in different metres and on new themes. It seems that he wrote his *Edda* as a treatise on traditional skaldic verse to try to keep interest in it alive and to encourage young poets to continue to compose in the traditional Scandinavian oral style, although in form the work itself is highly literary and owes much to the newly introduced tradition of Latin learned treatises.

Skaldic poems, it is true, were being extensively used and quoted by authors of sagas both as historical sources and to embellish the narrative. Snorri himself used them thus in his own Sagas of the Norse Kings (known as *Heimskringla* from the first words of one of the principal manuscripts), and so, particularly, did the authors of sagas about Icelandic poets, such as *Egils saga*, which may also have been written by Snorri. Indeed the majority of skaldic verse that has survived has been preserved as quotations in sagas. But the complex and difficult style of much skaldic verse, with its elevated and often obscure diction, made it hard to understand and limited its usefulness both to authors and readers of sagas. Such highly wrought art was coming to be less valued than literature that was simpler to understand and which could be enjoyed more easily by the uninitiated. If the practice of composing skaldic verse died, people would soon cease to understand most of it and it would soon be forgotten. A text-book was becoming necessary.

Snorri's *Edda* was written in the Icelandic language and is one of the very few medieval European treatises on poetry that is both written in a vernacular and is about vernacular verse. There is further testimony to an extensive and developed interest in the techniques of native poetry in the earlier exemplification of the range of skaldic verse forms, *Hattalykil* (key of metres), composed about 1145 by the Orkney earl Rognvald Kali and the Icelander Hall Thorarinsson. There are also many anecdotes in sagas about technical aspects of verse composition, such as King Harald Hardradi's complaint about a metrical fault in a verse of Thiodolf Arnorsson, and the king's own apparent preference for elaborate verse revealed in his compositions before the battle of Stamford Bridge.* Moreover there are references in many of the poems themselves to the details of their composition.

There is no direct evidence that Snorri or anyone else ever actually instituted a school to teach vernacular poetry (Latin verse composition was taught in at least one of the cathedral schools in Iceland), but several parts of his *Edda* are in the style of formal school treatises, as are the compilations of his successors Olaf Thordarson (another of his nephews) in the so-called *Third Grammatical Treatise*, and the anonymous author of the *Fourth Grammatical Treatise*, both of which are attempts to apply Latin rhetorical theory to Norse poetry.

It is the third part of the *Edda*, *Hattatal* (list of verse-forms) that is most like a formal school treatise. Snorri has provided a detailed commentary on his poem (or poems, since it is divided into three parts), and to begin with at least this is in the conventional form of a dialogue between master and pupil; it explains the formal devices of skaldic poetry (alliteration and rhyme) and the structure of the various stanza-forms used, and also briefly gives an account of some rhetorical devices. This commentary is in various ways reminiscent of Latin treatises on grammar and rhetoric, and

---

* See G. Turville-Petre, *Haraldr the Hard-ruler and His Poets*, London 1968, pp. 12–13; Snorri Sturluson, *Heimskringla*, Part two (Everyman's Library 847), pp. 230–31.

it is clear that Snorri was acquainted with the content of some Latin text-books, whether or not he could read Latin himself. He exemplifies a hundred varieties of verse-form, some of which, as he himself points out, are not metrical but rhetorical variants. He also admits that he has on occasion formalized what had earlier been a sporadic variation of style or metre, and used it in every line of a stanza to create a new verse form. There is little comment on content or overall structure; since he varies the metre in almost every stanza, a refrain or *stef* would have been hard to accommodate, though he mentions that feature of longer skaldic poems in one place. To the twentieth-century reader the content of the poem itself seems repetitious and uninspired, but it was usual for court poets to praise their kings in such generalized and conventional terms for their generosity and valour, and the poem with its commentary does give a valuable insight into the way an educated and self-conscious Icelander regarded the craft of poetry in the Middle Ages, and into how he looked upon the 'rules' of metrics and the norms of style.

Skaldskaparmal (the language of poetry), which may have been written after *Hattatal*, also begins in dialogue form, though this tails off towards the end. This time it is a conversation between two mythical characters, Ægir, god of the sea, and Bragi, god of poetry. Bragi at first tells some mythological stories that seem to be chosen at random, but this leads on to the myth of the origin of poetical inspiration which has so many interesting parallels in other cultures. Then the origin of some kennings (periphrastic descriptions, e.g. fire of the sea = gold) is given, and Bragi begins a systematic and fairly comprehensive survey of kennings for various beings and things, interspersed with a few narratives giving the supposed origin of some of them. Some of these narratives may have been added later by an interpolator, for this section of the work has been subject to a good deal of revision by various hands in different manuscripts. The illustrative quotations in this part of the work are not by Snorri himself but are from the work of earlier, sometimes much earlier, poets, some Norwegian, some Icelandic; many of the poems cited are only known from these quotations. They must mostly have been transmitted orally until Snorri wrote the extracts down, though some may have existed in written form. The longer extracts of skaldic poems on mythological themes are also known only from here, though these too may have been added by an interpolator since they are not closely related to the main topic of this section and are not in all manuscripts of it, though they obviously form part of the sources of the prose narratives and must have been known to Snorri. This section also includes a whole poem of the eddic type, *Grottasong*, which is quoted (in some manuscripts) in connection with the kennings for gold.

Then attention is turned to the second major aspect of poetical language (as Snorri has classified it), *heiti* (poetical words that do not involve periphrasis, like steed for horse). They are systematized in a similar way to the kennings, from which they are not kept entirely separate; it is also noteworthy that the systematization of poetical language in *Skaldskaparmal* is not quite the same as that presented near the beginning of *Hattatal*. This may be an indication not of multiple authorship, but that the author spent a long time, perhaps many years, on the work. In both sections the author shows a particular interest in word-play both for its own sake and as a way of explaining metaphors.

At the end of *Skaldskaparmal* there are a number of versified lists of names and words, again classified according to the concepts to which they relate. They were presumably included because they could be useful for poets in providing them with synonyms for the construction of kennings in their verse. They are a sort of primitive thesaurus. It is uncertain whether they were included in the work by Snorri himself, since they are not in all manuscripts, but a number of the lists are similar to those in *Skaldskaparmal* itself, and may be the source of them.

Gylfaginning may have been compiled after *Skaldskaparmal*. It comprises a systematic account of the whole of Norse mythology from the creation of the world to its end, thus following mainly the plan of *Voluspa*, the first of the mythological poems in the *Elder Edda*, which Snorri often quotes, as well as other mythological poems. The purpose of this part of Snorri's *Edda* was presumably to give an account of the mythology which is the background to so many of the kennings discussed in *Skaldskaparmal*, and which is important both in Christian and pre-Christian verse, although not all the stories told in *Gylfaginning* gave rise to kennings. Here too the stories are presented in the form of a dialogue, this time involving the fictional trinity of High, Just-as-high and Third, who answer questions put to them by Gylfi, a legendary king of Sweden. In this case the dialogue is maintained consistently right to the end of the section. It is made a contest of wisdom, and thus is more like the dialogue poems of the *Elder Edda*, such as *Vafthrudnismal*, than the text-book treatises that seem to have been the model for *Hattatal*. Gylfi's encounter with his informants is closed in the same way as the encounter they relate to him between Thor and the giant Utgarda-Loki. Like Thor, though he might be considered to have won the contest, he is tricked out of his victory (*Gylfaginning* means the tricking of Gylfi).

It is notable that little interpretation is given of the stories told in *Gylfaginning* and *Skaldskaparmal* other than the occasional aetiological aside (as for instance when Thor's drinking from the sea is said to have been the origin of the tides), and there is little sign of the usual medieval penchant for allegorization apart from a little indulgence in learned folk-etymology in commenting on the names of some goddesses, or in the account of Hel's household. On the whole the stories are told in a straightforward manner as if they are to be taken as factually true, though the continual use of fictional or mythical characters as narrators can be taken as a warning that this is not the author's intention. And in the prologue to *Gylfaginning* the author presents in general terms his overall interpretation of the significance of the heathen gods he had written about in the rest of the work. He himself was a Christian – in his time Christianity had been established in Iceland for a good two centuries – and did not believe in the heathen gods (indeed in *Skaldskaparmal* he explicitly warns the reader against such belief), but interpreted them as many other medieval historians did (and as he himself also did in *Ynglinga saga*, the first part of his *Heimskringla*) as kings of great power who came to be worshipped by ignorant people. He presents these kings as having originated in Asia Minor (the connection with the name Æsir is another example of learned folk-etymology), and as being descendants of King Priam of Troy who migrated with their peoples to Scandinavia in prehistoric times. At the end of the prologue and again at the end of *Gylfaginning* the process whereby these migrating kings came to be honoured as gods is described, and near the beginning of *Skaldskaparmal* the way in which historical events can give rise to myths is commented upon.

The migrating Æsir themselves, however, are depicted as worshipping gods, those gods about whom they tell Gylfi stories, and whose names they eventually assumed. An explanation of the origin of their religion is given in the opening paragraphs of the prologue, which state that it developed from worship of the earth and natural forces. Contemplation of these forces, according to the author's surprisingly rationalistic theory, led intelligent pagans to deduce the existence of an almighty creator, who had different names in different parts of the world but whom the Vikings called Odin.

Thus the author makes it clear that his view of the pagan religion is that it was a rational but misguided groping towards the truth. His account of its mythology is a scholarly and antiquarian attempt to record the beliefs of his ancestors without prejudice – beliefs which were outdated but still relevant for the proper understanding of an ancient kind of poetry which he wished should be preserved and continue to be produced as an important part of the contemporary culture of the Icelanders, Christian and literate though they now were.

Snorri's *Edda* is a unique and original work. It is the only comprehensive account of Norse mythology from the Middle Ages, and the only independent analysis of Norse poetic diction and metre. Though there were precedents for a treatise on each of these topics, Snorri took at most the idea for writing about them from his predecessors (who were mostly concerned with Latin literature); his work is in no way derivative. It is also notable for its detached and scholarly treatment both of religion and poetry, and the way in which sources and illustrations are extensively quoted and carefully attributed. Though it is clear that Snorri cared deeply about his material, he treats it with impartiality and humour, often mentioning two or more explanations of something without deciding between them. Especially interesting is the fact that in his discussions of both poetry and religion, he sees them in terms of an evolutionary process, contrasting the beliefs and practices of earlier times with those of his own. He even sees the development of language in historical terms, and speaks of languages 'branching' from each other.

Though like most writers on such topics in the Middle Ages, he believes in the authority of established writers, he also allows extensive use of 'licence' and innovation, provided that such use is in accordance with nature and probability. In the first part of the prologue to *Gylfaginning* where, as elsewhere in the work, he shows acquaintance with medieval Latin writings and the teachings of the medieval church, he also displays a remarkable capacity for independent rational thought and an inclination towards philosophical analysis, and his account of the kenning is a masterly piece of description. There are certainly inconsistencies and illogicalities in his work, but they arise from the complexity of his material rather than from the primitiveness of the author's mind.

It cannot be said that Snorri's *Edda* was very influential in the Middle Ages, or that he was successful in reviving interest in skaldic verse, if that was indeed his aim. Even so, his analysis of poetic diction was followed by the rather more derivative work of the authors of the *Third and Fourth Grammatical Treatises;* and *Skaldskaparmal* was adapted and copied by various people and came to be regarded as a guide to poetic language by composers of *rímur*, the peculiarly Icelandic genre of narrative poetry, half ballad, half romance, which became popular in Iceland in the later Middle Ages and continued to be produced and read down to modern times. But ever since the revival of learning in the late sixteenth and seventeenth centuries, when scholars began to rediscover the historical and mythological sources for the Viking Age, Snorri's *Edda* has been one of the principal quarries of historians of religion and poetry and one of the most widely read of early Icelandic texts. It is the mythological stories it contains that are the most immediately attractive part of the work, though it also contains a mine of information about Viking poetry, and the analysis of poetic diction and metre in *Skaldskaparmal* and *Hattatal* is of great importance, firstly because it tells us how a medieval poet regarded his art, and also because it gives the modern reader a lot of help in understanding the complicated diction and metre of skaldic poems (even though some of Snorri's explanations of kennings are clearly mistaken) and enables him to see what was held important in the technique of composition in early Iceland. As for the mythological stories, the fact that as

Snorri tells them they are more detailed and coherent than those in the *Elder Edda* and better told than those in Saxo Grammaticus's *History of the Danes* means that it is in this form that Norse mythology is most accessible and best known. It may be that Snorri's versions are less authentic than those less affected by Christianity and learning, but if the skill of the author gives his stories a plausibility which is misleading to the historian, it also makes them more rewarding for the student of literature.

The name *Edda* has been explained in various ways. The author was brought up by his foster-father Jon Loptsson at Oddi in the south of Iceland, and the name has been thought to mean 'the book of Oddi', though this is both linguistically and historically improbable (Snorri was not living at Oddi when he wrote the book). It has been connected with the poetry *óðr* which appears in the work itself with the meaning 'poetry', though without any connection being made with the title. It has been taken as a special use of the common noun *edda* which also appears in the work where it apparently means 'great-grandmother', again without any connection being made with the title. The semantic connection between the two meanings of the word is very problematical. *Edda* is also used in some Icelandic stories as a proper name for a woman. But in the Middle Ages *edda*, as well as being used as the title of Snorri's book, is also used as an abstract noun meaning 'poetics', and this latter may have been the original meaning of the word as a literary term. Since Snorri almost certainly had at least a smattering of Latin, he may have invented the term himself, deriving it from the Latin *edo*, one of the meanings of which is 'I compose', on the model of the Icelandic word *kredda*, 'creed, superstition', which is certainly derived from Latin *credo*, 'I believe'.

The name *Edda* later (in the seventeenth century) came to be applied also to the newly discovered collection of traditional and anonymous poems on legendary subjects that has since come to be known as the *Elder* or *Poetic Edda* (moreover this collection was for a while mistakenly attributed to the Icelandic scholar and priest Sæmund the Wise, and has sometimes been called *Sæmund's Edda*). The poetry in this collection is usually referred to as Eddic or Eddaic poetry to distinguish it from the poetry of the skalds, skaldic (scaldic) poetry, which is usually by named poets about contemporary people and events and characterized by more elaborate diction and metre. It is skaldic poetry that Snorri's *Edda* is most concerned with and which is most often quoted in the second and third parts of the work, though in *Gylfaginning* it is mostly eddic poetry that is quoted.

Note on the translation

There are seven manuscripts or manuscript fragments that contain independent texts of the *Prose Edda* or parts of it, six of them medieval, one written about 1600. None of them is quite complete. This translation follows mainly the text of the Codex Regius (GkS 2367, 4to), which is not the oldest manuscript, but seems to have fewest alterations from the original, and is nearest to being complete. It was written in the first quarter of the fourteenth century. Where there are gaps in the text of this manuscript, or illegible passages, or where what can be read is incoherent, the text is supplemented from one of the other manuscripts. Where words have been added in the translation corresponding to omissions in the manuscripts, they are enclosed in pointed brackets < >. In one place towards the end of *Hattatal* there is a verse that is only partly legible which is found in no other manuscript and so cannot be completed.

One of the most attractive features of the original work is its style, which is very different from that of normal modern English narrative prose. In order not to disguise this fact, and so as to give some flavour of the original style, the present translation has been made as literal as possible, and often the repetitions, allusiveness, abruptness and apparent illogicality of the Icelandic text have been reproduced; it is hoped that some of Snorri's characteristic irony remains apparent. The style of Icelandic poetry is even more remote from modern taste, and is often extremely artificial and obscure, and the verses too (though they have been translated into English prose) have been rendered literally, since in *Skaldskaparmal* at least the point of the inclusion of the quotations is to illustrate the use of kennings, which must therefore be translated as closely as possible. (It is, however, impossible to do this and at the same time reproduce the verse form.) The passages that are in verse in the original are indented. Where the meanings of kennings or words literally translated would not be clear to an English reader, and they are not clearly explained in the text itself, an explanation has been added in square brackets; further comment on proper names and the kennings involving them will often be found in the index. The texts of the verses, particularly in *Skaldskaparmal*, are often poorly preserved and there are many obscurities. The translations of these, as well as the equivalents given for some proper names and for words in the lists at the end of *Skaldskaparmal*, should be regarded as tentative and are often the result of guesswork, though the intention has been to render the apparent meaning of words as closely as possible. In translating the verses, I have relied heavily on the excellent explanations in the edition of *Edda Snorra Sturlusonar* by Magnús Finnbogason (Reykjavík 1952).

In *Hattatal*, where the verses illustrate different stanza forms and the number of syllables in a line and the placing of alliteration and internal rhyme is significant, as well as a literal prose translation with explanations in square brackets, the original text has been printed, though with some modifications to the usual standard spelling that were required by the type sorts available. Icelandic 'thorn' has been printed *th* and 'eth' or crossed *d* as *d*. Hooked *o* and *o* with a diagonal line through it are printed as in Modern Icelandic as ö, and both *æ* and *œ* are printed as *æ*. To assist with the correct pronunciation *i* has been used instead of *j*. Icelandic words quoted in the translation are printed in the same way and italicized. Though the treatment of consonants here is unconventional, none of these spellings is in fact alien to Icelandic manuscripts, and both the spellings *th* for 'thorn' and *d* for 'eth' are actually found in the Codex Regius. The text is included only to clarify the translation of the commentary, and is not intended as a substitute for a proper edition of the poem.

Proper names in the introduction and translation are treated in the conventional way, with accents and consonantal nominative singular endings (except when they follow a vowel) omitted, but again *i* has been used rather than *j*, both because it is the usual symbol in medieval manuscripts, and to emphasize that the sound is not like the English *j*. It should also be noted that the stress always falls on the first syllable of Icelandic words and names, and that *-ar, -ir, -ur* are in many cases plural endings.

At the top of each page of the Prologue, *Gylfaginning* and *Skaldskaparmal*, the numbers of the corresponding chapters of the edition of the text in *Edda Snorra Surlusonar* I (Copenhagen 1848) are printed, since it is by these chapter numbers that references to the text are usually made. In that edition some passages were included in the Prologue from a manuscript not used in the present translation, so that the chapter numbers are not always consecutive; and the first few chapters of *Skaldskaparmal* were counted as part of *Gylfaginning*. In *Hattatal* the numbers of the verses are given.

Select Bibliography

TEXTS AND TRANSLATIONS OF WORKS ATTRIBUTED
TO SNORRI STURLUSON:

Edda Snorra Sturlusonar, ed. Finnur Jónsson, Copenhagen 1931.

Snorri Sturluson, *Edda. Prologue and Gylfaginning*, ed. Anthony Faulkes, Oxford 1982.

The Prose Edda by Snorri Sturluson, tr. A.G. Brodeur, New York 1916 [omits *Hattatal* and parts of *Skaldskaparmal*].

The Prose Edda of Snorri Sturluson, tr. J.I. Young, Cambridge 1954 [omits *Hattatal* and much of *Skaldskaparmal*]. Reprinted University of California Press, Berkeley 1973.

Snorri Sturluson, *Heimskringla*, tr. Samuel Laing. Part one, *The Olaf Sagas*, Everyman's Library 717 and 722, 1964. Part two, *Sagas of the Norse Kings*, Everyman's Library 847, 1961.

Egils saga, tr. Christine Fell, Everyman 1975.

HISTORICAL BACKGROUND:

[Sturla Thórdarson], *The Saga of Hacon* [*Hákonar saga Hákonarsonar*], tr. G.W. Dasent, Rolls Series, Icelandic Sagas IV, London 1894.

Sturlunga saga I–II, tr. J.H. McGrew and R. George Thomas, New York 1970–74.

Einar Ó. Sveinsson, *The Age of the Sturlungs*, New York 1953 (Islandica XXXVI).

OTHER TEXTS:

The Poetic Edda, tr. H.A. Bellows, New York 1957.

Norse Poems [i.e. the *Elder Edda*], tr. W.H. Auden and P.B. Taylor, London 1981.

E.O.G. Turville-Petre, *Scaldic Poetry*, Oxford 1976.

R. Frank, *Old Norse Court Poetry*, New York 1978 (Islandica XLII).

The Saga of the Volsungs, ed. and tr. R.G. Finch, London 1965.

Saxo Grammaticus, *The History of the Danes* I–II, tr. P. Fisher, ed. H.E. Davidson, Cambridge 1979–80.

Prologue

Almighty God created heaven and earth and all things in them, and lastly two humans from whom generations are descended, Adam and Eve, and their stock multiplied and spread over all the world. But as time passed mankind became diverse: some were good and orthodox in faith, but many more turned aside to follow the lusts of the world and neglected God's commandments, and so God drowned the world in a flood together with all creatures in the world except those who were in the ark with Noah. After Noah's flood there lived eight people who inhabited the world and from them generations have descended, and it happened just as before that as the world came to be peopled and settled it turned out to be the vast majority of mankind that cultivated desire for wealth and glory and neglected obedience to God, and this reached such a pass that they refused to mention the name of God. But who was there then to tell their children of the mysteries of God? So it happened that they forgot the name of God and in most parts of the world there was no one to be found who knew anything about his creator. But even so God granted them earthly blessings, wealth and prosperity for them to enjoy in the world. He also gave them a portion of wisdom so that they could understand all earthly things and the details of everything they could see in the sky and on earth. They pondered and were amazed at what it could mean that the earth and animals and birds had common characteristics in some things, though there was a difference of quality. One of the earth's characteristics was that when it was dug into on high mountain tops, water sprang up there and there was no need to dig further for water there than in deep valleys. It is the same with animals and birds, that it is just as far to blood in the head as in the feet. It is a second property of the earth that every year there grows on the earth vegetation and flowers and the same year it all falls and fades. It is the same with animals and birds, that their hair and feathers grow and fall off every year. It is the third property of the earth, that when it is opened and dug, then vegetation grows on the soil which is uppermost on the earth. Rocks and stones they thought of as equivalent to teeth and bones of living creatures. From this they reasoned that the earth was alive and had life after a certain fashion, and they realized that it was enormously old in count of years and mighty in nature. It fed all creatures and took possession of everything that died. For this reason they gave it a name and traced their ancestry to it. Similarly they learned from their elderly relatives that after many hundreds of years had been reckoned there was the same earth, sun and heavenly bodies. But the courses of the heavenly bodies were various, some had a longer course and some a shorter. From such things they thought it likely that there must be some controller of the heavenly bodies who must be regulating their courses in accordance with his will, and he must be very powerful and mighty; and they assumed, if he ruled over the elements, that he must have existed before the heavenly bodies; and they realized that if he ruled the course of the heavenly bodies, he must rule the shining of the sun and the dew of the sky and the produce of the earth which is dependent on it, and similarly the wind of the sky and with it the storm of the sea. But they did not know where his kingdom was. And so they believed that he ruled all things on earth and in the sky, of heaven and the heavenly bodies, of the sea and the weathers. But so as to be better able to give an account of this and fix it in memory, they then gave a name among themselves to everything, and this religion has changed in many ways as nations became distinct and languages branched. But they understood everything with earthly understanding, for they were not granted spiritual wisdom. Thus they reasoned that everything was created out of some material.

The world was divided into three regions. From south to west and in up to the Mediterranean sea, this part was called Africa. The southern part of this section is hot and burned up by the sun. The second part from west and to the north and in up to the sea, this is called Europe or Enea. The northern part there is cold so that vegetation does not grow and habitation is impossible. From the north and over the eastern regions right to the south, that is called Asia. In that part of the world is all beauty and splendour and wealth of earthly produce, gold and jewels. The middle of the world is there too; and just as the earth there is more beautiful and better in all respects than in other places, so too mankind there was most honoured with all blessings, wisdom and strength, beauty and every kind of skill.

Near the middle of the world was constructed that building and dwelling which has been the most splendid ever, which was called Troy. We call the land there Turkey. This place was built much larger than others and with greater skill in many respects, using the wealth and resources available there. Twelve kingdoms were there and one high king, and many countries were subject to each kingdom. In the city there were twelve chief languages. The twelve rulers of the kingdoms were superior to other people who have lived in the world in all human qualities.

The name of one king there was Munon or Mennon. He was married to the daughter of the high king Priam; she was called Troan. They had a son, he was called Tror; we call him Thor. He was brought up in Thrace by a duke whose name was Loricus. When he was ten he inherited his father's weapons. He was as beautiful to look at when he came among other people as when ivory is inlaid in oak. His hair is more beautiful than gold. When he was twelve he had reached his full strength. Then he lifted from the ground ten bearskins all at once and then he killed his foster-father Loricus and his wife Lora or Glora and took possession of the realm of Thrace. We call this Thrudheim. Then he travelled through many countries and explored all quarters of the world and defeated unaided all berserks and giants and one of the greatest dragons and many wild animals. In the northern part of the world he came across a prophetess called Sibyl, whom we call Sif, and married her. No one is able to tell Sif's ancestry. She was the most beautiful of all women, her hair was like gold. Their son was Loridi, who took after his father; his son was Einridi, his son Vingethor, his son Vingenir, his son Moda, his son Magi, his son Sescef, his son Bedvig, his son Athra, whom we call Annar, his son Itrmann, his son Heremod, his son Scialdun, whom we call Skiold, his son Biaf, whom we call Biar, his son Iat, his son Gudolf, his son Finn, his son Friallaf, whom we call Fridleif. He had a son whose name was Woden, it is him that we call Odin. He was an outstanding person for wisdom and all kinds of accomplishments. His wife was called Frigida, whom we call Frigg. Odin had the gift of prophecy and so did his wife, and from this science he discovered that his name would be remembered in the northern part of the world and honoured above all kings. For this reason he became eager to set off from Turkey and took with him a very great following, young people and old, men and women, and they took with them many precious things. And whatever countries they passed through, great glory was spoken of them, so that they seemed more like gods than men. And they did not halt their journey until they came north to the country that is now called Saxony. Odin stayed there a long while and gained possession of large parts of that land.

There Odin put in charge of the country three of his sons; one's name was Veggdegg, he was a powerful king and ruled over East Saxony; his son was Vitrgils, his sons were Vitta, father of Hengest, and Sigar, father of Svebdegg, whom we call Svipdag. Odin's second son was called Beldegg, whom we call Baldr; he had the country that is now called Westphalia. His son was Brand, his son Friodigar, whom we call Frodi, his son was Freovin, his son Wigg, his son Gewis, whom we call Gavir. Odin's third son's name was Siggi, his son Rerir. This dynasty ruled over what is now called France, and from it is descended the family called the Volsungs. From all these people great family lines are descended. Then Odin set off north and came to a country that they called Reidgotaland and gained possession of all he wished in that land. He set over the area a son of his called Skiold; his son was called Fridleif. From them is descended the family called the Skioldungs; they are kings of Denmark, and what was then called Reidgotaland is now called Jutland.

After that Odin went north to what is now called Sweden. There was there a king whose name was Gylfi, and when he learned of the arrival of the men of Asia (who were called Æsir), he went to meet them and offered Odin as much power in his realm as he wished himself. And such was the success that attended their travels that in whatever country they stopped, there was then prosperity and good peace there, and everyone believed that they were responsible for it because the people who had power saw that they were unlike other people they had seen in beauty and wisdom. Odin found the conditions in the country attractive and selected as a site for his city the place which is now called Sigtunir. He also organized rulers there on the same pattern as had been in Troy, set up twelve chiefs in the place to administer the laws of the land, and he established all the legal system as it had previously been in Troy, and to which the Turks were accustomed.

After that he proceeded north to where he was faced by the sea, the one which they thought encircled all lands, and set a son of his over the realm which is now called Norway. He is called Sæming, and the kings of Norway trace their ancestry back to him, as do earls and other rulers, as it says in *Haleygiatal*. And Odin took with him a son of his whose name was Yngvi, who became king in Sweden, and from him are descended the family lines known as the Ynglings. These Æsir found themselves marriages within the country there, and some of them for their sons too, and these families became extensive, so that throughout Saxony and from there all over the northern regions it spread so that their language, that of the men of Asia, became the mother tongue over all these lands. And people think they can deduce from the records of the nàmes of their ancestors that those names belonged to this language, and that the Æsir brought the language north to this part of the world, to Norway and to Sweden, to Denmark and to Saxony; and in England there are ancient names for regions and places which one can tell come from a different language from this one.

gangłan ſpiʒr

The drawing depicts Gylfi (Gangleri) questioning his three informants in
Gylfaginning (Icelandic, ca.1300).
From the Uppsala manuscript of the *Prose Edda*, Uppsala University
Library, DG 11, f. 26v.

Gylfaginning

[The tricking of Gylfi]

King Gylfi was ruler in what is now called Sweden. Of him it is said that he gave a certain vagrant woman, as a reward for his entertainment, one plough-land in his kingdom, as much as four oxen could plough up in a day and a night. Now this woman was one of the race of the Æsir. Her name was Gefiun. She took four oxen from the north, from Giantland, the sons of her and a certain giant, and put them before the plough. But the plough cut so hard and deep that it uprooted the land, and the oxen drew the land out into the sea to the west and halted in a certain sound. There Gefiun put the land and gave it a name and called it Zealand. Where the land had been lifted from there remained a lake; this is now called Lake Mälar in Sweden. And the inlets in the lake correspond to the headlands in Zealand. Thus says the poet Bragi the Old:

> Gefiun drew from Gylfi, glad, a deep-ring of land [the island of Zealand] so that from the swift-pullers [oxen] steam rose: Denmark's extension. The oxen wore eight brow-stars [eyes] as they went hauling their plunder, the wide island of meadows, and four heads.

King Gylfi was clever and skilled in magic. He was quite amazed that the Æsir-people had the ability to make everything go in accordance with their will. He wondered whether this could be as a result of their own nature, or whether the divine powers they worshipped could be responsible. He set out to Asgard and travelled in secret and assumed the form of an old man and so disguised himself. But the Æsir were the wiser in that they had the gift of prophecy, and they saw his movements before he arrived, and prepared deceptive appearances for him. When he got into the city he saw there a high hall, so that he could scarcely see over it. Its roof was covered with gilded shields like tiles. Thiodolf of Hvinir refers thus to Val-hall being roofed with shields:

> On their backs they let shine — they were bombarded with

7

stones — Svafnir's [Odin's] hall-shingles [shields], those
sensible men.

In the doorway of the hall Gylfi saw a man juggling with knives,
keeping seven in the air at a time. This man spoke first and asked
him his name. He said it was Gangleri and that he had travelled
trackless ways; he requested that he might have a night's lodging
there and asked whose hall it was. The man replied that it
belonged to their king.

'And I can take you to see him. Then you can ask him his name
yourself.'

And the man turned ahead of him into the hall. Gylfi followed,
and the door immediately shut on his heels. He saw there many
apartments and many people, some engaged in games, some were
drinking, some were armed and were fighting. He looked around
and thought many of the things he saw were incredible. Then he
said:

> 'Every doorway, before you go through, should be peered
> round, for you cannot know for certain where enemies may
> be sitting waiting inside.'

He saw three thrones one above the other, and there were three
men, one sitting in each. Then he asked what the name of their
ruler was. The man who had brought him in replied that the one
that sat in the lowest throne was king and was called High, next to
him the one called Just-as-high, and the one sitting at the top was
called Third. Then High asked the newcomer whether he had any
further business, though he was welcome to food and drink like
everyone else there in the High one's hall. He said that he wished
first to find out if there was any learned person in there. High said
he would not get out unscathed unless he was more learned, and

> 'Stand out in front while you ask: he who tells shall sit.'

Gangleri began his questioning thus:
'Who is the highest and most ancient of all gods?'
High said: 'He is called All-father in our language, but in Old
Asgard he had twelve names. One is All-father, the second Herran
or Herian, the third Nikar or Hnikar, the fourth Nikuz or

8

Hnikud, the fifth Fiolnir, the sixth Oski, the seventh Omi, the eighth Biflidi or Biflindi, the ninth Svidar, the tenth Svidrir, the eleventh Vidrir, the twelfth Ialg or Ialk.'

Then Gangleri asked: 'Where is this god, what power has he, and what great works has he performed?'

High said: 'He lives throughout all ages and rules all his kingdom and governs all things great and small.'

Then spoke Just-as-high: 'He made heaven and earth and the skies and everything in them.'

Then spoke Third: 'But his greatest work is that he made man and gave him a soul that shall live and never perish though the body decay to dust or burn to ashes. And all men who are righteous shall live and dwell with him himself in the place called Gimle or Vingolf, but wicked men go to Hel and on to Niflhel; that is down in the ninth world.'

Then spoke Gangleri: 'What was he doing before heaven and earth were made?'

Then High replied: 'Then he was among the frost-giants.'

Gangleri spoke: 'What was the beginning? And how did things start? And what was there before?'

High replied: 'As it says in *Voluspa:*

> It was at the beginning of time, when nothing was; sand was
> not, nor sea, nor cool waves. Earth did not exist, nor heaven
> on high. The mighty gap was, but no growth.'

Then spoke Just-as-high: 'It was many ages before the earth was created that Niflheim was made, and in its midst lies a spring called Hvergelmir, and from it flow the rivers called Svol, Gunn-thra, Fiorm, Fimbulthul, Slidr and Hrid, Sylg and Ylg, Vid, Leiptr; Gioll is next to Hel-gates.'

Then spoke Third: 'But first there was the world in the southern region called Muspell. It is bright and hot. That area is flaming and burning and it is impassable for those that are foreigners there and are not native to it. There is one called Surt that is stationed there at the frontier to defend the land. He has a flaming sword and at the end of the world he will go and wage war and defeat all the gods and burn the whole world with fire. Thus it says in *Voluspa:*

Surt travels from the south with the stick-destroyer [fire].
Shines from his sword the sun of the gods of the slain.
Rock cliffs crash and troll-wives are abroad, heroes tread
the road of Hel and heaven splits.'

Gangleri spoke: 'What were things like before generations
came to be and the human race was multiplied?'

Then spoke High: 'These rivers, which are called Elivagar, when
they had got so far from their source that the poisonous flow
that accompanied them began to go hard like the clinker that comes
from a furnace, it turned to ice; and when this ice came to a halt
and stopped flowing, the vapour that was rising from the poison
froze on the top in the same direction and turned to rime, and this
rime increased layer upon layer right across Ginnungagap.'

Then spoke Just-as-high: 'Ginnungagap, the part that faces in a
northerly direction, was filled with the weight and heaviness of ice
and rime and there was vapour and a blowing inwards from it.
But the southerly part of Ginnungagap cleared up in the face of
the sparks and molten particles that came flying out of the world
of Muspell.'

Then spoke Third: 'Just as from Niflheim there arose coldness
and all things grim, so what was facing close to Muspell was hot
and bright, but Ginnungagap was as mild as a windless sky. And
when the rime and the blowing of the warmth met so that it
thawed and dripped, there was a quickening from these flowing
drops due to the power of the source of the heat, and it became
the form of a man, and he was given the name Ymir. But the
frost-giants call him Aurgelmir, and from him are descended
the generations of frost-giants, as it says in the *Shorter Voluspa*:

All sibyls are from Vidolf, all wizards from Vilmeid, all
sorcerers from Svarthofdi, all giants from Ymir come.

And here it is told by the giant Vafthrudnir

where Aurgelmir came from, together with the sons of
giants, first, that wise giant:

"When from Elivagar shot poison drops and grew until from
them came a giant in whom our ancestries all converge: thus
ever too terrible is all this." '

10

Then spoke Gangleri: 'How did generations grow from him, and how did it come about that other people came into being, or do you believe him to be a god whom you have just spoken of?'

Then High replied: 'Not at all do we acknowledge him to be a god. He was evil and all his descendants. We call them frost-giants. And it is said that when he slept, he sweated. Then there grew under his left arm a male and a female, and one of his legs begot a son with the other, and descendants came from them. These are frost-giants. The ancient frost-giant, him we call Ymir.'

Then spoke Gangleri: 'Where did Ymir live, and what did he live on?'

'The next thing, when the rime dripped, was that there came into being from it a cow called Audhumla, and four rivers of milk flowed from its teats, and it fed Ymir.'

Then spoke Gangleri: 'What did the cow feed on?'

High said: 'It licked the rime-stones, which were salty. And the first day as it licked stones there came from the stones in the evening a man's hair, the second day a man's head, the third day there was a complete man there. His name was Buri. He was beautiful in appearance, big and powerful. He begot a son called Bor. He married a wife called Bestla, daughter of the giant Bolthorn, and they had three sons. One was called Odin, the second Vili, the third Ve. And it is my belief that this Odin and his brothers must be the rulers of heaven and earth; it is our opinion that this must be what he is called. This is the name of the one who is the greatest and most glorious that we know, and you would do well to agree to call him that too.'

Then spoke Gangleri: 'How did they get on together, which group was the more powerful?'

Then High replied: 'Bor's sons killed the giant Ymir. And when he fell, so much blood flowed from his wounds that with it they drowned all the race of frost-giants, except that one escaped with his household. Giants call him Bergelmir. He went up on to his ark with his wife and was preserved there, and from them are descended the families of frost-giants, as it says here:

Countless winters before the earth was created, then was
Bergelmir born. That is the first I remember, when that wise
giant was laid on a box.'

Then Gangleri replied: 'What did Bor's sons do then, if you believe that they are gods?'

High said: 'There is not just a little to be told about that. They took Ymir and transported him to the middle of Ginnungagap, and out of him made the earth, out of his blood the sea and the lakes. The earth was made of the flesh and the rocks of the bones, stone and scree they made out of the teeth and molars and of the bones that had been broken.'

Then spoke Just-as-high: 'Out of the blood that came from his wounds and was flowing unconfined, out of this they made the sea with which they encompassed and contained the earth, and they placed this sea in a circle round the outside of it, and it will seem an impossibility to most to get across it.'

Then spoke Third: 'They also took his skull and made out of it the sky and set it up over the earth with four points, and under each corner they set a dwarf. Their names are Austri, Vestri, Nordri, Sudri. Then they took molten particles and sparks that were flying uncontrolled and had shot out of the world of Muspell and set them in the middle of the firmament of the sky both above and below to illuminate heaven and earth. They fixed all the lights, some in the sky, some moved in a wandering course beneath the sky, but they appointed them positions and ordained their courses. Thus it is said in ancient sources that by means of them days were distinguished and also the count of years, as it says in *Voluspa:*

> The sun did not know where her dwelling was. The moon did not know what power he had. The stars did not know where their places were.

That is what it was like above the earth before this took place.'

Then spoke Gangleri: 'This is important information that I have just heard. That is an amazingly large construction and skilfully made. How was the earth arranged?'

Then High replied: 'It is circular round the edge, and around it lies the deep sea, and along the shore of this sea they gave lands to live in to the races of giants. But on the earth on the inner side they made a fortification round the world against the hostility of giants, and for this fortification they used the giant Ymir's eyelashes, and they called the fortification Midgard. They also took his brains and threw them into the sky and made out of them the clouds, as it says here:

> From Ymir's flesh was earth created, and from blood, sea;
> rocks of bones, trees of hair, and from his skull, the sky.

> And from his eyelashes the joyous gods made Midgard for men's sons, and from his brains were those cruel clouds all created.'

Then spoke Gangleri: 'A great deal it seems to me they had achieved when earth and heaven were made and sun and stars were put in position and days were separated – and where did the people come from who inhabit the world?'

Then High replied: 'As Bor's sons walked along the sea shore, they came across two logs and created people out of them. The first gave breath and life, the second consciousness and movement, the third a face, speech and hearing and sight; they gave them clothes and names. The man was called Ask, the woman Embla, and from them were produced the mankind to whom the dwelling-place under Midgard was given. After that they made themselves a city in the middle of the world which is known as Asgard. We call it Troy. There the gods and their descendants lived and there took place as a result many events and developments both on earth and aloft. In the city there is a seat called Hlidskialf, and when Odin sat in that throne he saw over all worlds and every man's activity and understood everything he saw. His wife was called Frigg Fiorgvin's daughter, and from them is descended the family line that we call the Æsir race, who have resided in Old Asgard and the realms that belong to it, and that whole line of descent is of divine origin. And this is why he can be called All-father, that he is father of all the gods and of men and of everything that has been brought into being by him and his power. The earth was his daughter and his wife. Out of her he begot the first of his sons, that is Asa-Thor. He was possessed of power and strength. As a result he overcomes all living things.

'Norfi or Narfi was the name of a giant who lived in Giantland. He had a daughter called Night. She was black and dark in accordance with her ancestry. She was married to a person called

Naglfari. Their son was called Aud. Next she was married to someone called Annar. Their daughter was called Iord [Earth]. Her last husband was Delling, he was of the race of the Æsir. Their son was Day. He was bright and beautiful in accordance with his father's nature. Then All-father took Night and her son Day and gave them two horses and two chariots and set them up in the sky so that they have to ride around the earth every twenty-four hours. Night rides in front on the horse called Hrimfaxi, and every morning he bedews the earth with the drips from his bit. Day's horse is called Skinfaxi [shining-mane], and light is shed over all the sky and sea from his mane.'

Then spoke Gangleri: 'How does he control the course of the sun and moon?'

High said: 'There was a person whose name was Mundilfæri who had two children. They were so fair and beautiful that he called the one Moon and his daughter Sol [sun], and gave her in marriage to a person called Glen. But the gods got angry at this arrogance and took the brother and sister and set them up in the sky; they made Sol drive the horses that drew the chariot of the sun which the gods had created, to illuminate the worlds, out of the molten particle that had flown out of the world of Muspell. The names of these horses are Arvak and Alsvinn. Under the shoulders of the horses the gods put two bellows to cool them, and in some sources it is called ironblast. Moon guides the course of the moon and controls its waxing and waning. He took two children from the earth called Bil and Hiuki as they were leaving a well called Byrgir, carrying between them on their shoulders a tub called Sæg; their carrying-pole was called Simul. Their father's name is Vidfinn. These children go with Moon, as can be seen from earth.'

Then spoke Gangleri: 'The sun moves fast, almost as if she was afraid, and she would not be able to go any faster if she was in terror of her death.'

Then High replied: 'It is not surprising that she goes at great speed, he comes close who is after her. And she has no escape except to run away.'

Then spoke Gangleri: 'Who is it that inflicts this unpleasantness on her?'

High said: 'It is two wolves, and the one that is going after her is

called Skoll. She is afraid of him and he will catch her, and the one
that is running ahead of her is called Hati Hrodvitnisson, and he is
trying to catch the moon, and that will happen.'

Then spoke Gangleri: 'What is the origin of the wolves?'

High said: 'A certain giantess lives east of Midgard in a forest
called Ironwood. In that forest live trollwives called Iarnvidiur.
The ancient giantess breeds as sons many giants and all in wolf
shapes, and it is from them that these wolves are descended. And
they say that from this clan will come a most mighty one called
Moongarm. He will fill himself with the lifeblood of everyone that
dies, and he will swallow heavenly bodies and spatter heaven and
all the skies with blood. As a result the sun will lose its shine and
winds will then be violent and will rage to and fro. Thus it says in
Voluspa:

> In the east lives the old one, in Ironwood, and breeds there
> Fenrir's kind. Out of them all comes one in particular, sun's
> snatcher in troll's guise.
>
> He gorges the life of doomed men, reddens gods' halls with
> red gore. Dark is sunshine for summers after, all weathers
> hostile. Know you yet, or what?'

Then spoke Gangleri: 'What way is there to heaven from earth?'

Then High replied, laughing: 'That is not an intelligent ques-
tion. Has no one ever told you that the gods built a bridge to
heaven from earth called Bifrost? You must have seen it, maybe it
is what you call the rainbow. It has three colours and great
strength and is built with art and skill to a greater extent than
other constructions. And strong as it is, yet it will break when
Muspell's lads go and ride it, and their horses will have to swim
over great rivers. That is how they will advance.'

Then spoke Gangleri: 'It does not seem to me that the gods built
the bridge in good faith if it is liable to break, considering that they
can do as they please.'

Then spoke High: 'The gods are not deserving of blame for this
work. Bifrost is a good bridge, but there is nothing in this world
that will be secure when Muspell's sons attack.'

Then spoke Gangleri: 'What did All-father do then, when
Asgard was built?'

High spoke: 'In the beginning he established rulers and bade them decide with him the destinies of men and be in charge of the government of the city. This was in the place called Idavoll in the centre of the city. It was their first act to build the temple that their thrones stand in, twelve in addition to the throne that belongs to All-father. This building is the best that is built on earth and the biggest. Outside and inside it seems like nothing but gold. This place is called Gladsheim. They built another hall, this was the sanctuary that belonged to the goddesses, and it was very beautiful. This building is called Vingolf. The next thing they did was lay forges and for them they made hammer and tongs and anvil, and with these they made all other tools. After that they worked metal and stone and wood, using so copiously the metal known as gold that they had all their furniture and utensils of gold, and that age is known as the golden age, until it was spoiled by the arrival of the women. They came from Giantland. Next the gods took their places on their thrones and instituted their courts and discussed where the dwarfs had been generated from in the soil and down in the earth like maggots in flesh. The dwarfs had taken shape first and acquired life in the flesh of Ymir and were then maggots, but by decision of the gods they became conscious with intelligence and had the shape of men though they live in the earth and in rocks. Modsognir was a dwarf and the second was Durin. Thus it says in *Voluspa*:

> Then went all the powers to their judgment seats, most holy gods, and deliberated upon this, that a troop of dwarfs should be created from bloody surf and from Blain's bones. There man-forms many were made, dwarfs in the earth as Durin said.

And the names of these dwarfs, says the prophetess, are these:

> Nyi, Nidi, Nordri, Sudri, Austri, Vestri, Althiolf, Dvalin, Nar, Nain, Niping, Dain, Bifur, Bafur, Bombor, Nori, Ori, Onar, Oin, Modvitnir, Vig and Gandalf, Vindalf, Thorin, Fili, Kili, Fundin, Vali, Thror, Throin, Thekk, Lit, Vitr, Nyr, Nyrad, Rekk, Radsvinn.

But these are also dwarfs and live in rocks, whereas the previous ones lived in soil:

> Draupnir, Dolgthvari, Hor, Hugstari, Hlediolf, Gloin, Dori, Ori, Duf, Andvari, Heptifili, Har, Siar.

But these came from Svarinshaug to Aurvangar on Ioruvellir, and from them is descended Lofar; these are their names:

> Skirpir, Virpir, Skafinn, Ai, Alf, Ingi, Eikinskialdi, Fal, Frosti, Finn, Ginnar.'

Then spoke Gangleri: 'Where is the chief centre or holy place of the gods?'

High replied: 'It is at the ash Yggdrasil. There the gods must hold their courts each day.'

Then spoke Gangleri: 'What is there to tell about that place?'

Then said Just-as-high: 'The ash is of all trees the biggest and best. Its branches spread out over all the world and extend across the sky. Three of the tree's roots support it and extend very, very far. One is among the Æsir, the second among the frost-giants, where Ginnungagap once was. The third extends over Niflheim, and under that root is Hvergelmir, and Nidhogg gnaws the bottom of the root. But under the root that reaches towards the frost-giants, there is where Mimir's well is, which has wisdom and intelligence contained in it, and the master of the well is called Mimir. He is full of learning because he drinks of the well from the horn Giallarhorn. All-father went there and asked for a single drink from the well, but he did not get one until he placed his eye as a pledge. Thus it says in *Voluspa:*

> I know it all, Odin, where you deposited your eye, in that renowned well of Mimir. Mimir drinks mead every morning from Val-father's pledge. Know you yet, or what?

The third root of the ash extends to heaven, and beneath that root is a well which is very holy, called Weird's well. There the gods have their court. Every day the Æsir ride there up over Bifrost. It is also called As-bridge. The names of the Æsir's horses are as follows: best is Sleipnir, he is Odin's, he has eight legs. Second is

Glad, third Gyllir, fourth Glær, fifth Skeidbrimir, sixth Silfrtopp, seventh Sinir, eighth Gils, ninth Falhofnir, tenth Gulltopp, Lettfeti eleventh. Baldr's horse was burned with him. And Thor walks to the court and wades rivers whose names are:

> Kormt and Ormt and two Kerlaugs, these shall Thor wade every day when he is to judge at the ash Yggdrasil, for As-bridge burns all with flame, the holy waters boil.'

Then spoke Gangleri: 'Does fire burn over Bifrost?'

High said: 'The red you see in the rainbow is burning fire. The frost-giants and mountain-giants would go up into heaven if Bifrost was crossable by everyone that wanted to go. There are many beautiful places in heaven and everywhere there has divine protection round it. There stands there one beautiful hall under the ash by the well, and out of this hall come three maidens whose names are Weird, Verdandi, Skuld. These maidens shape men's lives. We call them norns. There are also other norns who visit everyone when they are born to shape their lives, and these are of divine origin, though others are of the race of elves, and a third group are of the race of dwarfs, as it says here:

> Of very diverse parentage I think the norns are, they do not have a common ancestry. Some are descended from Æsir, some are descended from elves, some are daughters of Dvalin.'

Then spoke Gangleri: 'If norns determine the fates of men, they allot terribly unfairly, when some have a good and prosperous life, and some have little success or glory, some a long life, some short.'

High said: 'Good norns, ones of noble parentage, shape good lives, but as for those people that become the victims of misfortune, it is evil norns that are responsible.'

Then spoke Gangleri: 'What other particularly notable things are there to tell about the ash?'

High said: 'There is a great deal to tell of it. There is an eagle sits in the branches of the ash, and it has knowledge of many things, and between its eyes sits a hawk called Vedrfolnir. A squirrel called Ratatosk runs up and down through the ash and carries malicious messages between the eagle and Nidhogg. Four stags run in the branches of the ash and feed on the foliage. Their names are: Dain, Dvalin, Duneyr, Durathror. And there are so many snakes in Hvergelmir with Nidhogg that no tongue can enumerate them. As it says here:

> The ash Yggdrasil suffers hardships more than people realize. Stag bites above, and at the sides it rots, Nidhogg eats away at it below.

Also it is said:

> More snakes lie beneath the ash Yggdrasil than any old fool thinks. Goin and Moin — they are Grafvitnir's sons — Grabak and Grafvollud, Ofnir and Svafnir I think will for ever mar the tree's twigs.

It is also said that the norns that dwell by Weird's well take water from the well each day and with it the mud that lies round the well and pour it up over the ash so that its branches may not rot or decay. And this water is so holy that all things that come into that well go as white as the membrane called the skin that lies round the inside of an eggshell, as it says here:

> I know an ash — its name is Yggdrasil, high tree, holy — drenched with white mud. From it come the dews that fall in the valleys. It stands forever green above Weird's well.

The dew that falls from it on to the earth, this is what people call honeydew, and from it bees feed. Two birds feed in Weird's well. They are called swans, and from these birds has come that species of bird that has that name.'

Then spoke Gangleri: 'You are able to give a great deal of information about the heavens. What other chief centres are there besides the one at Weird's well?'

High said: 'Many splendid places are there. There is one place that is called Alfheim. There live the folk called light-elves, but dark-elves live down in the ground, and they are unlike them in appearance, and even more unlike them in nature. Light-elves are fairer than the sun to look at, but dark elves are blacker than pitch. One place there is called Breidablik, and no fairer place is there. Also there is the one called Glitnir, and its walls and columns and pillars are of red gold, and its roof of silver. There also is a place called Himinbiorg. It stands at the edge of heaven at the bridge's end where Bifrost reaches heaven. There also is a great place called Valaskialf. This place is Odin's. The gods built it and roofed it with pure silver, and it is there in this hall that Hlidskialf is, the throne of that name. And when All-father sits on that throne he can see over all the world. At the southernmost end of heaven is the hall which is fairest of all and brighter than the sun, called Gimle. It shall stand when both heaven and earth have passed away, and in that place shall live good and righteous people for ever and ever. Thus it says in *Voluspa*:

> I know a hall standing fairer than the sun, better than gold, at Gimle. There shall virtuous men dwell, and for all ages enjoy delight.'

Then spoke Gangleri: 'What will protect this place when Surt's fire burns heaven and earth?'

High said: 'They say there is another heaven south of and above this heaven of ours, and that heaven is called Andlang; and that there is a third heaven still further above that one, and that is called Vidblain, and it is in that heaven that we believe this place to be. But we believe it is only light-elves that inhabit these places for the time being.'

Then spoke Gangleri: 'Where does the wind come from? It is so strong it stirs great seas and whips up fire, but strong as it is, it cannot be seen. Thus it is marvellously made.'

Then said High: 'I can easily tell you that. At the northernmost end of heaven there sits a giant called Hræsvelg. He has eagle form. And when he starts to fly winds arise from beneath his wings. It says so here:

> He is called Hræsvelg who sits at heaven's end, giant in eagle form. From his wings they say wind comes over all men.'

Then spoke Gangleri: 'Why is there such a great difference between the warmth of summer and the cold of winter?'

High said: 'So wise a man should not need to ask, for everyone is able to tell that, but if you have got to be the only one so ill-informed that you have never heard it, then I will look on it kindly that you should for once show your ignorance in asking rather than that you should continue unaware of what you ought to know. Svasud is the name of the one that is father of Summer, and he is so blissful in his life that it is from his name that what is pleasant is called *svaslig* [delightful]. And Winter's father is called either Vindloni or Vindsval. He is Vasad's son, and members of this family have been grim and cold-hearted, and Winter inherits their nature.'

Then spoke Gangleri: 'Which are the Æsir that men ought to believe in?'

High said: 'There are twelve Æsir whose nature is divine.'

Then spoke Just-as-high: 'No less holy are the Asyniur, nor is their power less.'

Then spoke Third: 'Odin is highest and most ancient of the Æsir. He rules all things, and mighty though the other gods are, yet they all submit to him like children to their father. Frigg is his wife, and she knows men's fates though she does not prophesy, as it says here that Odin himself spoke to the As called Loki:

"Mad you are Loki, and out of your wits; why will you not be silent, Loki? All fates I believe Frigg knows, though she herself does not pronounce."

'Odin is called All-father, for he is father of all gods. He is also called Val-father [father of the slain], since all those who fall in battle are his adopted sons. He assigns them places in Val-hall and Vingolf, and they are then known as Einheriar. He is also called Hanga-god [god of the hanged] and Hapta-god [god of prisoners], Farma-god [god of cargoes], and he called himself by various other names on his visit to King Geirrod:

"I call myself Grim and Ganglari, Herian, Hialmberi, Thekk, Third, Thunn, Unn, Helblindi, High, Sann, Svipal, Sanngetal, Herteit, Hnikar, Bileyg, Baleyg, Bolverk, Fiolnir, Grimnir, Glapsvinn, Fiolsvinn, Sidhott, Sidskegg, Sig-father, Hnikud, All-father, Atrid, Farmatyr, Oski, Omi, Just-as-high, Blindi, Gondlir, Harbard, Svidur, Svidrir, Ialk,

21

Kialar, Vidur, Thror, Ygg, Thund, Vakr, Skilfing, Vafud, Hropta-Tyr, Gaut, Veratyr." '

Then spoke Gangleri: 'What a terrible lot of names you have given him! By my faith, one would need a great deal of learning to be able to give details and explanations of what events have given rise to each of these names.'

Then said High: 'It is very instructive to go closely into all this. But to put it in a word, most names have been given him as a result of the fact that with all the branches of languages in the world, each nation finds it necessary to adapt his name to their language for invocation and prayers for themselves, but some events giving rise to these names have taken place in his travels and have been made the subject of stories, and you cannot claim to be a wise man if you are unable to tell of these important happenings.'

Then spoke Gangleri: 'What are the names of the other Æsir? And what do they do? And what glorious works have they done?'

High said: 'Thor is the most outstanding of them; he is known as Asa-Thor [Thor of the Æsir] or Oku-Thor [driving-Thor]. He is strongest of all the gods and men. His realm is a place called Thrudvangar, and his hall is called Bilskirnir. In that hall there are five hundred and forty apartments. It is the biggest building that has ever been built. Thus it says in *Grimnismal:*

> Five hundred apartments and yet forty more I think are in Bilskirnir in all. Of the buildings whose roofs I know, I know my son's is the greatest.

Thor has two goats whose names are Tanngniost and Tanngrisnir, and a chariot that he drives in, and the goats draw the chariot. From this he is known as Oku-Thor. He also has three special possessions. One of them is the hammer Miollnir, well known to frost-giants and mountain-giants when it is raised aloft, and that is not to be wondered at: it has smashed many a skull for their fathers and kinsmen. He has another possession that is very valuable, a girdle of might, and when he buckles it on his As-strength is doubled. He has a third thing that is a most important possession. This is a pair of iron gloves. He must not be without these when he grips the hammer. But there is no one so wise that can recount all his exploits, though I can tell you so many stories about him that much time will be taken up before all I know is told.'

Then spoke Gangleri: 'I would like to hear information about more Æsir.'

High said: 'Odin's second son is Baldr, and there is good to be told of him. He is best and all praise him. He is so fair in appearance and so bright that light shines from him, and there is a plant so white that it is called after Baldr's eyelash. It is the whitest of all plants, and from this you can tell his beauty both of hair and body. He is the wisest of the Æsir and most beautifully spoken and most merciful, but it is one of his characteristics that none of his decisions can be fulfilled. He lives in a place called Breidablik. This is in heaven. No unclean thing is permitted to be there, as it says here:

> It is called Breidablik where Baldr has made himself a dwelling, in that land where I know to be fewest evil intents.

'The third As is the one called Niord. He lives in heaven in a place called Noatun. He rules over the motion of wind and moderates sea and fire. It is to him one must pray for voyages and fishing. He is so rich and wealthy that he can grant wealth of lands or possessions to those that pray to him for this. Niord is not of the race of the Æsir. He was brought up in the land of the Vanir, but the Vanir gave him as hostage to the gods and took in exchange as an Æsir-hostage the one called Hænir. He came to be the pledge of truce between the gods and the Vanir.

'Niord has a wife called Skadi, daughter of the giant Thiassi. Skadi wants to have the home her father had had — this is in some mountains, a place called Thrymheim — but Niord wants to be near the sea. They agreed on this, that they should stay nine nights in Thrymheim and then alternate nines at Noatun. But when Niord came back to Noatun from the mountain he said this:

> "I hate mountains — not long was I there, just nine nights:
> wolves' howling I thought ugly compared with the swans'
> song."

Then Skadi said this:

"I could not sleep on the sea's beds for the birds' screaming;
he wakes me who comes from out at sea every morning, that
gull."

Then Skadi went up into the mountain and lived in Thrymheim
and generally travels on skis and carries a bow and shoots game.
She is called ski-deity or ski-lady. As it says:

> It is called Thrymheim where Thiassi dwelt, that most
> mighty giant, but now Skadi, bright bride of gods, inhabits
> her father's old abode.

'Niord of Noatun had afterwards two children. The son was
called Freyr and the daughter Freyia. They were beautiful in
appearance and mighty. Freyr is the most glorious of the Æsir. He
is ruler of rain and sunshine and thus of the produce of the earth,
and it is good to pray to him for prosperity and peace. He also
rules over the wealth of men. And Freyia is the most glorious of
the Asyniur. She has a dwelling in heaven called Folkvangar, and
wherever she rides to battle she gets half the slain, and the other
half Odin, as it says here:

> There is a place called Folkvang, and there Freyia is in
> charge of allotting seats in the hall. Half the slain she
> chooses each day, and half has Odin.

Sessrumnir, her hall, it is large and beautiful. And when she
travels she drives two cats and sits in a chariot. She is the most
approachable one for people to pray to, and from her name is
derived the honorific title whereby noble ladies are called *frovur*
[noble ladies]. She was very fond of love songs. It is good to pray
to her concerning love affairs.'

Then spoke Gangleri: 'Most important these Æsir seem to me
to be, and it is not surprising that great power is with you when
you claim to know details about the gods and know which one
must be prayed to for every prayer. But are there yet more gods?'

High said: 'There is also an As called Tyr. He is the bravest and
most valiant and he has great power over victory in battles. It is
good for men of action to pray to him. There is a saying that a man
is *ty*-valiant who surpasses other men and does not hesitate. He

was so clever that a man who is clever is said to be *ty*-wise. It is one proof of his bravery that when the Æsir were luring Fenriswolf so as to get the fetter Gleipnir on him, he did not trust them that they would let him go until they placed Tyr's hand in the wolf's mouth as a pledge. And when the Æsir refused to let him go then he bit off the hand at the place that is now called the wolf-joint [wrist], and he is one-handed and he is not considered a promoter of settlements between people.

'There is one called Bragi. He is renowned for wisdom and especially for eloquence and command of language. Especially he is knowledgeable about poetry, and because of him poetry is called *brag*, and from his name a person is said to be a *brag* [chief] of men or women who has eloquence beyond others, whether it is a woman or a man. Idunn is his wife. She keeps in her casket apples which the gods have to feed on when they age, and then they all become young, and so it will go on right up to Ragnarok.'

Then spoke Gangleri: 'It seems to me that the gods are staking a great deal on Idunn's care and trustworthiness.'

Then spoke High, laughing: 'It nearly led to disaster on one occasion. I could tell you about that, but first you must hear the names of some more Æsir.

'There is one called Heimdall. He is known as the white As. He is great and holy. Nine maidens bore him as their son, all of them sisters. He is also called Hallinskidi and Gullintanni: his teeth were of gold. His horse is called Gulltopp. He lives in a place called Himinbiorg by Bifrost. He is the gods' watchman and sits there at the edge of heaven to guard the bridge against mountain-giants. He needs less sleep than a bird. He can see, by night just as well as by day, a distance of a hundred leagues. He can also hear grass growing on the earth and wool on sheep and everything that sounds louder than that. He has a trumpet called Giallarhorn and its blast can be heard in all worlds. The head is referred to as Heimdall's sword. Thus it is said here:

> There is a place called Himinbiorg, and there they say it is Heimdall who is ruler of the holy places. There the gods' watchman drinks in the pleasant hall, merry, the good mead.

And moreover he says himself in *Heimdalargaldr:*

25

"Offspring of nine mothers am I, of nine sisters am I the son."

'Hod is the name of one As. He is blind. Only too strong is he. And the gods would prefer that this As did not need to be named, for the work of his hands will long be kept in mind among gods and men.

'Vidar is the name of one, the silent As. He has a thick shoe. He is almost equal in strength to Thor. He is a source of great support to the gods in all dangers.

'Ali or Vali is the name of one, the son of Odin and Rind. He is bold in battles and a very good shot.

'Ull is the name of one, son of Sif, stepson of Thor. He is such a good archer and skier that no one can compete with him. He is also beautiful in appearance and has a warrior's accomplishments. He is a good one to pray to in single combat.

'Forseti is the name of the son of Baldr and Nanna Nep's daughter. He has a hall in heaven called Glitnir, and whoever comes to him with difficult legal disputes, they all leave with their differences settled. It is the best place of judgment among gods and men. Thus it says here:

> There is a hall called Glitnir, it is held up by golden pillars and likewise roofed with silver. There Forseti dwells most days and settles all disputes.

'That one is also reckoned among the Æsir whom some call the Æsir's calumniator and originator of deceits and the disgrace of all gods and men. His name is Loki or Lopt, son of the giant Farbauti. Laufey or Nal is his mother. Byleist and Helblindi are his brothers. Loki is pleasing and handsome in appearance, evil in character, very capricious in behaviour. He possessed to a greater degree than others the kind of learning that is called cunning, and tricks for every purpose. He was always getting the Æsir into a complete fix and often got them out of it by trickery. Sigyn is the name of his wife, Nari or Narfi their son. And Loki had other offspring too. There was a giantess called Angrboda in Giantland. With her Loki had three children. One was Fenriswolf, the second Iormungand (i.e. the Midgard serpent), the third is Hel. And when the gods realized that these three siblings were being brought up in

Giantland, and when the gods traced prophecies stating that from these siblings great mischief and disaster would arise for them, then they all felt evil was to be expected from them, to begin with because of their mother's nature, but still worse because of their father's.

'Then All-father sent the gods to get the children and bring them to him. And when they came to him he threw the serpent into that deep sea which lies round all lands, and this serpent grew so that it lies in the midst of the ocean encircling all lands and bites on its own tail. Hel he threw into Niflheim and gave her authority over nine worlds, such that she has to administer board and lodging to those sent to her, and that is those who die of sickness or old age. She has great mansions there and her walls are exceptionally high and the gates great. Her hall is called Eliudnir, her dish Hunger, her knife Famine, the servant Ganglati, serving-maid Ganglot, her threshold where you enter Stumbling-block, her bed Sick-bed, her curtains Gleaming-bale. She is half black and half flesh-covered – thus she is easily recognizable – and rather downcast and fierce-looking.

'The Æsir brought up the wolf at home, and it was only Tyr who had the courage to approach the wolf and give it food. And when the gods saw how much it was growing each day, and all prophecies foretold that it was destined to cause them harm, then the Æsir adopted this plan, that they made a very strong fetter which they called Leyding and brought it to the wolf and suggested he should try his strength with the fetter. The wolf decided that it was not beyond its strength and let them do what they wished with it. At the first kick that the wolf made at it this fetter broke. Thus he loosed himself from Leyding. Next the Æsir made a second fetter twice as strong which they called Dromi, and asked the wolf again to try this fetter and declared that he would achieve great fame for his strength if such mighty pieces of engineering could not hold him. The wolf thought to himself that this fetter was very strong, but also that his strength had grown since he broke Leyding. It occurred to him that he would have to take some risks if he was to achieve fame, and allowed the fetter to be put on him. And when the Æsir declared they were ready, the wolf shook himself and knocked the fetter on the ground and strained hard, kicked with his feet, broke the fetter so that the fragments flew far away. Thus he struck himself out of Dromi. Since then it has been used as a saying to loose from Leyding or strike out of Dromi when something is achieved with great effort. After this the Æsir began to fear that they would not manage to get the wolf bound. Then All-father sent some one called Skirnir, Freyr's messenger, down into the world of black-elves to some dwarfs and had a fetter called Gleipnir made. It was made of six ingredients: the sound of the cat's footfall and the woman's beard, the mountain's roots and the bear's sinews and the fish's breath and bird's spittle. And even if you did not know this information before, you can now discover true proofs that you are not being deceived in the following: you must have seen that a woman has no beard and there is no noise from a cat's running and there are no roots under a mountain, and I declare now by my faith that everything I have told you is just as true even if there are some things that you cannot test.'

Then spoke Gangleri: 'I can indeed see that this is true. I can understand the things that you have given as proofs, but what was the fetter made like?'

High said: 'I can easily tell you that. The fetter was smooth and soft like a silken ribbon, but as firm and strong as you shall now hear. When the fetter was brought to the Æsir, they thanked the messenger heartily for carrying out their errand. Then the Æsir went out on to a lake called Amsvartnir, onto an island called Lyngvi, and summoned with them the wolf, showed him the silky band and bade him tear it and declared it was rather firmer than seemed likely, judging from its thickness, and passed it to each other and tried it by pulling at it with their hands, and it did not tear; yet the wolf, they said, would tear it. Then the wolf replied:

' "It looks to me with this ribbon as though I will gain no fame from it if I do tear apart such a slender band, but if it is made with art and trickery, then even if it does look thin, this band is not going on my legs."

'Then the Æsir said that he would soon tear apart a slender silken band, seeing that he had earlier broken great iron fetters, – "but if you cannot manage to tear this band then you will present no terror to the gods, and so we will free you."

'The wolf said: "If you bind me so that I am unable to release myself, then you will be standing by in such a way that I should have to wait a long time before I got any help from you. I am reluctant to have this band put on me. But rather than that you question my courage, let some one put his hand in my mouth as a pledge that this is done in good faith."

'But all the Æsir looked at each other and found themselves in a dilemma and all refused to offer their hands until Tyr put forward his right hand and put it in the wolf's mouth. And now when the wolf kicked, the band grew harder, and the harder he struggled, the tougher became the band. Then they all laughed except for Tyr. He lost his hand. When the Æsir saw that the wolf was thoroughly bound they took the cord that was hanging from the fetter, which is called Gelgia, and threaded it through a great stone slab – this is called Gioll – and fastened the slab far down in the ground. Then they took a great rock and thrust it even further into the ground – this is called Thviti – and used this rock as an anchoring-peg. The wolf stretched its jaws enormously and reacted violently and tried to bite them. They thrust into its mouth a certain sword; the hilt touches its lower gums and the point its upper ones. This is its gum-prop. It howls horribly and saliva runs from its mouth. This forms the river called Hope. There it will lie until Ragnarok.'

Then spoke Gangleri: 'It was a pretty terrible family that Loki begot, and all these siblings are important. But why did not the Æsir kill the wolf since they can expect evil from him?'

High replied: 'So greatly did the gods respect their holy places and places of sanctuary that they did not want to defile them with the wolf's blood even though the prophecies say that he will be the death of Odin.'

Then spoke Gangleri: 'Who are the Asyniur?'

High said: 'The highest is Frigg. She has a dwelling called Fensalir and it is very splendid. Second is Saga. She dwells at Sokkvabekk, and that is a big place. Third is Eir. She is an extremely good physician. Fourth is Gefiun. She is a virgin, and is attended by all who die virgins. Fifth is Fulla. She too is a virgin and goes around with hair flowing free and has a gold band around her head. She carries Frigg's casket and looks after her footwear and shares her secrets. Freyia is highest in rank next to Frigg. She was married to someone called Od. Hnoss is the name of their daughter. She is so beautiful that from her name whatever is beautiful and precious is called *hnossir* [treasures]. Od went off on long travels, and Freyia stayed behind weeping, and her tears are red gold. Freyia has many names, and the reason for this is that she adopted various names when she was travelling among strange peoples looking for Od. She is called Mardoll and Horn, Gefn, Syr. Freyia owned the Brisings' necklace. She is known as Lady of the Vanir. Seventh is Siofn. She is much concerned to direct people's minds to love, both women and men. It is from her name that affection is called *siafni*. Eighth Lofn: she is so kind and good to pray to that she gets leave from All-father or Frigg for people's union, between women and men, even if before it was forbidden or refused. Hence it is from her name that it is called *lof* [permission], as well as when something is praised (*lofat*) greatly by people. Ninth Var: she listens to people's oaths and private agreements that women and men make between each other. Thus these contracts are called *varar*. She also punishes those who break them. Tenth Vor: she is wise and enquiring, so that nothing can be concealed from her. There is a saying that a woman becomes aware (*vor*) of something when she finds it out. Eleventh Syn: she guards the doors of the hall and shuts them against those who are not to enter, and she is appointed as a defence at assemblies against matters that she wishes to refute. Thus there is a saying that a denial (*syn*) is made when one says no. Twelfth Hlin: she is given the function of protecting people whom Frigg wishes to save from some danger. From this comes the saying that someone who escapes finds refuge (*hleinir*). Thirteenth Snotra: she is wise and courteous. From her name a woman or man who is a wise person is called *snotr*. Fourteenth Gna: she is sent by Frigg into various worlds to carry out her business. She has a horse that gallops across sky and sea, called Hofvarpnir. It happened once as she was riding that some Vanir saw her travelling through the sky. Then said one:

> "What is it flying there? What is it travelling there, passing through the sky?"

'She said:

> "I am not flying, though I travel and pass through the sky on Hofvarpnir whom Hamskerpir begot on Gardrofa."

'From Gna's name a thing is said to tower (*gnæfa*) when it goes
high up. Sol and Bil are reckoned among the Asyniur, but their
characteristics have been mentioned above. There are still others,
whose function it is to wait in Val-hall, serve drink and look after
the tableware and drinking vessels. Thus are they named in
Grimnismal:

> Hrist and Mist I desire should bring me a horn, Skeggiold
> and Skogul, Hild and Thrud, Hlokk and Herfiotur, Goll
> and Geirahod, Randgrid and Radgrid and Reginleif. These
> serve ale to the Einheriar.

These are called valkyries. Odin sends them to every battle. They
allot death to men and govern victory. Gunn and Rota and the
youngest norn, called Skuld, always ride to choose who shall be
slain and to govern the killings. Thor's mother Iord and Vali's
mother Rind are reckoned among the Asyniur.

'There was someone called Gymir, and his wife Aurboda. She
was of the race of mountain-giants. Gerd is their daughter, the
most beautiful of all women. It happened one day that Freyr had
gone into Hlidskialf and was looking over all worlds, and when he
looked to the north he saw on a certain homestead a large and
beautiful building, and to this building went a woman, and when
she lifted her arms and opened the door for herself, light was shed
from her arms over both sky and sea, and all worlds were made
bright by her. And his punishment for his great presumption in
having sat in that holy seat was that he went away full of grief.
And when he got home he said nothing, he neither slept nor
drank; no one dared to try to speak with him. Then Niord sent for
Freyr's servant Skirnir, and bade him go to Freyr and try to get
him to talk and ask who he was so angry with that he would not
speak to anyone. Skirnir said he would go though he was not
keen, and said unpleasant answers were to be expected from him.
And when he got to Freyr he asked why Freyr was so downcast
and would not speak to anyone. Then Freyr replied and said he
had seen a beautiful woman and for her sake he was so full of grief
that he would not live long if he were not to have her.

' "And now you must go and ask for her hand on my behalf and
bring her back here whether her father is willing or not, and I shall
reward you well for it."

31

'Then Skirnir replied, saying that he would undertake the mission, but Freyr must give him his sword. This was such a good sword that it would fight on its own. But Freyr did not let the lack of that be an obstacle and gave him the sword. Then Skirnir went and asked for the woman's hand for him and received the promise from her, and nine nights later she was to go to the place called Barey and enter into marriage with Freyr. But when Skirnir told Freyr the result of his errand he said this:

> "Long is a night, long is a second, how can I suffer for three? Often has a month seemed shorter to me than half this wedding-eve."

'This is the reason for Freyr so being unarmed when he fought Beli, killing him with a stag's antler.'

Then spoke Gangleri: 'It is very strange that such a prince as Freyr should want to give away his sword when he did not have another that was as good! This would have been a terrible handicap for him when he fought with the one called Beli. I dare swear by my faith that he must then have regretted this gift.'

Then High replied: 'It did not matter much when he and Beli met. Freyr could have killed him with his fist. There will come a time when Freyr will find being without the sword a greater disadvantage when Muspell's sons come and wage war.'

Then spoke Gangleri: 'You say that all those men that have fallen in battle since the beginning of the world have now come to Odin in Val-hall. What has he got to offer them for food? I should have thought that there must be a pretty large number there.'

Then High replied: 'It is true what you say, there is a pretty large number there, and many more have yet to arrive, and yet there will seem too few when the wolf comes. But there will never be such a large number in Val-hall that the meat of the boar called Sæhrimnir will not be sufficient for them. It is cooked each day and whole again by evening. But this question that you are now asking, it seems to me very likely that there can be few so wise as to be able to give the correct answer to it. The cook is called Andhrimnir and the pot Eldhrimnir. Thus it says here:

> Andhrimnir has Sæhrimnir cooked in Eldhrimnir, best of meats. But there are few that know on what the Einheriar feed.'

Then spoke Gangleri: 'Does Odin have the same fare as the Einheriar?'

High said: 'The food that stands on his table he gives to two wolves of his called Geri and Freki. He himself needs no food: wine is for him both drink and meat. Thus it says here:

> Geri and Freki the battle-accustomed father of hosts feeds,
> but on wine alone splendidly weaponed Odin ever lives.

Two ravens sit on his shoulders and speak into his ear all the news they see or hear. Their names are Hugin and Munin. He sends them out at dawn to fly over all the world and they return at dinner-time. As a result he gets to find out about many events. From this he gets the name raven-god. As it says:

> Hugin and Munin fly each day over the mighty earth. I fear
> for Hugin lest he come not back, yet I am afraid more about
> Munin.'

Then spoke Gangleri: 'What do the Einheriar have as drink that lasts them as plentifully as the food? Is water drunk there?'

Then said High: 'This is a strange question you are asking, whether All-father would invite kings and earls and other men of rank to his house and would give them water to drink, and I swear by my faith that there comes many a one to Val-hall who would think he had paid a high price for his drink of water if there were no better cheer to be got there, when he had previously endured wounds and agony leading to his death. I can tell you a different story about this. There is a goat called Heidrun standing on top of Val-hall feeding on the foliage from the branches of that tree whose name is well known, it is called Lerad, and from the goat's udder flows mead with which it fills a vat each day. This is so big that all the Einheriar can drink their fill from it.'

Then spoke Gangleri: 'That is a terribly handy goat for them. It must be a jolly good tree that it is feeding on.'

Then spoke High: 'There is a matter of even more note regarding the stag Eikthyrnir which stands on Val-hall and feeds on the branches of this tree, and from its horns comes such a great dripping that it flows down into Hvergelmir, and from there flow the rivers whose names are: Sid, Vid, Sekin, Ekin, Svol, Gunnthro, Fiorm, Fimbulthul, Gipul, Gopul, Gomul, Geirvimul; these flow through where the Æsir live. These are the names of others: Thyn, Vin, Tholl, Boll, Grad, Gunnthrain, Nyt, Not, Nonn, Hronn, Vina, Veg, Svinn, Thiodnuma.'

Then spoke Gangleri: 'That is amazing information that you have just given. Val-hall must be a terribly large building, it must often be pretty crowded around the doorways.'

Then High replied: 'Why don't you ask how many doors there are in Val-hall, and how wide they are? If you hear about this then what you will say is that on the contrary it is amazing if everyone cannot go out and in that wants to. But to tell the truth it is not more crowded when it is occupied than when it is being entered. You can hear about it here in *Grimnismal*:

> Five hundred doors and yet forty more, that is what I think
> are in Val-hall. Eight hundred Einheriar will go at once
> through one doorway when they and the wolf go to fight.'

Then spoke Gangleri: 'There is a very large number of people in Val-hall. I declare by my salvation that Odin is a very great lord when he commands such a great troop. But what entertainment do the Einheriar have when they are not drinking?'

High said: 'Each day after they have got dressed they put on war-gear and go out into the courtyard and fight each other and they fall each upon the other. This is their sport. And when dinner-time approaches they ride back to Val-hall and sit down to drink, as it says here:

> All Einheriar in Odin's courts fight one another each day.
> They select their victims and from battle ride, sit the more at
> peace together.

But it is true what you said: a mighty one is Odin. There is much evidence that points to this. Thus it says here in the words of the Æsir themselves:

> "The ash Yggdrasil, this is the foremost of trees, and
> Skidbladnir of ships, Odin of the Æsir, of horses Sleipnir,
> Bifrost of bridges, and Bragi of poets, Habrok of hawks and
> of dogs Garm." '

Then spoke Gangleri: 'Whose is the horse Sleipnir? And what is there to tell about it?'

High said: 'You do not know details of Sleipnir and are not acquainted with the circumstances of its origin! – but you will find this worth listening to. It was right at the beginning of the gods' settlement, when the gods had established Midgard and built Val-hall, there came there a certain builder and offered to build them a fortification in three seasons so good that it would be reliable and secure against mountain-giants and frost-giants even though they should come in over Midgard. And he stipulated as his payment that he should get Freyia as his wife, and he wished to have the sun and moon. Then the Æsir went into discussion and held a conference, and this bargain was made with the builder that he should get what he demanded if he managed to build the fortification in one winter, but on the first day of summer if there was anything unfinished in the fortification then he should forfeit his payment. He was to receive from no man help with the work. And when they told him these terms, then he asked that they should permit him to have the help of his stallion called Svadil-færi. And it was Loki that was responsible for this being granted him. He set to work the first day of winter to build the fortification, and at night he hauled up stone with the stallion. And the Æsir thought it a great marvel what enormous rocks this stallion hauled, and the stallion performed twice the deed of strength that the builder did. But at their agreement there had been mighty witnesses invoked and many oaths, for the giants did not think it safe to be among the Æsir without a guarantee of safety if Thor were to return home, but at the time he was gone away into eastern parts to thrash trolls. And as winter passed the building of the fortification advanced rapidly and it was so high and strong that it could not be stormed. And when summer was three days away then he had almost got round to the entrance of the fortification. Then the gods took their places on their judgment seats and tried to think of what to do and asked each other who had been responsible for the decision to marry Freyia into Giant-land and to spoil the sky and heaven by taking away sun and moon and giving them to giants. And there was agreement among them all that he must have been responsible for this decision who is responsible for most evil, Loki Laufeyiarson, and declared he

35

would deserve an evil death if he did not find a scheme whereby the builder would forfeit his payment, and they offered to attack Loki. And he, being afraid, swore oaths that he would manage things so the builder would forfeit his payment, whatever it cost him to do it. And the same evening, when the builder drove out for stone with his stallion Svadilfæri, there ran out of a certain wood a mare up to the stallion and neighed at it. And when the stallion realized what kind of horse it was, it went frantic and tore apart the tackle and ran towards the mare, and she away to the wood and the builder after them, trying to catch the stallion, and these horses ran around all night and the building work was held up for that night. The next day not as much building was done as had been the case previously. And when the builder realized that the work was not going to be completed, then the builder got into a giant rage. But when the Æsir saw for certain that it was a mountain-giant that they had there, then the oaths were disregarded and they called upon Thor and he came in a trice and the next thing was that Miollnir was raised aloft. Then he paid the builder's wages and it wasn't the sun and moon, instead he stopped him from living in Giantland and struck the first blow so that his skull was shattered into fragments and sent him down beneath Niflhel. But Loki had had such dealings with Svadilfæri that somewhat later he gave birth to a foal. It was grey and had eight legs, and this is the best horse among gods and men. Thus it says in *Voluspa*:

> Then went all the powers to their judgment seats, most holy gods, and deliberated upon this, who had tainted all the sky with darkness and to the family of giants given Od's beloved.

> Oaths were gone back on, pledged words and promises, all the solemn vows that passed between them. Thor achieved this alone, bursting with wrath. He seldom sits idle when he learns of such things.'

Then spoke Gangleri: 'What is there to be told about Skidbladnir if it is the best of ships? Is there no other ship as good as it or as big?'

High said: 'Skidbladnir is the best ship and constructed with greatest ingenuity, but the biggest ship is Naglfari, it belongs to Muspell. It was certain dwarfs, sons of Ivaldi, that made Skidbladnir and gave Freyr the ship. It is big enough for all the Æsir to be able to go aboard it with weapons and war gear, and it gets a fair wind as soon as the sail is hoisted, wherever it is required to go. And when it is not to be taken to sea, then it is made of so many parts and with such great art that it can be folded up like a cloth and put in one's pocket.'

Then spoke Gangleri: 'Skidbladnir is a good ship, but it must require a very great deal of magic to make something like that. Has Thor never got into such a situation that he has come up against such great power or might that he has found it more than he could manage because of strength or magic?'

Then spoke High: 'I expect there are few people that can tell about that, though he has found many situations hard to deal with. But even if it has happened that something or other has been so powerful or strong that Thor has not managed to defeat it, yet there is no need to speak of it, for there is much evidence to show, and everyone is bound to believe, that Thor is mightiest.'

Then spoke Gangleri: 'It looks to me as though I must have asked you something that none of you is capable of telling me.'

Then spoke Just-as-high: 'We have heard tell of some events which it seems to us impossible to believe can be true, but I guess there is one sitting not far off who will be able to give a true account of it, and you can be confident that he will not lie now for the first time who never lied before.'

Then spoke Gangleri: 'Here I shall stand and listen whether anyone offers a solution to this matter, and if not I declare you are overcome if you are not able to tell what I ask.'

Then spoke Third: 'It is clear now that he is determined to know this story even though it does not seem to us nice to tell. But you are not to interrupt.

'The beginning of this business is that Oku-Thor set off with his goats and chariot and with him the As called Loki. In the evening they arrived at a peasant's house and were given a night's lodging there. During the evening Thor took his goats and slaughtered them both. After this they were skinned and put in the pot. When it was cooked Thor sat down to his evening meal, he and his companion. Thor invited the peasant and his wife and their children to share the meal with him. The farmer's son was called Thialfi, his daughter Roskva. Then Thor placed the goatskins on the other side of the fire and instructed the peasant and his household to throw the bones on to the goatskins. Thialfi, the peasant's son, took hold of the goat's ham-bone and split it open with his knife and broke it to get at the marrow. Thor stayed the night there, and in the small hours before dawn he got up and dressed, took the hammer Miollnir and raised it and blessed the goatskins. Then the goats got up and one of them was lame in the hind leg. Thor noticed this and declared that the peasant or one of his people must have not treated the goat's bones with proper care. He realized that the ham-bone was broken. There is no need to make a long tale about it, everyone can imagine how terrified the peasant must have been when he saw Thor making his brows sink down over his eyes; as for what could be seen of the eyes themselves, he thought he would collapse at just the very sight. Thor clenched his hands on the shaft of the hammer so that the knuckles went white, and the peasant did as one might expect, and all his household, they cried out fervently, begged for grace, offered to atone with all their possessions. And when he saw their terror then his wrath left him and he calmed down and accepted from them in settlement their children Thialfi and Roskva, and they then became Thor's bondservants and they have attended him ever since. He left the goats behind there and started on his journey east to Giantland and all the way to the sea, and then he went out across the great deep sea. And when he reached land he went ashore and with him Loki and Thialfi and Roskva. When they had gone a little way they were faced by a huge forest. They walked all that day until dark. Thialfi was the fastest of runners. He carried Thor's knapsack, but there was not much in the way of lodgings to be found. When it had got dark they looked for somewhere to spend the night and came upon a certain very large building. There was an entrance at one end and it was the full width of the building. Here they sought night-quarters for themselves. But at midnight there was a great earthquake, the ground moved under them in shudders and the building shook. Then Thor got up and called to his companions and they searched around and found a side-chamber on the right hand side half-way down the building and went in. Thor positioned himself in the doorway and the others were further in behind him and they were fearful, but Thor clasped the shaft of his hammer and planned to defend himself. Then they heard a great rumbling and groaning. And when dawn came Thor went out and saw someone lying a little way from him in the forest, and he was no midget. He was asleep and snoring mightily. Then Thor realized what the cause of the noise in the night had been. He clasped on his girdle of might and his As-strength grew, but at that moment the person awoke and stood up quickly. And then they say that Thor for once was afraid to strike him with the hammer, and asked him his name. And he said his name was Skrymir.

' "But I do not need," he said, "to ask you your name. I can tell that you are Thor of the Æsir. But have you been making off with my glove?"

'Then Skrymir reached over and picked up his glove. Then Thor realized that this was what he had been using during the night as a building, and the side-chamber, that was the thumb of the glove. Skrymir asked if Thor would like to have his company, and Thor agreed. Then Skrymir went and undid his knapsack and got ready to eat breakfast, and so did Thor and his companions in a separate place. Then Skrymir suggested that they pool their food, and Thor agreed. So Skrymir tied up all their provisions in one bag and put it on his back. He went ahead during the day and took rather long strides. And then in the evening Skrymir found them a place to spend the night under a certain large oak, – "but you take the knapsack and get on with your supper."

'Then Skrymir went to sleep and snored hard, and Thor took the knapsack and was about to undo it, and the story goes, incredible though it must seem, that no knot could he get undone and no strap-end moved so as to make it less tight than it was already. And when he realized that this labour was going to get nowhere, he got angry, grasped the hammer Miollnir in both hands and stepped forward with one foot to where Skrymir was lying and struck at his head. Skrymir awoke and asked whether some leaf of foliage had fallen on his head, and whether they had finished eating and were ready for bed. Thor said they were just about to go to sleep. They then went under another oak. To tell you the truth, it was not possible to sleep without fear.

'But at midnight Thor heard that Skrymir was snoring and

sleeping deeply so that the forest resounded. Then he stood up and went up to him, swung the hammer quickly and hard and struck down in the centre of his crown. He felt the face of the hammer sink deep into the head. And at that moment Skrymir woke and said:

' "What's the matter now? Did an acorn or something fall on my head? And what are you doing, Thor?"

'But Thor backed away quickly and replied that he had just woken up, said that it was now midnight and still time to sleep. Then Thor resolved that if he got an opportunity to strike him a third blow, he would never open his eyes again; he now lay waiting to see if Skrymir fell fast asleep. And a little before dawn, then he could hear that Skrymir must have fallen asleep, and he got up and ran at him, swung the hammer with all his might and struck at the temple that was facing upwards. Then the hammer sank in up to the handle, but Skrymir sat up and stroked his cheek and said:

' "Can there be some birds sitting in the tree above me? I am sure as I awoke that some rubbish from the branches fell on my head. Are you awake, Thor? It must be time to get up and dress. And you do not now have very far to go on to the castle called Utgard. I have heard you whispering among yourselves that I am a person of no small build, but you will see bigger men there if you get into Utgard. Now I will give you some good advice: don't act big. Utgarda-Loki's men will not easily put up with cheekiness from babies like you. Otherwise turn back, and that I think will be the better course for you to take. But if you are determined to go on, then make for the east, but my road now lies to the north to these mountains that you should be able to see."

'Skrymir took the knapsack and threw it on his back and turned abruptly away from them into the forest, and there is no report that the Æsir expressed hope for a happy reunion.

'Thor continued his journey with his companions and went on until midday. Then they saw a castle standing on some open ground and had to bend their heads back to touch their spines before they could see up over. They approached the castle and there was a gate across the entrance and it was shut. Thor went to the gate and was unable to open it, but by struggling to get into the castle they squeezed between the bars and thus got in, and then saw a great hall and went up to it. The door was open. They went in and saw there many people on two benches, most of them a fair size. Next they came before the king, Utgarda-Loki, and addressed him, but he was slow to turn to them and bared his teeth in a smile and said:

' "News travels slowly over long distances. But am I wrong in thinking that this little fellow is Oku-Thor? You must be bigger than you look to me. And what are the feats that your party thinks they can perform? No one is allowed to stay here with us who does not have some art or skill in which he is superior to most people."

'Then the one who was in the rear of the party, which was Loki, said:

' "I know a feat that I am quite prepared to have a go at, that there is no one inside here who can eat his food quicker than I."

'Then Utgarda-Loki replied: "That is a feat if you can perform it, and we must try out these feats," – called down the bench that some one called Logi was to come out on to the floor and compete with Loki. Then a trencher was fetched and brought in on to the floor of the hall and filled with meat. Loki sat down at one end and Logi at the other, and each ate as quickly as he could and they met in the middle of the trencher. Loki had then eaten all the meat off the bones, but Logi had also eaten all the meat and the bones too and also the trencher, and it seemed to everyone now that Loki had lost the contest.

'Then Utgarda-Loki asked what that young man there could perform, and Thialfi said that he would attempt to run a race of some kind with anyone Utgarda-Loki put forward. He said, Utgarda-Loki, that this was a good feat and declared he would indeed have to be good at running if he was to achieve this feat, and yet he said he would soon put it to the test. Then Utgarda-Loki got up and went out, and there was a good course there for running over level ground. Then Utgarda-Loki called to him a certain little fellow called Hugi and bade him run a race with Thialfi. Then they began the first race, and Hugi was so far ahead that he turned back to meet him at the end of the race. Then said Utgarda-Loki:

' "You will have to make a greater effort, Thialfi, if you are going to win the contest, and yet it is true that never before have people come here that have seemed to me able to run faster than that."

'Then they began again another race, and when Hugi got to the end of the course and turned back, Thialfi was still a good arrow-shot behind. Then said Utgarda-Loki:

' "Thialfi has I think run a good race, but I no longer have any confidence in him that he will win the contest. But we shall see now when they run the third race."

'Then they started another race. And when Hugi had got to the end of the course and turned back, then Thialfi had not reached half-way. Then everyone said that this contest was decided.

'Then Utgarda-Loki asked Thor which of his accomplishments it was that he would be willing to display before them, such great stories as people had made of his exploits. Then Thor said that he would most willingly undertake to compete at drinking with someone. Utgarda-Loki said that would be fine and went inside the hall and called for his butler, bade him get the forfeit-horn that the men of his court were accustomed to drink from. Next the butler came forward with the horn and handed it to Thor. Then said Utgarda-Loki:

' "From this horn it is considered to be well drunk if it is drained in one draught, but some people drain it in two draughts. But no one is such a poor drinker that it is not emptied in three."

'Thor looked at the horn, and it did not seem all that big, though it was rather long. But he was very thirsty, began to drink and took great gulps and intended that it should not be necessary to address the horn again for the time being. But when he ran out of breath and straightened up from the horn and saw how his drinking was progressing, it seemed to him as though there could be very little difference by which the level in the horn was now lower than before. Then Utgarda-Loki spoke:

' "That was a good drink, and not excessive. I would not have believed it if anyone had told me that Thor of the Æsir would not have drunk a greater draught, but still I know that you will be intending to drink it off in the second draught."

'Thor made no reply, put the horn to his mouth and was determined now that he was going to drink a bigger draught and struggled with the drink as long as his breath held out, and found still that the point of the horn would not go as far up as he wanted.

And when he took the horn from his mouth and looked in, it now seemed to him as though it had gone down less than the previous time. The level was now far enough down for the horn to be carried easily without spilling. Then spoke Utgarda-Loki:

' "What's the matter now, Thor? Are you not keeping back for one drink more than you will find easy to manage? It seems to me that if you are going to drain the horn with the third draught, then this must be intended to be the biggest one. But here among us you will not be able to be reckoned as great a person as the Æsir say you are, if you do not give a better account of yourself in other contests than it seems to me you are going to do with this one."

'Then Thor got angry, put the horn to his mouth and drank as hard as he could and struggled as long as possible with the drink. And when he looked into the horn, this time it had made most of all some difference. And then he handed back the horn and would drink no more. Then spoke Utgarda-Loki:

' "It is obvious now that your might is not as great as we thought. Do you want to have a try at more contests? It is clear that you are going to get nowhere with this one."

'Thor replied: "I may as well have a try at yet more contests. But I would have been surprised when I was back home with the Æsir if such drinks had been reckoned so slight. And what game do you want to offer me now?"

'Then spoke Utgarda-Loki: "What the young lads here do, though it may not seem of great significance, is lift up my cat off the ground. But I would not know how to mention such a thing to Thor of the Æsir if I had not previously seen that you are a much less impressive person than I thought."

'Next a kind of grey cat ran out on to the hall floor, and it was rather big. Thor went up and took hold with his hand down under the middle of its belly and lifted it up. But the cat arched its back as much as Thor stretched up his hand. And when Thor reached as high up as the furthest he could, then the cat raised just one paw and Thor was not able to perform this feat. Then spoke Utgarda-Loki:

' "This game went just as I expected: the cat is rather big, but Thor is short and small in comparison with the big fellows here with us."

'Then spoke Thor: "Small as you say I am, just let someone come out and fight me! Now I am angry!"

'Then Utgarda-Loki replied, looking round the benches, and said: "I do not see anyone in here who will not think it demeaning to fight with you." And then he went on: "Let's see a moment. Call here to me the old woman, my nurse Elli, and let Thor fight with her if he likes. She has brought down people who have seemed to me no less strong-looking than Thor is."

'Next there came into the hall an old crone. Then Utgarda-Loki said that she was to have a wrestling match with Thor of the Æsir. There is not a great deal to be told about it. What happened in this match was that the harder Thor strained in the wrestling, the firmer she stood. Then the old woman started to try tricks, and then Thor began to lose his footing, and there was some very hard pulling, and it was not long before Thor fell on to the knee of one leg. Then Utgarda-Loki went up, told them to stop the wrestling, and said this, that there was no point in Thor challenging any more people in his hall to a fight. It was also now late into the night. Utgarda-Loki showed Thor and his companions to places and they spent the night there with hospitable treatment. And in the morning as soon as it dawned Thor got up and so did his companions, they got dressed and were about to be off. Then Utgarda-Loki appeared and had a table laid for them. There was no lack of good cheer, food and drink. And when they had finished eating then they set off. Utgarda-Loki went out with them, and accompanied them on their road out of the castle. And as they parted, Utgarda-Loki spoke to Thor and asked how he thought his expedition had gone, and whether he had come up against any person more powerful than himself. Thor said that he could not claim that he had not suffered great loss of face in their encounter.

' "And moreover I know that you will say that I am a person of little account, and it is that which irks me."

'Then spoke Utgarda-Loki: "Now you shall be told the truth, now you have come outside the castle, which is that if I live and can have my way you shall never again come into it. And I swear by my faith that you never would have come into it if I had known before that you had such great strength in you, and that you were going to bring us so close to great disaster. But I have deceived you

44

by appearances, so that the first time when I discovered you in the forest it was I that came and met you. And when you tried to undo the knapsack I had fastened it with trick wire, and you could not find where it had to be unfastened. And next you struck me three blows with your hammer, and the first was the smallest and yet it was so hard that it would have been enough to kill me if it had struck its mark. But where you saw near my hall a table-mountain, and down in it you saw three square valleys, one deepest of all, these were the marks of your hammer. I moved the table-mountain in front of your blows, but you did not notice. So it was too with the games in which you competed with my men. The first was the one that Loki engaged in. He was very hungry and ate fast, but the one who is called Logi [flame], that was wildfire, and it burned the trencher just as quickly as the meat. And when Thialfi competed at running with the one called Hugi [thought], that was my thought, and Thialfi was not likely to be able to compete with its speed. And when you were drinking from the horn and it seemed to you that it was going slowly — I swear by my faith that then there took place a miracle that I would not have believed possible: the other end of the horn was out in the sea, and you did not notice, but now when you come to the sea then you will see what a lowering of the level you have made in the sea by your drinking."

'This is now known as the tides. And he went on:

' "It did not seem to me any less impressive either when you lifted up the cat, and to tell you the truth everyone that was watching was terrified when you raised one of its feet from the ground. For that cat was not what it appeared to you: it was the Midgard serpent which lies encircling all lands, and its length was hardly enough for both its head and its tail to touch the ground. And so far did you reach up that you were not far from the sky. And that also was a great miracle with the wrestling when you stood so long and fell no further than on to the knee of one leg when you were fighting Elli [old age], for there never has been anyone, and there never will be anyone, if they get so old that they experience old age, that old age will not bring them all down. And the truth I must tell you now is that we must part, and it will now be better on both sides that you do not come to see me again. I shall again next time defend my castle with similar tricks or with others so that you will not get any power over me."

'And when Thor heard this speech he snatched up his hammer and swung it in the air, but when he was about to bring it down then he found he could nowhere see Utgarda-Loki. And then he turned back towards the castle, intending to smash the castle. Then all he saw there was a wide and beautiful open landscape, but no castle. Then he turned back and went on his way until he got back to Thrudvangar. But the fact is that he had then made up his mind to seek an opportunity for a meeting to take place between him and the Midgard serpent, as later occurred. Now I think there is no one that can give you a truer account of this expedition of Thor's.'

Then spoke Gangleri: 'Very powerful is Utgarda-Loki, and he uses a great deal of trickery and magic. It is clear that he is powerful when he had men in his following who have great might. But did Thor never get his own back for this?'

High replied: 'It is no secret, even among those who are not scholars, that Thor achieved redress for this expedition that has just been recounted, and did not stay at home long before setting out on his journey so hastily that he had with him no chariot and no goats and no companionship. He went out across Midgard having assumed the appearance of a young boy, and arrived one evening at nightfall at a certain giant's; his name was Hymir. Thor stayed there as a guest for the night. And at dawn Hymir got up and dressed and got ready to row out to sea fishing. And Thor sprang up and was soon ready and asked Hymir to let him row out to sea with him. But Hymir said there would not be much advantage in having him along since he was small and just a youth.

' "And you'll get cold if I stay out as long and as far as I am used to do."

'But Thor said he need not hesitate to row out from shore since it was not certain whether it would be he that would first beg to row back; and Thor got angry with the giant so that he was on the point of letting the hammer crash down on him straight away, but he decided to hold back since he was planning to try his strength elsewhere. He asked Hymir what they were to use as bait, but Hymir told him to get his own bait. Then Thor went off to where he could see a certain herd of oxen belonging to Hymir. He took the biggest ox, called Himinhriot, and tore off its head and took it down to the sea. Hymir had now launched the boat. Thor went aboard and took his seat in the well of the boat, took two oars and rowed, and Hymir thought there was some impetus from his rowing. Hymir was rowing forward in the bows and the rowing progressed fast. Then Hymir said they had reached the fishing ground where he usually sat catching flat fish, but Thor said he wanted to row much further, and they did another spurt of rowing. Then Hymir said they had got so far out that it was dangerous to be further out because of the Midgard serpent. But Thor said he would row on a bit and did so, but Hymir was then very unhappy. And when Thor had shipped his oars, he got out a line that was pretty strong, and the hook was no smaller or less mighty-looking. On to this hook Thor fastened the ox-head and threw it overboard, and the hook went to the bottom. And then it is true to say that Thor fooled the Midgard serpent no less than Utgarda-Loki had made a laughing-stock of Thor when he was lifting the serpent up with his hand. The Midgard serpent stretched its mouth round the ox-head and the hook stuck into the roof of the serpent's mouth. And when the serpent felt this, it jerked away so hard that both Thor's fists banged down on the gunwale. Then Thor got angry and summoned up his As-strength, pushed down so hard that he forced both feet through the boat and braced them against the sea-bed, and then hauled the serpent up to the gunwale. And one can claim that a person does not know what a horrible sight is who did not get to see how Thor fixed his eyes on the serpent, and the serpent stared back up at him spitting poison. It is said that then the giant Hymir changed colour, went pale, and panicked when he saw the serpent and how the sea flowed out and in over the boat. And just at the moment when Thor was grasping his hammer and lifting it in the air, the giant fumbled at his bait-knife and cut Thor's line from the gunwale, and the serpent sank into the sea. But Thor threw his hammer after it, and they say that he struck off its head by the sea-bed. But I think in fact the contrary is correct to report to you that the Midgard serpent lives still and lies in the encircling sea. But Thor swung his fist and struck at Hymir's ear so that he plunged overboard and one could see the soles of his feet. But Thor waded ashore.'

Then spoke Gangleri: 'Have any greater events taken place among the Æsir? It was a very great exploit that Thor achieved on this expedition.'

High replied: 'There are events to be related that would have been thought more significant by the Æsir. And the beginning of this story is that Baldr the Good dreamed great dreams boding peril to his life. And when he told the Æsir the dreams they took counsel together and it was decided to request immunity for Baldr from all kinds of danger, and Frigg received solemn promises so that Baldr should not be harmed by fire and water, iron and all kinds of metal, stones, the earth, trees, diseases, the animals, the birds, poison, snakes. And when this was done and confirmed, then it became an entertainment for Baldr and the Æsir that he should stand up at assemblies and all the others should either shoot at him or strike at him or throw stones at him. But whatever they did he was unharmed, and they all thought this a great glory. But when Loki Laufeyiarson saw this he was not pleased that Baldr was unharmed. He went to Fensalir to Frigg and changed his appearance to that of a woman. Then Frigg asked this woman if she knew what the Æsir were doing at the assembly. She said that everyone was shooting at Baldr, and moreover that he was unharmed. Then said Frigg:

' "Weapons and wood will not hurt Baldr. I have received oaths from them all."

'Then the woman asked: "Have all things sworn oaths not to harm Baldr?"

'Then Frigg replied: "There grows a shoot of a tree to the west of Val-hall. It is called mistletoe. It seemed young to me to demand the oath from."

'Straight away the woman disappeared. And Loki took mistletoe and plucked it and went to the assembly. Hod was standing at the edge of the circle of people, for he was blind. Then Loki said to him:

' "Why are you not shooting at Baldr?"

'He replied: "Because I cannot see where Baldr is, and secondly because I have no weapon."

'Then said Loki: "Follow other people's example and do Baldr honour like other people. I will direct you to where he is standing. Shoot at him this stick."

'Hod took the mistletoe and shot at Baldr at Loki's direction. The missile flew through him and he fell dead to the ground, and this was the unluckiest deed ever done among gods and men. When Baldr had fallen, then all the Æsir's tongues failed them, as did their hands for lifting him up, and they all looked at each other and were all of one mind towards the one who had done the deed. But no one could take vengeance, it was a place of such sanctuary. When the Æsir tried to speak then what happened first was that weeping came out, so that none could tell another in words of his grief. But it was Odin who took this injury the hardest in that he had the best idea what great deprivation and loss the death of Baldr would cause the Æsir. And when the gods came to themselves then Frigg spoke, and asked who there was among the Æsir who wished to earn all her love and favour and was willing to ride the road to Hel and try if he could find Baldr, and offer Hel a ransom if she would let Baldr go back to Asgard. Hermod the Bold, Odin's boy, is the name of the one who undertook this journey. Then Odin's horse Sleipnir was fetched and led forward and Hermod mounted this horse and galloped away. So the Æsir took Baldr's body and carried it to the sea. Hringhorni was the name of Baldr's ship. It was the biggest of all ships. This the Æsir planned to launch and perform on it Baldr's funeral. But the ship refused to move. So they sent to Giantland for a giantess called Hyrrokkin. And when she arrived, riding a wolf and using vipers as reins, she dismounted from her steed, and Odin summoned four berserks to look after the mount, and they were unable to hold it without knocking it down. Then Hyrrokkin went to the prow of the boat and pushed it out with the first touch so that flame flew from the rollers and all lands quaked. Then Thor became angry and grasped his hammer and was about to smash her head until all the gods begged for grace for her. Then Baldr's body was carried out on to the ship, and when his wife Nanna Nep's daughter saw this she collapsed with grief and died. She was carried on to the pyre and it was set fire to. Then Thor stood by and consecrated the pyre with Miollnir. But a certain dwarf ran in front of his feet. His name was Lit. Thor kicked at him with his foot and thrust him into the fire and he was burned.

'This burning was attended by beings of many different kinds: firstly to tell of Odin, that with him went Frigg and valkyries and his ravens, while Freyr drove in a chariot with a boar called Gullinbursti or Slidrugtanni. But Heimdall rode a horse called Gulltopp, and Freyia her cats. There came also a great company of frost-giants and mountain-giants. Odin laid on the pyre a gold arm-ring called Draupnir. It afterwards had the property that every ninth night there dripped from it eight gold rings of the same weight. Baldr's horse was led on to the pyre with all its harness. But there is this to tell of Hermod that he rode for nine nights through valleys dark and deep so that he saw nothing until he came to the river Gioll and rode on to Gioll bridge. It is covered with glowing gold. There is a maiden guarding the bridge called Modgud. She asked him his name and lineage and said that the other day there had ridden over the bridge five battalions of dead men.

' "But the bridge resounds no less under just you, and you do not have the colour of dead men. Why are you riding here on the road to Hel?"

'He replied: "I am to ride to Hel to seek Baldr. But have you seen anything of Baldr on the road to Hel?"

'And she said that Baldr had ridden there over Gioll bridge, "but downwards and northwards lies the road to Hel."

'Then Hermod rode on until he came to Hel's gates. Then he dismounted from the horse and tightened its girth, mounted and spurred it on. The horse jumped so hard and over the gate that it came nowhere near. Then Hermod rode up to the hall and dismounted from his horse, went into the hall, saw sitting there in the seat of honour his brother Baldr; and Hermod stayed there the night. In the morning Hermod begged from Hel that Baldr might ride home with him and said what great weeping there was among the Æsir. But Hel said that it must be tested whether Baldr was as beloved as people said in the following way,

' "And if all things in the world, alive and dead, weep for him, then he shall go back to the Æsir, but be kept with Hel if any objects or refuses to weep."

'Then Hermod got up and Baldr went with him out of the hall and took the ring Draupnir and sent it to Odin as a keepsake, and Nanna sent Frigg a linen robe and other gifts too; to Fulla a finger-ring. Then Hermod rode back on his way and came to Asgard and told all the tidings he had seen and heard.

'After this the Æsir sent over all the world messengers to request that Baldr be wept out of Hel. And all did this, the people and animals and the earth and the stones and trees and every metal, just as you will have seen that these things weep when they come out of frost and into heat. When the envoys were travelling back having well fulfilled their errand, they found in a certain cave a giantess sitting. She said her name was Thanks. They bade her weep Baldr out of Hel. She said:

> "Thanks will weep dry tears for Baldr's burial. No good got
> I from the old one's son either dead or alive. Let Hel hold
> what she has."

'It is presumed that this was Loki Laufeyiarson, who has done most evil among the Æsir.'

Then spoke Gangleri: 'It was quite an achievement of Loki's when he brought it about first of all that Baldr was killed, and also that he was not redeemed from Hel. But was he punished at all for this?'

High said: 'He was requited for this in such a way that he will not soon forget it. The gods having become as angry with him as one might expect, he ran away and hid in a certain mountain, built a house there with four doors so that he could see out of the house in all directions. But in the daytime he often turned himself into the form of a salmon and hid in a place called Franangr waterfall. Then he pondered what sort of device the Æsir would be likely to think up to catch him in the waterfall. And as he sat in the house he took some linen thread and tied knots in it in the way in which ever since a net has been. A fire was burning in front of him. Then he noticed that the Æsir were only a short distance away from him, and Odin had seen where he was from Hlidskialf. He immediately jumped up and out into the river throwing the net down into the fire. And when the Æsir reached the house then the first to enter was the wisest of all, called Kvasir. And when he saw in the fire the shape in the ashes where the net had burned he realized that it must be a device to catch fish, and told the Æsir. After that they went and made themselves a net just like what they saw in the ashes that Loki had made. And when the net was finished the Æsir went to the river and threw the net into the waterfall. Thor held one end and all the Æsir held the other and they dragged the net. But Loki went along in front and lay down between two stones. They dragged the net over him and could tell there was something live there and went a second time up to the waterfall and threw out the net and weighted it down so heavily that nothing would be able to go underneath. Then Loki went along in front of the net, and when he saw that it was only a short way to the sea then he leaped up over the top of the net and slipped up into the waterfall. This time the Æsir saw where he went, they went back up to the waterfall and divided their party into two groups, and Thor waded along the middle of the river and thus they advanced towards the sea. And when Loki saw there were two alternatives – it was mortal danger to rush into the sea, but so it was also to leap again over the net – and this is what he did, leaped as swiftly as he could over the top of the net. Thor grabbed at him and got his hand round him and he slipped in his hand so that the hand caught hold at the tail. And it is for this reason that the salmon tapers towards the tail.

'Now Loki was captured without quarter and taken to a certain cave. Then they took three stone slabs and set them on edge and knocked a hole in each slab. Then Loki's sons Vali and Nari or Narfi were fetched. The Æsir turned Vali into the form of a wolf and he tore his brother Narfi to pieces. Then the Æsir took his guts and bound Loki with them across the three stones – one under his shoulders, one under his loins, the third under the backs of his knees – and these bonds turned to iron. Then Skadi got a poisonous snake and fixed it up over him so that the poison would drip from the snake into his face. But his wife Sigyn stands next to him holding a basin under the drops of poison. And when the basin is full she goes and pours away the poison, but in the meantime the poison drips into his face. Then he jerks away so hard that the whole earth shakes. That is what you call an earthquake. There he will lie in bonds until Ragnarok.'

Then spoke Gangleri: 'What information is there to be given about Ragnarok? I have not heard tell of this before.'

High said: 'There are many important things to be told about it. First of all that a winter will come called *fimbul*-winter [mighty or mysterious winter]. Then snow will drift from all directions. There will then be great frosts and keen winds. The sun will do no good. There will be three of these winters together and no summer between. But before that there will come three other winters during which there will be great battles throughout the world. Then brothers will kill each other out of greed and no one will show mercy to father or son in killing or breaking the taboos of kinship. Thus it says in *Voluspa*:

> Brothers will fight and kill each other, cousins will break the bonds of their relationship. It will be harsh for heroes, much depravity, age of axes, age of swords, shields cloven, age of winds, age of wolves, until the world is ruined.

Then something will happen that will be thought a most significant event, the wolf will swallow the sun, and people will think this a great disaster. Then the other wolf will catch the moon, and he also will cause much mischief. The stars will disappear from the sky. Then there will take place another event, the whole earth and mountains will shake so much that trees will become uprooted from the earth and the mountains will fall, and all fetters and bonds will snap and break. Then Fenriswolf will get free. Then the ocean will surge up on to the lands because the Midgard serpent will fly into a giant rage and make its way ashore. Then it will also happen that Naglfar will be loosed from its moorings, the ship of that name. It is made of dead people's nails, and it is worth taking care lest anyone die with untrimmed nails, since such a person contributes much material to the ship Naglfar which gods and men wish would take a long time to finish. And in this flood Naglfar will be carried along. There is a giant called Hrym who will captain Naglfar. But Fenriswolf will go with mouth agape and its upper jaw will be against the sky and its lower one against the earth. It would gape wider if there was room. Flames will burn from its eyes and nostrils. The Midgard serpent will spit so much poison that it will bespatter all the sky and sea, and it will be very terrible, and it will be on one side of the wolf. Amid this turmoil the sky will open and from it will ride the sons of Muspell. Surt will ride in front, and both before and behind him there will be burning fire. His sword will be very fine. Light will shine from it more brightly than from the sun. And when they ride over Bifrost it will break, as was said above. Muspell's lads will advance to the field called Vigrid. Then there will also arrive there Fenriswolf and the Midgard serpent. By then Loki will also have arrived there and Hrym and with him all the frost-giants, but with Loki will be all Hel's people. But Muspell's sons will have their own battle array; it will be very bright. The field Vigrid is a hundred leagues in each direction.

'And when these events take place, Heimdall will stand up and blow mightily on Giallarhorn and awaken all the gods and they will hold a parliament together. Then Odin will ride to Mimir's well and consult Mimir on his own and his people's behalf. Then the ash Yggdrasil will shake and nothing will then be unafraid in heaven or on earth. The Æsir will put on their war gear, and so will all the Einheriar, and advance on to the field. Odin will ride in front with golden helmet and fine coat of mail and his spear called Gungnir. He will make for Fenriswolf, and Thor will advance at his side and be unable to aid him because he will have his hands full fighting the Midgard serpent. Freyr will fight Surt and there will be a harsh conflict before Freyr falls. The cause of his death will be that he will be without the good sword that he gave Skirnir. Then will also have got free the dog Garm, which is bound in front of Gnipahellir. This is the most evil creature. He will have a battle with Tyr and they will each be the death of the other. Thor will be victorious over the Midgard serpent and will step away from it nine paces. Then he will fall to the ground dead from the poison which the serpent will spit at him. The wolf will swallow Odin. That will be the cause of his death. And immediately after Vidar will come forward and step with one foot on the lower jaw of the wolf. On this foot he will have a shoe for which the material has been being collected throughout all time: it is the waste pieces that people cut from their shoes at the toe and heel. Therefore anyone that is concerned to give assistance to the Æsir must throw these pieces away. With one hand he will grasp the wolf's upper jaw and tear apart its mouth and this will cause the wolf's death. Loki will have a battle with Heimdall and they will cause each other's death. After that Surt will fling fire over the earth and burn the whole world. Thus it is related in *Voluspa*:

> Loud blows Heimdall, his horn is aloft. Odin speaks with Mim's head. The ash Yggdrasil shakes as it stands, the ancient tree groans, and the giant gets free.

What is it with the Æsir? What is it with the elves? All Giantland resounds. Æsir are in council. Dwarfs groan before rock doorways, frequenters of rock-walls. Know you yet, or what?

Hrym drives from the east holding his shield before him, Iormungand writhes in a giant rage. The serpent churns the waves, the eagle will screech with joy, darkly pale it tears corpses, Naglfar is loosed.

A bark sails from the east, across the sea will come Muspell's troops with Loki at the helm. All that monstrous brood are there with the wolf. In company with them is Byleist's brother.

Surt travels from the south with the stick-destroyer [fire]. Shines from his sword the sun of the gods of the slain. Rock cliffs crash and troll-wives are abroad, heroes tread the road of Hel and heaven splits.

Then Hlin's second sorrow comes to pass as Odin goes to fight the wolf, and Beli's bright slayer against Surt. There shall fall Frigg's delight.

Odin's son goes to fight the wolf, Vidar on his way against the slaughterous beast. With his hand he lets his blade pierce Hvedrung's son's heart. So is his father avenged.

Goes the great son of Hlodyn, dying, to the serpent who shrinks from no shame. All heroes shall leave the world when Midgard's protector strikes in wrath.

The sun will go dark, earth sink in the sea. From heaven vanish bright stars. Steam surges and life's warmer [fire], high flame flickers against the very sky.

It also says here:

There is a field called Vigrid where shall meet in battle Surt and the sweet gods. A hundred leagues each way it is; this field is marked out for them.'

Then spoke Gangleri: 'What will happen then after heaven and earth and all the world is burned and all the gods and all Einheriar and all mankind are dead? You said previously that everyone shall live in some world or other for ever and ever.'

Then said Third: 'There will then be many mansions that are good, and many that are bad. The best place to be in heaven then will be Gimle, and there will be plenty of good drink for those that take pleasure in it in the hall called Brimir. That is also in heaven. That is also a good hall which is situated on Nidafioll, built of red gold. It is called Sindri. In these halls shall dwell good and virtuous people. On Nastrands is a large and unpleasant hall, and its doors face north. It is also woven out of snakes' bodies like a wattled house, and the snakes' heads all face inside the house and spit poison so that rivers of poison flow along the hall, and wading those rivers are oathbreakers and murderers, as it says here:

I know a hall that stands far from the sun on Nastrand.
North face the doors. Poison drops flow in through the
smoke-hole. This hall is woven from snakes' backs. There
shall wade heavy streams men who are perjured and
murderers.

But it is worst in Hvergelmir:

There Nidhogg torments the bodies of the dead.'

Then spoke Gangleri: 'Will there be any gods alive then? And will there be any kind of earth or sky?'

High said: 'The earth will shoot up out of the sea and will then be green and fair. Crops will grow unsown. Vidar and Vali will be alive, the sea and Surt's fire not having harmed them, and they will dwell on Idavoll, where Asgard had been previously. And then Thor's sons Modi and Magni will arrive, bringing Miollnir. After that Baldr and Hod will arrive from Hel. Then they will all sit down together and talk and discuss their mysteries and speak of the things that had happened in former times, of the Midgard serpent and Fenriswolf. Then they will find in the grass the golden playing pieces that had belonged to the Æsir. Thus it is said:

Vidar and Vali will dwell in the gods' holy places when
Surt's flame goes dark. Modi and Magni shall have Miollnir
when Vingnir fights no more.

And in a place called Hoddmimir's holt two people will lie hid during Surt's fire called Life and Leifthrasir, and their food will be the dews of morning. And from these people there will be descended such a great progeny that all the world will be inhabited. As it says here:

> Life and Leifthrasir, and they shall lie hid in Hoddmimir's holt. Dews of morning they shall have as their food, and from them shall grow mankind.

And this also will seem amazing to you, that the sun will have begotten a daughter no less fair than she is, and she shall follow the paths of her mother, as it says here:

> A daughter shall Alfrodul bear before Fenrir catches her. She shall ride, when the powers die, the maiden, her mother's road.

And now if you know any more questions to ask further into the future, I do not know where you will find answers, for I have heard no one relate the history of the world any further on in time. And may the knowledge you have gained do you good.'

Next Gangleri heard great noises in every direction from him, and he looked out to one side. And when he looked around further he found he was standing out on open ground, could see no hall and no castle. Then he went off on his way and came back to his kingdom and told of the events he had seen and heard about. And from his account these stories passed from one person to another.

But the Æsir sat down to discuss and hold a conference and went over all these stories that had been told him, and assigned those same names that were mentioned above to the people and places that were there [in Sweden], so that when long periods of time had passed men should not doubt that they were all the same, those Æsir about whom stories were told above and those who were now given the same names. So someone there was given the name Thor – and this means the ancient Thor of the Æsir, that is Oku-Thor – and to him are attributed the exploits which Thor

(Hec-tor) performed in Troy. And it is believed that the Turks told tales about Ulysses and that they gave him the name Loki, for the Turks were especially hostile to him.

Skaldskaparmal

[The language of poetry]

There was a person whose name was Ægir or Hler. He lived on an island which is now called Hlesey. He was very skilled in magic. He set out to visit Asgard, and when the Æsir became aware of his movements, he was given a great welcome, though many things had deceptive appearances. And in the evening when they were about to start the drinking, Odin had swords brought into the hall and they were so bright that light shone from them, and no other light was used while they sat drinking. Then the Æsir instituted their banquet and twelve Æsir who were to be judges took their places in their thrones and their names are as follows: Thor, Niord, Freyr, Tyr, Heimdall, Bragi, Vidar, Vali, Ull, Hænir, Forseti, Loki; similarly the Asyniur, Frigg, Freyia, Gefiun, Idunn, Gerd, Sigyn, Fulla, Nanna. Everything there seemed to Ægir magnificent to look at. The wall-panels were all hung with splendid shields. There was also strong mead there and great quantities were drunk. The person sitting next to Ægir was Bragi, and they drank and conversed together. Bragi related to Ægir many events in which the Æsir had been involved.

He began his account where three Æsir set out – Odin and Loki and Hænir – and crossed mountains and wildernesses, and food was difficult to come by. And when they came down into a certain valley they saw a herd of oxen and took one of the oxen and set it in an earth oven. And when they thought it must be cooked they opened the earth oven and it was not cooked. And a second time when they opened the oven after some time had passed, it was still not cooked. Then they discussed among themselves what could be the reason. Then they heard someone talking in the oak tree up above them, saying that the one that was sitting there claimed to be responsible for the oven not cooking. They looked up and it was an eagle sitting there, and no small one. Then said the eagle:

'If you will grant me my fill of the ox, then the oven will cook.'

They agreed to this. Then it let itself drop from the tree and sat on the oven and to begin with immediately put away the ox's two hams and both shoulders. Then Loki got angry and snatched up a great pole and swung it with all his strength and drove it at the eagle's body. The eagle jerked away at the blow and flew up. Then the pole was stuck to the eagle's body and Loki's hands to the other end. The eagle flew at such a height that Loki's feet banged down against the stones and gravel and trees, and his arms he thought were going to be wrenched from his shoulders. He shouted and begged the eagle most earnestly for a truce but it said that Loki would never get free unless he vowed solemnly to get Idunn to come outside Asgard with her apples, and Loki accepted. Then he got free and went up to his comrades. And nothing else noteworthy was told on this occasion of their expedition until they got home. But at the agreed time Loki lured Idunn out through Asgard into a certain forest, saying that he had found some apples that she would think worth having, and told her she should bring her apples with her and compare them with these. Then giant Thiassi arrived in eagle shape and snatched Idunn and flew away with her to his home in Thrymheim.

But the Æsir were badly affected by Idunn's disappearance and soon became grey and old. Then the Æsir held a parliament and asked each other what was the last that was known about Idunn, and the last that had been seen was that she had gone outside Asgard with Loki. Then Loki was arrested and brought to the parliament and he was threatened with death or torture. Being filled with terror, he said he would go in search of Idunn in Giantland if Freyia would lend him a falcon shape of hers. And when he got the falcon shape he flew north to Giantland and arrived one day at giant Thiassi's; he was out at sea in a boat, but Idunn was at home alone. Loki turned her into the form of a nut and held her in his claws and flew as fast as he could. When Thiassi got home and found Idunn was not there he got his eagle shape and flew after Loki and he caused a storm-wind by his flying. And when the Æsir saw the falcon flying with the nut and where the eagle was flying, they went out under Asgard and brought there loads of wood-shavings, and when the falcon flew in over the fortification, it let itself drop down by the wall of the fortification. Then the Æsir set fire to the wood-shavings and the eagle was unable to stop when it missed the falcon. Then the eagle's feathers caught fire and his flight was ended. Then the Æsir were close by and killed giant Thiassi within the As-gates, and this killing is greatly renowned.

But Skadi, daughter of giant Thiassi, took helmet and mail-coat and all weapons of war and went to Asgard to avenge her father. But the Æsir offered her atonement and compensation, the first item of which was that she was to choose herself a husband out of the Æsir and choose by the feet and see nothing else of them. Then she saw one person's feet that were exceptionally beautiful and said:

'I choose that one; there can be little that is ugly about Baldr.'

But it was Niord of Noatun.

It was also in her terms of settlement that the Æsir were to do something that she thought they would not be able to, that was to make her laugh. Then Loki did as follows: he tied a cord round the beard of a certain nanny-goat and the other end round his testicles, and they drew each other back and forth and both squealed loudly. Then Loki let himself drop into Skadi's lap, and she laughed. Then the atonement with her on the part of the Æsir was complete.

It is said that Odin, as compensation for her, did this: he took Thiassi's eyes and threw them up into the sky and out of them made two stars.

Then spoke Ægir: 'Thiassi seems to me to have been very powerful, what was his origin?'

Bragi replied: 'His father was called Olvaldi, and you will find what I have to say about him remarkable. He was very rich in gold, and when he died and his sons had to divide their inheritance, they measured out the gold when they divided it by each in turn taking a mouthful, all of them the same number. One of them was Thiassi, the second Idi, the third Gang. And we now have this expression among us, to call gold the mouth-count of these giants, and we conceal it in secret language or in poetry by calling it speech or words or talk of these giants.'

Then spoke Ægir: 'This seems to me a very good way to conceal it in secret language.' And Ægir went on: 'How did this craft that you call poetry originate?'

Bragi replied: 'The origin of it was that the gods had a dispute with the people called Vanir, and they appointed a peace-conference and made a truce by this procedure, that both sides went up to a vat and spat their spittle into it. But when they dispersed, the gods kept this symbol of truce and decided not to let it be wasted, and out of it made a man. His name was Kvasir, he was so wise that no one could ask him any questions to which he did not know the answer. He travelled widely through the world teaching people knowledge, and when he arrived as a guest to some dwarfs, Fialar and Galar, they called him to a private discussion with them and killed him. They poured his blood into two vats and a pot, and the latter was called Odrerir, but the vats were called Son and Bodn. They mixed honey with the blood and it turned into the mead whoever drinks from which becomes a poet or scholar. The dwarfs told the Æsir that Kvasir had suffocated in intelligence because there was no one there educated enough to be able to ask him questions.

'Then these dwarfs invited to stay with them a giant called Gilling and his wife. Then the dwarfs invited Gilling to go out to sea in a boat with them. But as they went along the coast the dwarfs rowed on to a shoal and the boat capsized. Gilling could not swim and was drowned, but the dwarfs righted their boat and rowed to land. They told his wife what had happened and she was greatly distressed and wept loudly. Then Fialar asked her if it would be some consolation for her if she looked out to the sea where he had drowned, and she agreed. Then he told his brother Galar that he was to go up above the doorway she was going out of and drop a millstone on her head, and declared he was weary of her howling; and Galar did so. When Gilling's son Suttung found out about this, he went there and seized the dwarfs and took them out to sea and put them on a skerry below high-water level. They begged Suttung for quarter and offered him as atonement in compensation for his father the precious mead, and they were reconciled on these terms. Suttung took the mead home with him and put it for safe keeping in a place called Hnitbiorg, setting his daughter Gunnlod in charge of it. That is why we call poetry Kvasir's blood or dwarfs' drink or the contents or some term for liquid of Odrerir or Bodn or Son, or dwarfs' transportation, because this mead brought them deliverance from the skerry, or Suttung's mead or the liquid of Hnitbiorg.'

Then spoke Ægir: 'I think it is an obscure way to talk to call poetry by these names, but how did the Æsir get hold of Suttung's mead?'

Bragi replied: 'There is this story about it, that Odin set out from home and came to where nine slaves were mowing hay. He asked if they would like him to hone their scythes. They said yes. Then he took a whetstone from his belt and honed, and they thought the scythes were cutting very much better and asked if they could buy the whetstone. The price he set on it was that he who wished to buy must give what was reasonable for it, and they all said they wanted to and bade him sell it to them, but he threw the whetstone up in the air, and when all tried to catch it they dealt with each other in such a way that they all cut each other's throats with the scythes. Odin sought lodging for the night with a giant called Baugi, Suttung's brother. Baugi reckoned his economic affairs were going badly, and said his nine slaves had killed each other, and declared he did not know where he was going to get workmen from. Odin told him his name was Bolverk; he offered to take over the work of nine men for Baugi, and stipulated as his payment one drink of Suttung's mead. Baugi said he had no say in the disposal of the mead, said that Suttung wanted to have it all to himself, but he said he would go with Bolverk and try whether they could get the mead. Bolverk did the work of nine men for Baugi during the summer, and when winter came he asked Baugi for his hire. Then they both set off. Baugi told his brother Suttung of his agreement with Bolverk, but Suttung flatly refused a single drop of the mead. Then Bolverk told Baugi that they would have to try some stratagems to see if they could get hold of the mead, and Baugi said that was a good idea. Then Bolverk got out an auger called Rati and instructed Baugi to bore a hole in the mountain, if the auger would cut. He did so. Then Baugi said that the mountain was bored through, but Bolverk blew into the auger-hole and the bits flew back up at him. Then he realized that Baugi was trying to cheat him, and told him to bore through the mountain. Baugi bored again. And when Bolverk blew a second time, the bits flew inwards. Then Bolverk turned himself into the form of a snake and crawled into the auger-hole, and Baugi stabbed after him with the auger and missed him. Bolverk went to where Gunnlod was and lay with her for three nights and then she let him drink three draughts of the mead. In the first draught he drank everything out of Odrerir, and in the second out of Bodn, in the third out of Son, and then he had all the mead. Then he turned himself into the form of an eagle and flew as hard as he could. And when Suttung saw the eagle's flight he got his own eagle shape and flew after him. And when the Æsir saw Odin flying they put their containers out in the courtyard, and when Odin came in over Asgard he spat out the mead into the containers, but it was such a close thing for him that Suttung might have caught him that he sent some of the mead out backwards, and this was disregarded. Anyone took it that wanted it, and it is what we call the rhymester's share. But Odin gave Suttung's mead to the Æsir and to those people who are skilled at composing poetry. Thus we call poetry Odin's booty and find, and his drink and his gift and the Æsir's drink.'

Then spoke Ægir: 'In how many ways do you vary the vocabulary of poetry, and how many categories are there in poetry?'

Then spoke Bragi: 'There are two categories into which all poetry is divided.'

Ægir asked: 'Which two?'

Bragi said: 'Language and verse-forms.'

'What choice of language is used in poetry?'

'There are three categories in the language of poetry.'

'What are they?'

'To call everything by its name; the second category is the one called substitution; and the third category of language is what is called kenning [description], and this category is constructed in this way, that we speak of Odin or Thor or Tyr or one of the Æsir or elves, in such a way that with each of those that I mention, I add a term for the attribute of another As or make mention of one or other of his deeds. Then the latter becomes the one referred to, and not the one that was named; for instance when we speak of Victory-Tyr or Hanged-Tyr or Cargo-Tyr, these are expressions for Odin, and these we call periphrastic terms; similarly if one speaks of Chariot-Tyr [i.e. Thor].'

But these things have now to be told to young poets who desire to learn the language of poetry and to furnish themselves with a wide vocabulary using traditional terms; or else they desire to be able to understand what is expressed obscurely. Then let such a one take this book as scholarly inquiry and entertainment. But these stories are not to be consigned to oblivion or demonstrated to be false, so as to deprive poetry of ancient kennings which major poets have been happy to use. Yet Christian people must not believe in heathen gods, nor in the truth of this account in any other way than that in which it is presented at the beginning of this book, where it is told what happened when mankind went astray from the true faith, and after that about the Turks, how the people of Asia, known as Æsir, distorted the accounts of the events that took place in Troy so that the people of the country would believe that they were gods.

King Priam in Troy was a great ruler over all the host of Turks, and his sons were the highest in rank in his whole host. That magnificent hall that the Æsir called Brimir's hall or beer-hall, was King Priam's hall. And whereas they give a long account of Ragnarok, this is the Trojan war. The story goes that Oku-Thor used an ox-head as bait and pulled the Midgard serpent up to the gunwale, but the serpent survived by sinking into the sea. This story is based on the one about how Hector killed the splendid hero Volucrontes while the great Achilles was looking on, and thus lured Achilles towards him with the head of the slain man whom they saw as corresponding to the ox from which Thor had taken the head. And when Achilles had been drawn into this dangerous situation by his impetuosity, then the only way for him to save his life was to run away from Hector's deadly stroke, wounded though he was. It is also said that Hector pressed his attack so violently, and that his valour was raised to such a pitch when he saw Achilles that there was nothing strong enough to stand before him. And when he missed Achilles and he had fled, he slaked his wrath by killing a hero called Roddrus. In the same way the Æsir said that when Oku-Thor missed the serpent, he killed giant Hymir; and at Ragnarok the Midgard serpent came with frightening suddenness against Thor and blew poison on him and struck him his death-blow, but the Æsir did not like to admit that Oku-Thor had died as a result of one person overthrowing him in death even though such had been the case, and they exaggerated the story beyond what was true, when they said that the Midgard serpent suffered death there. But they adduced this, that though Achilles gained victory over Hector, yet he was to lie dead on the same field as a result. This was achieved by Helenus and Alexander. This Helenus was called Ali by the Æsir. They say that he avenged his brother and survived when all the gods were dead and the fire, with which Asgard and all the possessions of the gods were burned, was extinguished. As for Pyrrhus, they saw him as corresponding to Fenriswolf; it killed Odin, and Pyrrhus could be said to be a wolf according to their religion, for he paid no respect to places of sanctuary when he killed the king in the temple in front of Thor's altar. What they call Surt's fire was when Troy burned. And Oku-Thor's sons, Modi and Magni, came to claim lands from Ali or Vidar. The latter is Aeneas, he escaped from Troy and later achieved great deeds. Similarly it is also said that Hector's sons arrived in the land of Phrygia and established themselves in that kingdom, driving Helenus out.

We shall present further examples of how major poets have found it fitting to compose using these kinds of terms and kennings, as for instance Arnor, the earls' poet, who gives Odin the name All-father:

> Now plan I to tell men — long takes my pain to ease — the virtues of the hostile earl — All-father's malt-surf [the mead of poetry] pounds [resounds].

Here he also calls his poetry All-father's malt-surf. Havard the halt said this:

> Now for sea-steeds' [ships'] trunks [warriors] there is eagles' flight over land in store [i.e. the birds of prey are gathering, a battle is taking place]. I guess they are getting Hanged-god's [Odin's] hospitality [in Val-hall] and rings [plunder].

Viga-Glum said this:

> The host with Hanged-Tyr's [Odin's] hoods [helmets] held back — they thought it not pleasant to venture – from going down the slopes.

Ref said this:

> Often the kind man brought me to the raven-god's [Odin's] holy drink [instructed me in poetry]. Baldr [this man] of the prow-land's [sea's] flashes [gold] is departed from the poet [i.e. dead].

Eyvind Skaldspillir said this:

And Sigurd, he who gave raven-beer [blood] from the flower of the Haddings to Cargo-Tyr's [Odin's] swans [ravens], him land-rulers deprived of life at Oglo.

Glum Geirason said this:

It was Victory-Tyr [Odin] himself there in the attacking elf [viking] of Atal's beasts [ships]. There were gods guiding that wind-beam [ship] Beimi [viking].

Eyvind also said this:

Gauta-Tyr [Odin] sent Gondul and Skogul to choose among kings which of Yngvi's line should go with Odin and be in Val-hall.

Ulf Uggason said this:

Far-famed Hropta-Tyr [Odin] rides to the mighty broad pyre of his son, and from my jaws flow words of praise.

Thiodolf of Hvinir said this:

The fallen lay there on the sand, destined for the one-eyed dweller in Frigg's embrace [ie. for her husband Odin in Val-hall]. We rejoice in such achievement.

Hallfrod said this:

The keen wind-steed-[ship-]taker [sea-farer, Earl Hakon] lures under himself [wins] with the true language of swords [battle] the pine-haired deserted wife of Third [Odin; his deserted wife is Iord, earth, i.e. the land of Norway].

Here there is an example of land being called Odin's wife in poetry. And we have here what Eyvind said:

'Hermod and Bragi,' said Hropta-Tyr [Odin], 'go to meet the prince, for a king is coming who is to be considered a hero, here to this hall.'

Kormak said this:

The land-getter, who binds the mast-top straight, honours the provider of the deities' fiord [the mead of poetry, whose provider is the poet] with a head-band. Ygg [Odin] won Rind by spells.

Steinthor said this:

I am mightily proud of my ancient horn-cascade [mead of poetry] of the meanness-avoiding cargo of Gunnlod's embrace [Odin], though it be meagre.

Ulf Uggason said this:

There I perceive valkyries and ravens accompanying the wise victory-tree [Odin] to the drink of the holy offering [Baldr's funeral feast]. Within have appeared these motifs.

Egil Skallagrimsson said this:

I do not worship Vilir's brother [Odin], god of earth, because I am eager; yet has Mim's friend [Odin] granted me a grief-comforter which I count better — gave me, too, wolf's enemy [Odin] battle-accustomed, skill without blemish.

Here he is called god of earth and Mim's friend and wolf's enemy. Ref said this:

To you we owe Fal's cup [the mead of poetry], noble Slaughter-Gaut [Odin], practised controller of wave-horse's [ship's] snow-road's [sea's] hall [sky].

Einar Skalaglamm said this:

I shall succeed in pouring the draught of Host-Tyr's [Odin's] wine-vessel [the mead of poetry] before the ship-impellers [seamen] — I need no urging to that.

As Ulf Uggason said:

Splendid Heimdall rides to the pyre raised by gods for the fallen son [Baldr] of the strangely wise raven-tester [Odin], on his horse.

In *Eiriksmal* it says this:

> What sort of dream is that, Odin? I dreamed I rose up before
> dawn to clear up Val-hall for slain people. I aroused the
> Einheriar, bade them get up to strew the benches, clean the
> beer-cups, the valkyries to serve wine for the arrival of a
> prince.

Kormak said this:

> I who am young bid the excellent power-wielder of Yngvi's
> folk hold over me his quivering bow-land [hand]. Hropt
> [Odin] took Gungnir.

Thorolf said this:

> Hlidskialf's king [Odin], shy of [reluctant to use] shield,
> told the man himself his thoughts where Harek's troops
> were cut down.

Eyvind said this:

> ... <the mead of poetry> which the speedy one [Odin]
> flying bore from Surt's deep vales.

Bragi said this:

> It is conveyed to me that the son [Thor] of the father of
> mankind [Odin] was determined soon to test his strength
> against the water-soaked earth-band [Midgard serpent].

Einar said this:

> For most highly-gifted rulers achieve less in most matters
> with Bestla's son [Odin] than you. I have attempted poetry
> about battle.

Thorvald Blonduskald said this:

> Now have I snatched much of the mead [made a lot of
> poetry] of Buri's heir Bor's son [Odin].

Now examples will be given of how the poets have referred to poetry using such terms as were noted above, as when it is called Kvasir's blood and dwarfs' ship, dwarfs' mead, giants' mead, Suttungi's mead, Odin's mead, Æsir's mead, recompense for giants' father, liquid of Odrerir and Bodn and Son and their contents, liquid of Hnitbiorg, Odin's booty and find and cargo and gift. Thus in this following verse composed by Einar Skalaglamm:

> Land's magnanimous guardian I bid hear — hear, earl, Kvasir's blood — fiord-bone's [stone's] men's [dwarfs'] yeast-surf [mead].

And as Einar Skalaglamm also said:

> There flows over all Ull's ash-ship's crew [shield-warriors] who follow him who excites the activity of strife's defence-trouble [battle] the dwarfs' mountain-kept liquid.

As Orm Steinthorsson said:

> ... that the beer-plank's [woman's] body and mine to one room be brought when dead; let men receive Dvalin's drink [the mead of poetry].

And as Ref said:

> I offer Thorstein feast [the mead] of rock-men's [giants'] thought-land [breast]; fell-Mærir's [giants'] wave [the mead] crashes [poetry resounds], I bid mankind listen.

As Egil said:

> The prince offered me hospitality; praise is for me a duty. I bore Odin's mead to the land of the English.

And as Glum Geirason said:

> Listen! I begin the feast [the mead, a poem] of the gods' ruler [Odin] for princes. We crave silence, for we have heard of the loss of men.

And as Eyvind said:

> I desire silence for Har's ale [Odin's mead, poetry] while I
> raise Gilling's payment [the mead], while his descent in
> pot-liquid [the mead, poetry] of gallows-cargo [Odin] we
> trace to gods.

As Einar Skalaglamm said:

> Wave of time's sea rushes before the prince. Rognir's
> [Odin's] deeds [poetry] benefit me. Swell of Odrerir pounds
> against song's skerry [my teeth].

And as he also said:

> Now it is that Bodn's wave [poetry] starts to swell. In the
> hall let the king's men make silence and hear rock Saxons'
> [dwarfs'] ship.

And as Eilif Gudrunarson said:

> You must decide about kindly gifts, since about High kin [=
> Hakon] Son's seed [the mead of poetry] grows on our
> word-meadow [tongue].

As Volu-Stein said:

> Hear, Egil, my streams [the mead] of Mim's friend's
> [Odin's] joy-hill [breast] echo against gum-skerries [teeth].
> Thund's [Odin's] find is granted me.

Orm Steinthorsson said this:

> No need for men to nurse fear about my poetry. In Vidur's
> [Odin's] booty I use no spite. We know how to order
> praise-works.

Ulf Uggason said this:

> I bring heart-glad Olaf Hild's noise-maker's [Odin's] mind-
> fiord-[breast-]liquid [mead]. Him will I greet with Grim-
> nir's [Odin's] gift.

Poetry is called sea or liquid of the dwarfs, because the liquid in Odrerir was Kvasir's blood before the mead was made, and it was made in that cauldron, and hence it is called Odin's pot-liquid, as in the poem of Eyvind quoted above:

> . . . while his descent in pot-liquid of gallows-cargo we trace to gods.

Poetry is also called the dwarfs' vessel or *lid*. *Lid* is a word for ale and *lid* is a word for ships. This is the origin of the expression whereby poetry is now as a result called dwarfs' ship, as it says here:

> I have ready both swollen wind of rock-earl's [giant's] bride [troll-wife's wind is 'thought'] and unforgettable dwarfs' ship to send the same way.

How shall Thor be referred to? By calling him son of Odin and Iord, father of Magni and Modi and Thrud, husband of Sif, stepfather of Ull, ruler and owner of Miollnir and the girdle of might, of Bilskirnir, defender of Asgard, Midgard, enemy and slayer of giants and troll-wives, killer of Hrungnir, Geirrod, Thrivaldi, lord of Thialfi and Roskva, enemy of the Midgard serpent, foster-son of Vingnir and Hlora. The poet Bragi said this:

> Vidrir's [Odin's] heir's [Thor's] line lay by no means slack on Eynæfir's ski [boat] when Iormungand uncoiled on the sand.

Olvir Hnufa said this:

> The encircler of all lands [Midgard serpent] and Iord's son became violent.

Eilif said this:

> Roskva's brother [Thialfi] stood enraged, Magni's father struck a victorious blow. Neither Thor nor Thialfi's power-stone [heart] shakes with terror.

And as Eystein Valdason said:

Thrud's father looked with piercing eyes on steep-way's [land's] ring [Midgard serpent] until red-fish's dwelling [sea] surged over the boat.

Eystein also said:

Sif's beloved quickly brought out his fishing gear with the old fellow. We can stir Hrimnir's [giant's] horn-flow [mead].

And he also said:

The coal-fish of the earth [Midgard serpent] responded thus, that Ull's relative's [Thor's] fists banged out on the gunwale; broad planks pushed forward.

Bragi said this:

Oflugbardi's terrifier [Thor] lifted his hammer in his right hand when he recognized the coal-fish that bounds all lands [the Midgard serpent].

Gamli said this:

While Bilskirnir's lord, who never nursed treachery in his heart, did quickly destroy the sea-bed-fish [Midgard serpent] with gorge-whale's [giant's] bane [Miollnir].

Thorbiorn Disarskald said this:

Thor has with Ygg's [Odin's] angels [the Æsir] defended Asgard with might.

Bragi said this:

And the ugly ring [serpent] of the side-oared ship's road [sea] stared up spitefully at Hrungnir's skull-splitter.

Bragi also said:

Well have you, cleaver apart of Thrivaldi's nine heads, held back your steeds with notorious giant-feast drinker [Thrym = thunder].

Eilif said this:

> The oppressor [Thor] of the kinfolk [trolls] of evening-
> faring women [troll-wives] yawned with his arm's mouth
> [fist] over the heavy red lump of tong-weed [iron].

Bragi said this:

> The stockily built stumpy one [Hymir] is said to have
> thought tremendous danger in the goat-possessor's [Thor's]
> enormous heavy haul.

Ulf said this:

> The most mighty fell-Gaut's [giant's] feller made his fist
> crash on the reed-bed-bone [rock] frequenter's [giant's] ear.
> A mighty hurt was that.

Ulf also said:

> Vidgymnir of Vimur's ford struck the ear-bed [head] from
> the shining snake by the waves. Within have appeared these
> motifs.

Here he is called giant of Vimur's ford. Vimur is the name of a
river that Thor waded when he was on his way to Geirrod's
courts. And Vetrlidi said this:

> You broke Leikn's bones, you pounded Thrivaldi, you cast
> down Starkad, you stood over the dead Gialp.

And Thorbiorn Disarskald said this:

> There was a clang on Keila's crown, you broke Kiallandi
> completely, before that you slew Lut and Leidi, you made
> Buseyra bleed, you halted Hengiankiapta, Hyrrokkin died
> previously, yet was the dusky Svivor's life taken earlier.

How shall Baldr be referred to? By calling him son of Odin and
Frigg, husband of Nanna, father of Forseti, owner of Hringhorni
and Draupnir, enemy of Hod, Hel's companion, god of lamen-
tations. Ulf Uggason composed a long passage in *Husdrapa* based

on the story of Baldr, and an account of the events which were the
origin of Baldr's being referred to in this way was written above
[in *Gylfaginning*].

How shall Niord be referred to? By calling him god of chariots
or descendant of Vanir or a Van and father of Freyr and Freyia,
the giving god. Thord Siareksson says this:

> Gudrun became herself her son's slayer; the wise god-bride
> [Skadi] could not love the Van; Kialar [Odin] trained horses
> pretty well; Hamdir is said not to have held back sword-
> play.

Here reference is made to Skadi's leaving of Niord, which was
written about above.

How shall Freyr be referred to? By calling him son of Niord,
brother of Freyia and him also a Vanir god and descendant of
Vanir and a Van, and harvest god and wealth-giver. Egil Skalla-
grimsson said this:

> For Freyr and Niord have endowed Griotbiorn with a
> power of wealth.

Freyr can be called Beli's enemy, as Eyvind Skaldaspillir said:

> When the earls' opponent wished to live on Beli's enemy's
> outlying land.

He is possessor of Skidbladnir and of the boar known as Gullin-
bursti, as it says here:

> Ivaldi's sons set to work in days of yore to construct
> Skidbladnir, best of ships, for bright Freyr, bounteous son
> of Niord.

Ulf Uggason said this:

> Battle-skilled Freyr rides in front to Odin's son's [Baldr's]
> pyre on golden-bristled boar and governs hosts.

It is also called Slidrugtanni.

How shall Heimdall be referred to? By calling him son of nine mothers, guardians of the gods, as was written above, or the white As, Loki's enemy, recoverer of Freyia's necklace. A sword is called Heimdall's head; it is said he was struck through with a man's head. He is the subject of the poem *Heimdalargaldr*, and ever since the head has been called Heimdall's doom: man's doom is an expression for sword. Heimdall is the owner of Gulltopp. He is also the visitor to Vagasker and Singastein; on that occasion he contended with Loki for the Brisingamen. He is also known as Vindhler. Ulf Uggason composed a long passage in *Husdrapa* based on this story, and it is mentioned there that they were in the form of seals. Also son of Odin.

How shall Tyr be referred to? By calling him the one-handed As and feeder of the wolf, battle-god, son of Odin.

How shall Bragi be referred to? By calling him Idunn's husband, inventor of poetry (*brag*) and the long-bearded As. It is from his name that the expression 'beard-*bragi*' comes for someone who has a big beard. Also son of Odin.

How shall Vidar be referred to? He may be called the silent As, possessor of the iron shoe, enemy and slayer of Fenriswolf, the gods' avenging As, father's homestead-inhabiting As and son of Odin, brother of the Æsir.

How shall Vali be referred to? By calling him son of Odin and Rind, stepson of Frigg, brother of the Æsir, Baldr's avenging As, enemy of Hod and his slayer, father's homestead-inhabiter.

How shall Hod be referred to? By calling him the blind As, Baldr's slayer, shooter of mistletoe, son of Odin, Hel's companion, Vali's enemy.

How shall Ull be referred to? By calling him son of Sif, stepson of Thor, ski-As, bow-As, hunting As, shield-As.

How shall Hænir be referred to? By calling him Odin's table-companion or comrade or confidant and the swift As and the long foot and mud-king.

How shall Loki be referred to? By calling him son of Farbauti and Laufey, of Nal, brother of Byleist and Helblindi, father of Vanargand, i.e. Fenriswolf, and of Iormungand, i.e. the Midgard serpent, and Hel's and Nari's and Ali's relative and father, brother, comrade and table-companion of Odin and the Æsir, Geirrod's visitor and casket-ornament, thief from giants, of goat and Brisingamen and Idunn's apples, relative of Sleipnir, husband of Sigyn, enemy of gods, Sif's hair-harmer, maker of mischief, the cunning As, accuser and tricker of the gods, contriver of Baldr's death, the bound one, wrangler with Heimdall and Skadi. As Ulf Uggason says here:

> Renowned defender [Heimdall] of the powers' way [Bif-rost], kind of counsel, competes with Farbauti's terribly sly son at Singastein. Son of eight mothers plus one, mighty of mood, is first to get hold of the beautiful sea-kidney [jewel, Brisingamen]. I announce it in strands of praise.

Here it is mentioned that Heimdall is son of nine mothers.

Now there shall be told more of the underlying stories from which those kennings just listed have originated, and of which the origins have not already been told, just as Bragi told Ægir how Thor had gone to eastern parts to thrash trolls, but Odin rode Sleipnir into Giantland and arrived at a giant's called Hrungnir. Then Hrungnir asked what sort of person this was with the golden helmet riding sky and sea, and said he had a marvellously good horse. Odin said he would wager his head on it that there would be no horse as good to be found in Giantland. Hrungnir said it was a good horse, but declared he had a horse that must be much longer-paced, it was called Gullfaxi. Hrungnir had got angry and leaped up on his horse and galloped after Odin, intending to pay him back for his boasting. Odin galloped so hard that he kept ahead on the next rise in the ground, and Hrungnir was in such a great giant fury that the first thing he knew was that he had rushed in through the As-gates. And when he got to the hall doors, Æsir invited him in for a drink. He went into the hall and demanded that he should be given a drink. Then the goblets that Thor normally drank out of were brought out, and Hrungnir drained each one. And when he became drunk there was no lack of big words: he said he was going to remove Val-hall and take it to Giantland, but bury Asgard and kill all the gods, except that he was going to take Freyia and Sif home with him, and Freyia was the only one then who dared to bring him drink, and he declared he was going to drink all the Æsir's ale. And when the Æsir got tired of his boasting they invoked the name of Thor. Immediately Thor entered the hall with hammer raised up and in great anger and asked who was responsible for cunning giants being there drinking, and who had guaranteed Hrungnir safety while he was in Val-hall and why Freyia should be serving him drink as if at the Æsir's banquet. Then Hrungnir replied, looking at Thor with no friendly eyes, and said that Odin had invited him to a drink and that he was under his protection. Then Thor said that Hrungnir was going to regret that invitation before he got out. Hrungnir said it would be no honour to Asa-Thor to kill him when he was unarmed, whereas it would be a greater proof of his valour if he dared to fight with him on the frontier at Griotunagardar.

'And it has been a very foolish thing for me to do,' he said, 'to leave behind at home my shield and whetstone, but if I had my weapons here, we would hold the duel now, but as it is I declare you will be guilty of baseness if you go and kill me when I am unarmed.'

Thor was eager not to let anything stop him from going to single combat when he had been challenged to a duel, for no one had ever done that to him before. Then Hrungnir went off on his way and galloped mightily until he got into Giantland, and his journey was very widely talked of among the giants, together with the fact that an appointment had been made between him and Thor. The giants felt there was a great deal at stake for them as to which one won the victory. They would have little good to look forward to from Thor if Hrungnir died, for he was the strongest of them. Then the giants made a person at Griotunagardar of clay, and he was nine leagues high and three broad beneath the arms, but they could not get a heart big enough to suit him until they took one out of a certain mare, and this turned out not to be steady in him when Thor came. Hrungnir had a heart that is renowned, made of solid stone and spiky with three points just like the symbol for carving called Hrungnir's heart has ever since been made. His head was also of stone. His shield was also stone, broad and thick, and he held the shield before him as he stood at Griotunagardar waiting for Thor, and he had a whetstone as weapon and rested it on his shoulder and he did not look at all pleasant. On one side of him stood the clay giant, whose name was Mokkurkalfi, and he was quite terrified. They say he wet himself when he saw Thor. Thor went to keep his appointment for the duel, and with him Thialfi. Then Thialfi ran on ahead to where

Hrungnir was standing and said to him:

'You are standing unguardedly, giant, you've got your shield in front of you, but Thor has seen you and he is travelling by the lower route underground, and he is going to come at you from below.'

Then Hrungnir shoved the shield beneath his feet and stood on it, and held the whetstone with both hands. Next he saw lightnings and heard great thunders. Then he saw Thor in an As-rage, he was travelling at an enormous rate and swung his hammer and threw it from a great distance at Hrungnir. Hrungnir raised the whetstone with both hands, threw it in return. It met the hammer in flight, the whetstone, and the whetstone broke in two. One piece fell to the ground, and from it have come all whetstone rocks. The other piece flew into Thor's head so that he fell forwards to the ground, but the hammer Miollnir hit the middle of Hrungnir's head and shattered his skull into small fragments, and he fell forwards over Thor so that his leg lay across Thor's neck. Thialfi attacked Mokkurkalfi, and he fell with little glory. Then Thialfi went up to Thor and went to remove Hrungnir's leg from him and was unable to manage it. Then all the Æsir came up when they found out that Thor had fallen, and went to remove the leg from him and could not move it at all. Then Magni, son of Thor and Iarnsaxa, arrived. He was then three years old. He threw Hrungnir's leg off Thor and said:

'Isn't it a terrible shame, father, that I arrived so late. I think I would have knocked this giant into Hel with my fist if I had come across him.'

Then Thor stood up and welcomed his son warmly and said he would grow up to be a powerful person.

'And I have decided,' he said, 'to give you the horse Gullfaxi, which used to be Hrungnir's.'

Then spoke Odin and said it was wrong of Thor to give that fine horse to the son of a giantess and not to his own father.

Thor returned home to Thrudvangar and the whetstone remained in his head. Then there arrived a sorceress called Groa, wife of Aurvandil the Bold. She chanted her spells over Thor until the whetstone began to come loose. When Thor felt this and it seemed likely that the whetstone was going to be got out, he wanted to repay Groa for her treatment and give her pleasure. He told her these tidings that he had waded south across Elivagar carrying Aurvandil in a basket on his back south from Giantland, and there was this proof, that one of his toes had been sticking out of the basket and had got frozen, so Thor broke it off and threw it up in the sky and made out of it the star called Aurvandil's toe. Thor said it would not be long before Aurvandil was home, and Groa was so pleased that she could remember none of her spells, and the whetstone got no looser and is still stuck in Thor's head. And this is something that is taboo, throwing whetstones across a room, for then the whetstone in Thor's head stirs. Thiodolf of Hvinir has composed a passage based on this story in *Haustlong*. It says there:

Also can be seen on the circle [of the shield], O cave-fire-[gold-]tree [man], how the terror of giants [Thor] made a visit to the mound of Griotun. The son of Iord drove to the game of iron [battle] and the moon's way [sky] thundered beneath him. Wrath swelled in Meili's brother [Thor].

All the hawks' sanctuaries [skies] found themselves burning because of Ull's stepfather, and the ground all low was battered with hail, when the goats drew the temple-power [Thor] of the easy-chariot forward to the encounter with Hrungnir. Svolnir's widow [Iord, earth] practically split apart.

Baldr's brother [Thor] did not spare there the greedy enemy of men [Hrungnir]. Mountains shook and rocks smashed; heaven above burned. I have heard that the watcher [Hrungnir] of the dark bone [rock] of the land [sea] of Haki's carriages [ships] moved violently in opposition when he saw his warlike slayer.

Swiftly flew the pale ring-ice [shield] beneath the soles of the rock-guarder [giant]. The bonds [gods] caused this, the ladies of the fray [valkyries] wished it. The rock-gentleman [giant] did not have to wait long after that for a swift blow from the tough multitude-smashing friend [Thor] of hammer-face-troll [Miollnir].

The life-spoiler of Beli's bale-troops [giants] made the bear [giant] of the noisy storms' secret refuge [mountain fastnesses] fall on the shield-islet. There sank down the gully-land [mountain] prince [giant] before the tough hammer and the rock-Dane-breaker [Thor] forced back the mighty defiant one.

And the hard fragment of the whetstone of the visitor [giant] of the woman of Vingnir's people [the race of giants] whizzed at ground's [earth, Iord's] son into his brain-ridge, so that the steel-pumice [whetstone] still stuck in Odin's boy's skull, stood there spattered with Eindridi's [Thor's] blood.

Until ale-Gefiun [Groa] began to enchant the red boaster of being rust's bale [whetstone] from the inclined slopes of the wound-giving god's hair. Clearly I see these deeds on Geitir's fence [the shield]. I received the border's moving cliff [shield] decorated with horrors from Thorleif.

Then Ægir said: 'Hrungnir seems to me to have been very mighty. Did Thor achieve any greater exploit in his dealings with trolls?'

Then Bragi replied: 'The story of how Thor went to Geirrod's courts is worth detailed treatment. On that occasion he did not have the hammer Miollnir or the girdle of might or the iron gauntlets, and that was Loki's doing. He went with him, for it had befallen Loki, having gone flying once for fun with Frigg's falcon form, that out of curiosity he had flown into Geirrod's courts and saw there a great hall, and he alighted and looked in through the window. But Geirrod looked out at him and ordered that the bird should be caught and brought to him. The person sent got with difficulty up on to the wall of the hall, it was so high; Loki was pleased that it caused him trouble to get at him, and planned to delay flying up until the man had performed the whole of the difficult climb. But when the fellow came at him, he beat his wings and jumped hard upwards, and found his feet were stuck. Loki was captured there and brought to giant Geirrod. And when he saw his eyes, he had a feeling it must be a person and demanded that he answer him, but Loki remained silent. Then Geirrod locked Loki in a chest and starved him there for three months. And when Geirrod took him out and demanded that he speak, Loki said who he was, and to redeem his life he swore Geirrod oaths that he would get Thor to come to Geirrod's courts without his bringing either his hammer or girdle of might. Thor lodged for the night with a giantess called Grid. She was Vidar the silent's mother. She told Thor the truth about Geirrod, that he was a cunning giant and awkward to deal with. She lent him a girdle of might and some iron gauntlets of hers, and her staff, called Grid's pole. Then Thor approached the river called Vimur, greatest of all rivers. Then he buckled on the girdle of might and pressed down on Grid's pole on the side away from the current, while Loki held on beneath the girdle of might. And when Thor got to the middle of the river, the river rose so much that it washed up over his shoulders. Then Thor spoke this:

"Rise not thou now, Vimur, since I desire to wade thee into the giants' courts. Know thou that if thou risest then will rise the As-strength in me up as high as heaven."

'Then Thor saw up in a certain cleft that Geirrod's daughter Gialp was standing astride the river and she was causing it to rise. Then Thor took up out of the river a great stone and threw it at her and said:

' "At its outlet must a river be stemmed."

'He did not miss what he was aiming at, and at that moment he found himself close to the bank and managed to grasp a sort of rowan-bush and thus climbed out of the river. Hence comes the saying that Thor's salvation is a rowan. And when Thor got to Geirrod's, he and his companion were first of all shown into a goat-shed as their lodging, and inside there was a single seat to sit on and it was Thor who sat on it. Then he realized that the seat was lifting under him up towards the roof. He pushed Grid's pole up into the rafters and pressed himself hard down on the seat. Then there was a great crack accompanied by a great scream. Under the seat it had been Geirrod's daughters Gialp and Greip and he had broken both their backs. Then Geirrod had Thor called into the hall for games. There were great fires there along the length of the hall. And when Thor came into the hall opposite Geirrod, Geirrod picked up with tongs a glowing lump of molten iron and threw it at Thor, and with the iron gauntlets Thor caught and raised the molten lump into the air, while Geirrod ran to the shelter of an iron pillar for protection. Thor flung the molten lump and it crashed through the pillar and through Geirrod and through the wall and so into the ground outside.'

Eilif Gudrunarson has composed a passage based on this story in *Thorsdrapa*:

The sea-thread's [Midgard serpent's] father [Loki] set out to urge the feller [Thor] of flight-ledge-gods' [giants'] life-net from home. Lopt was proficient at lying. The not very trustworthy trier [Loki] of the mind of war-thunder-Gaut [Thor] said that green paths led to Geirrod's wall-steed [house].

The mind-tough Thor let vulture-way [air = *lopt*; Lopt is a name for Loki] urge him only a little time to go — they were eager to crush Thorn's kin [giants] — when Idi's yard-visitor [Thor], mightier than White Sea Scots [giants], set out once from Third's [Odin's, Asgard] to the seat of Ymsi's kind [Giantland].

Full of perjury, the cargo [Loki] of incantation-fetter's [Sigyn's] arms was on his way sooner with the company's leader than the battle-Rognir [Thialfi]. I recite Grimnir's [Odin's] lip-streams [mead of poetry]. The entrapper [Thor] of the shrill-crier-[eagle-]hall [mountain] Endil's [giant's] girls [troll-wives] made his sole-palms [feet] span the heath [walked].

And the ones accustomed to the course [battle] of the battle-wolf [sword] travelled; the heaven-targe-[sun-]dwelling's [sky's] blood [water] of the women [Gialp and Greip] of Frid's first defiler [giant] was reached [i.e. the river Vimur], when Loki's bale-averter [Thor], guilty of hastiness, wished, deed-unsparing, to open hostilities with the bride [Gialp] of rush-Grimnir's [giant's] kinsmen.

And the honour-lessener [Thor] of the wake-hilt-[rock-]Nanna [troll-wife] caused the swollen rivers, rolling with hail over the lynx's sea [mountains], to be foot-crossed. The violent scree-villain-[giant-]scatterer very much disturbed the broad staked-track-way [river] where mighty rivers spewed poison.

There they pushed shooting-snakes [spears] in the fish-trap

forest [river] against the talkative [noisy] fish-trap-forest wind [current]. The slippery wheel-knobs [stones] did not lie asleep. The clanging-file [ferrule] did bang on stones, and the mountains' falling-noise [river] rushed along, beaten by storm, with Fedia's anvil [rock].

The stone-land's [sword's] impeller [warrior, Thor], possessor of the strength-girdle, let the mightily-grown waters fall over him. One could have found no better course for oneself. The diminisher of Morn's children [giants] said his might would grow as high as the world's roof unless the violent Thorn's [Ymir's] neck blood [water] diminished.

The fine oath-bound Gaut's [Odin's] residence [Asgard] vikings [Æsir], battle-wise, waded hard while the sward-flowing fen [river] flowed. The earth-drift-[mountain-]wave [river] raged mightily, blown by stormy weather, at the ridge-land [mountain] room-[cave-]dwellers' [giants'] trouble-worsener [Thor].

Until Thialfi came flying on the shield-strap with the helper of men [Thor]; this was a mighty achievement for the heaven-king. Mischief-Mimir's [giant's] widows [Gialp and Greip] made the harsh current violent against the pole. The feller of the dolphins of the steeps [giants] advanced with violent temper with Grid's pole.

Their hostility-acorns [hearts] did not fail these people, firmly opposed to evil, at the wolf-home-league's [mountain's] deep-fall [river-gorge]. Atli [Thor] gained more battle-bold, relentless purpose. Neither Thor's nor Thialfi's valour-stone [heart] shook with fear.

And then the allied sword's help haters waged shield's hard-fetter-[strap-]board's [shield's] din [battle] against slope-Hords [giants], before the pool-riders [river-crossers, Thor and Thialfi], destroyers of the strand-people [giants], performed Hedin's parting-bowl-[helmet-]game [battle] with the cave's kindred-Briton [Geirrod].

The hostile troop [giants] of Sweden of frost [Scythia] scattered before the ness-court [giants] shatterer. The slab-court [giants] took to flight in terror when the kin of Iolnir's [Odin's] blaze-wielder [sword-wielder, warrior] stood firm;

the Danes [giants] of the distant flood-rib [rock] sanctuary [Giantland] had to bow before them.

Where the chieftains, filled with valorous purpose, went forward into the Thorn-[giant-]building, there was uproar among the Cumbrians [giants] of the cave's circular wall. The heaper of peak-Lister [mountain] reindeer [giants] was brought into dire straits on the hat of the wife of giants [Gialp's head]. That was a black disturbance of the peace.

And they pressed their eye-lash-moon-flame-[eye-]sky [skull] against the roof-battens of the stone-plain's [mountain's] hall [cave]. The females were trodden down by long swords. The driver [Thor] of the hull of the storm's hover-chariot broke each of the cave-women's age-old laughter-ship-[breast-]keels [backbones].

Iord's son began to display unusual knowledge [skill], and the men [giants] of the fiord-apple-[rock-]moor-lair [mountain cave] did not suppress their ale-joy. The bow-string-troubler [warrior, Geirrod], relative of Sudri, struck with forge-heated tongs-morsel [glowing lump of iron] at the mouth of Odin's sorrow-stealer [helper, Thor].

So that the speedy-hastener of battle [Thor], the old friend of Throng [Freyia], swallowed in the quick bite of his hands the raised drink of molten metal in the air, when the sparkling cinder flew furiously from the grip's breast [palm] of the passionate desirer [Geirrod] of Hrimnir's lady towards the one who longs for Thrud in his heart [Thor].

Thrasir's hall [giant's cave] shook when Heidrek's [giant's] broad head was brought under the old wall-leg [pillar] of the platform-bear [house]. Ull's splendid stepfather struck the hurting-pin [piece of iron] hard down in the middle of the belt of the fishing-line-way-[sea-]tooth [rock] villain [giant].

Extremely angry, he destroyed with bloody hammer Glaum's descendants [giants]. The beater [Thor] of the frequenter [giant] of hearth-stone-Syn's [giantess's] dwelling gained victory. No lack of support befell the double-wood-stave [bow-tree, warrior], the god of the wagon, who inflicted grief on the giant's bench-fellows.

Worshipped by multitudes, he who overcomes the calves [giants] of the secret cave of elf-world's shine [in the darkness of mountains] wielded the forest's handy fragment [Grid's pole] mightily. Nor could the Rugians of falcon-lair-Lister [mountain-giants] stand up to the trusty stone-Ella-[giant-]people's life-curtailer.

How shall Frigg be referred to? By calling her daughter of Fiorgyn, wife of Odin, mother of Baldr, rival of Iord and Rind and Gunnlod and Gerd, mother-in-law of Nanna, queen of Æsir and Asyniur, of Fulla and falcon form and Fensalir.

How shall Freyia be referred to? By calling her daughter of Niord, sister of Freyr, wife of Od, mother of Hnoss, possessor of the fallen slain and of Sessrumnir and tom-cats, of Brisingamen, Van-deity, Van-lady, fair-tear deity. All Asyniur can be referred to by naming the name of another one and referring to them by their possession or deeds or descent.

How shall Sif be referred to? By calling her wife of Thor, mother of Ull, the fair-haired deity, rival of Iarnsaxa, mother of Thrud.

How shall Idunn be referred to? By calling her wife of Bragi and keeper of the apples, and the apples the Æsir's old-age cure. She is also giant Thiassi's booty in accordance with the story told above about his abducting her from the Æsir. Thiodolf of Hvinir composed a passage based on that story in *Haustlong*:

How can I provide a repayment for the war-wall-bridge [shield]? <I received a well-decorated . . .> voice-cliff [shield] from Thorleif. I can see the uncertain situation of three god-bold dieties and Thiassi on the brightly-finished side of the battle-sheet [shield].

The lady-wolf [Thiassi] flew noisily to meet the commanders of the crew [the Æsir] no short time ago in an old old-one's [eagle's] form. Long ago the eagle alighted where the Æsir put their meat in an earth-oven. The rock-Gefn-[giantess-]refuge-[cave-]god [giant] was not found guilty of cowardice.

Middlingly free of deceit, he was a slow provider of service to the gods. The helmet-capped educator [Odin] of the fetters [gods] declared there was something behind it. The much-wise corpse-heap-wave-[blood-]gull [eagle] began to speak from an ancient fir. Hænir's friend [Loki] was not well disposed to him.

The mountain-wolf [giant] asked step-Meili [Hænir] to share out to him his fill from the holy table. The raven-god's [Odin's] friend [Loki] had to blow [the fire]. The battle-bold Rognir [Odin, i.e. chief] of land-whales [giants] let himself drop down where the guileless defenders of gods were sitting.

The gracious lord of earth [Odin] bade Farbauti's son [Loki] quickly share the bow-string-Var's [Skadi's] whale [ox] among the fellows. But the cunning unyielding opponent of Æsir thereupon snatched up from the broad table four ox-parts.

And Morn's hungry father [the giant] was then eating horribly the yoke-bear [ox] at the roots of an oak — that was long ago — until the deep-minded war-booty-withholding god struck the most terrible enemy of earth [giant] down between the shoulders with a pole.

Then the burden of Sigyn's arms [Loki], whom all the powers eye in his bonds, got stuck to the ski-deity's [Skadi's] fosterer [father, Thiassi]. The pole clung to the mighty haunter of Giantland and the hands of Hænir's good friend [Loki] to the end of the rod.

The bird of blood [eagle], happy with its booty, flew a long distance with the wise god, so that the wolf's father [Loki] was about to rip in two. Then Thor's friend — heavy Lopt [Loki] had collapsed — was forced to beg Midiung's mate [the giant] as hard as he could for quarter.

The scion of Hymir's race [giants] instructed the crew-guider, crazy with pain, to bring to him the maid who knew the Æsir's old-age cure [Idunn]. The thief of Brising's girdle [Brisingamen] afterwards caused the gods' lady [Idunn] to go into the rock-Nidud's [giant's] courts to Brunnakr's bench.

The bright-shield-dwellers [giants] were not unhappy after

this, now Idunn was among the giants, newly arrived from the south. All Ingi-Freyr's kin [Æsir] became old and grey in their assembly; the powers were rather ugly in form,

— until they found ale-Gefn's [Idunn's] flowing corpse-sea [blood] hound [wolf, thief, i.e. Loki] and bound the thief, that tree of deceit, who had led ale-Gefn off. 'You shall be trapped, Loki,' the angry one spoke thus, 'unless by some scheme you bring back the renowned maid, enlarger of the fetters' [gods'] joy.'

I have heard this, that the trier of Hænir's mind [Loki] afterwards tricked back the Æsir's girl-friend with the help of a hawk's flight-skin; and with deceitful mind Morn's father [the giant], energetic power of feather-blade-play [wing-beating], directed a storm-wind against the hawk's offspring [Loki in eagle form].

Shafts soon began to burn, for the great powers [gods] had shaved them; and the son of Greip's wooer [a giant] is scorched. There is a sudden swerve in his travel. This is depicted on my mountain-Finn's [giant's, Hrungnir's] sole-bridge [pedestal, shield]. I received the border's moving cliff [shield] decorated with horrors from Thorleif.

It is also normal to refer to Æsir by calling one by the name of another and referring to him by his deeds or possession or descent.

How shall the sky be referred to? By calling it Ymir's skull and hence giant's skull and toil or burden of the dwarfs or helmet of Vestri and Austri, Sudri, Nordri, land of sun and moon and stars, constellations and winds, helmet or house of air and earth and sun. Arnor the earls' poet said this:

Never will as generous a young ruler step on to shield-plank [ship] — this prince's magnificence was ample — under Ymir's old skull.

And as he also said:

The bright sun will become a black one, earth will sink into dark sea, Austri's toil will split, all the sea will crash on the fells.

And also as Kolli said:

> Never any battle-keen land-ruler beneath the sun's ground
> will be more excellent or better than Ingi's brother.

And as Thiodolf of Hvinir said:

> Iord's son drove to iron-game [battle], and the moon's way
> thundered under him. Meili's brother's rage swelled.

As Orm Barreyiarskald said:

> However mighty, goddess of Draupnir's band [lady], I learn
> the lord is — he rules his realm — the ruler of the constel-
> lation's path will welcome me.

As the poet Bragi said:

> He who threw into the wide winds' basin the ski-goddess's
> [Skadi's] father's eyes above the dwellings of the multitude
> of men.

And as Markus said:

> It is beyond expectation that there could be born a nobler
> defender of seafarers on the ocean-bounded storm-vat's
> [sky's] base [earth]. Each man praises the ring-thrower's
> [generous ruler's] elevated life.

As Stein Herdisarson said:

> I greet the holy ruler of the world's high tent [sky] with this
> poetry — praise is brought forth — rather than men, for he
> is more worthy.

And as Arnor the earls' poet said:

> Save, O thou dear king of day's base [sky], the dear Her-
> mund.

And as Arnor also said:

True ruler of sun's tents [sky], save brave Rognvald.

And as Hallvard said:

Knut protects the land as the lord of all [defends] the splendid hall of the mountains [sky].

As Arnor said:

Michael, full of wisdom, weighs what seems misdone and all the good. The ruler of sun's helmet [sky] on his judgment seat then divides men up.

How shall earth be referred to? By calling it Ymir's flesh and mother of Thor, daughter of Onar, bride of Odin, rival of Frigg and Rind and Gunnlod, mother-in-law of Sif, floor and base of winds' hall, sea of the animals, daughter of Night, sister of Aud and Day. As Eyvind Skaldaspillir said:

Now the river's elf-disc [sun of river = gold] is hidden in the body of giants' enemy's [Thor's] mother [Iord, earth]. Mighty are the undertakings of a powerful people.

As Hallfrod the troublesome poet said:

The match was later consummated by which that wise-ruling king's crony [the earl] married [gained possession of] the tree-grown only daughter of Onar [Iord, earth, the country of Norway].

And he also said:

The guider [earl] of harbour-horses [ships] managed to draw to himself Baleyg's [Odin's] broad-faced bride [Iord, earth, Norway] by the politics of steel [battle].

Compare the verse written above, 'It is beyond expectation that there could be born . . .'. As Thiodolf said:

The gladdener of lords [king] fastens men's vessels around elk-sea's [land's] edge on the pure ocean's hull-rowed bay.

As Hallfrod said:

> So I think the famed distributor [ruler] — land comes under
> necklet-diminisher [generous ruler] — very reluctant to
> leave Aud's splendid sister alone.

Thiodolf said this:

> The spear-shy [unwarlike] wretch kept far off when the
> battle-gleam-[sword-]impeller [warrior, ruler] once took
> Rind's rival [Iord, the land] without bride-price [by vio-
> lence].

How shall sea be referred to? By calling it Ymir's blood, visitor
to the gods, husband of Ran, father of Ægir's daughters, whose
names are Himinglæva, Dufa, Blodughadda, Hefring, Unn,
Hronn, Bylgia, Bara, Kolga; land of Ran and of Ægir's daughters
and of ships and of terms for sea-ship, of keel, stem, planks,
strake, of fish, ice; sea-kings' way and roads, no less ring of the
islands, house of the sands and seaweed and skerries, land of
fishing-tackle and of sea-birds, of sailing wind. As Orm Bar-
reyiarskald said:

> Out on the sand-bank of good vessels Ymir's blood roars.

Ref said this:

> The tame mast-top-beast [ship] bears wave-pressed shoul-
> ders eastwards over the sea — I expect land over the prow
> — the whale-roof-ridge [wave] sprays.

As Svein said:

> When hard gusts from white mountain-range teased apart
> and wove together the storm-happy daughters of Ægir,
> bred on frost.

And as Ref said:

> Gymir's spray-cold spae-wife often brings the twisted-rope-
> bear [ship] into Ægir's jaws [under the waves] where the
> wave breaks.

Here it is implied that they are all the same, Ægir and Hler and Gymir. And he also said:

> But sea-crest-Sleipnir [ship], spray-driven, tears his breast, covered with red paint, out of white Ran's mouth [the sea's grasp].

As Einar Skulason said:

> A hard storm-wind has driven the ship fast from land. The swan-bank-steed [ship] makes snow-ground [Iceland] sink in surf [beneath the horizon].

And as he also said:

> Many a firm rowlock lifts and the fishing-tackle's sounding strand [sea] drives into bends in the land. Stays are sometimes made tight by men's grasps.

And he also said:

> The stems of the king's warships have golden ornaments. This expedition is glorious for the prince. The island-fetter [sea] pushes forward Heiti's horse [the ship].

As he also said:

> Autumn-cold holm-circle [sea] impels frosted wake-ski [ship].

And also:

> Cool lands' roaring belt [sea] springs aside before the prows.

As Snæbiorn said:

> They say the nine skerry-brides [Ægir's daughters, waves] turn fast the most hostile island-box-mill [churning sea] out beyond the land's edge, they who long ago ground Hamlet's meal-ship [Hamlet's mill = sea]. The ring-damager [generous ruler] cuts with ship's prow the dwelling [sea] of the ships' slopes [waves].

Here the sea is called Hamlet's mill. As Einar Skulason also said:

> The firm-driven nail flexes in the driving current where
> Rakni's moving ground [sea] whitens. Sail's enemy [wind]
> pushes reefs against stay.

How shall the sun be referred to? By calling it daughter of
Mundilfæri, sister of Moon, wife of Glen, fire of sky and air. As
Skuli Thorsteinsson said:

> God-blithe bedfellow of Glen steps to her divine sanctuary
> with brightness; then descends the good light of grey-clad
> moon.

Einar Skulason said this:

> Wherever the world's hall's [sky's] high wandering flame
> [sun] hovers above our precious friend, most cruel to the
> flame [gold] of Beiti's stronghold [sea; cruel to gold =
> generous].

How shall wind be referred to? By calling it son of Forniot,
brother of Ægir and of fire, breaker of tree, harmer and slayer or
dog or wolf of tree or sail or rigging. In *Nordrsetudrapa* Svein said
this:

> Forniot's ugly sons began first to send snow.

How shall fire be referred to? By calling it brother of wind and
of Ægir, slayer and damager of tree and houses, Half's killer, sun
of the houses.

How shall winter be referred to? By calling it son of Vindsval
and snakes' death, storm-season. Orm Steinthorsson said this:

> I shall devise joy for the blind man this Vindsval's son.

Asgrim said this:

> The gold-generous battle-promoter was then that snake
> woe [winter] in Thrandheim. The world knows your true
> achievements.

How shall summer be referred to? By calling it son of Svasud and comfort of the snakes, growth of men. As Egil Skallagrimsson said:

> Stainer of wolf's teeth [with blood, i.e. warrior], we shall
> wave our swords in the sun, we have something to achieve
> in the valley-fish's [snakes'] mercy [summer].

How shall a man be referred to? He shall be referred to by his actions, what he gives or receives or does. He can also be referred to by his property, what he owns and also if he gives it away; also by the family lines he is descended from, also those that have descended from him. How shall he be referred to by these things? By calling him achiever or performer of his expeditions or activities, of killings or voyages or huntings, or with weapons or ships. And because he is a trier (*reynir*) of the weapons and doer (*vidr*) of the killings, which is the same thing as achiever – *vidr* is also a word for tree, there is a tree called *reynir* [rowan] – on the basis of these terms poets have called men ash or maple, *lund* [grove, tree] or other masculine tree-names, and made reference to killings or ships or wealth. It is also normal to refer to a man using all the names of Æsir. Names of giants are also used, and this is mostly as satire or criticism. Using names of elves is thought complimentary. A woman shall be referred to by all female adornment, gold and jewels, ale or wine or other drink that she serves or gives, also by ale-vessels and by all those things that it is proper for her to do or provide. It is proper to refer to her by calling her dealer (*selia*) or consumer (*lóg*) of what she hands out, but *selia* [willow] and log are trees. Hence woman is called in kennings by all feminine tree-names. And the reason a woman is referred to by gemstones or beads is that there was in antiquity a female adornment that was called 'stone-chain' that they wore round their necks. Now it is made into a kenning, so that woman is now referred to in terms of stone and all words for stone. Woman is also referred to in terms of all Asyniur or valkyries or norns or *disir* [(divine) ladies]. It is also normal to refer to a woman by any of her activities or by her possession or descent.

How shall gold be referred to? By calling it Ægir's fire and Glasir's foliage, Sif's hair, Fulla's snood, Freyia's weeping, mouth-count and voice and words of giants, dripping from Draupnir and rain or shower from Draupnir or from Freyia's eyes, otter-payment, Æsir's forced payment, seed of Fyri plains, Holgi's mound-roof, fire of all kinds of waters and of the arm, stones and rocks or gleam of the arm.

Why is gold called Ægir's fire? The origin of it is this story: Ægir, as was told before, went as a guest to Asgard, and when he was about to return home, he invited Odin and all the Æsir to visit him after an interval of three months. Undertaking this journey were first of all Odin and Niord, Freyr, Tyr, Bragi, Vidar, Loki, and then Asyniur, Frigg, Freyia, Gefiun, Skadi, Idunn, Sif. Thor was not there; he was away in eastern parts killing trolls. And when the gods had taken their places, Ægir had glowing gold brought into the middle of the hall which illuminated and lit up the hall like fire, and this was used as lights at his feast just as in Val-hall there had been swords instead of fire. Then Loki wrangled with all the gods there and killed a slave of Ægir's called Fimafeng. The name of another of his slaves is Eldir. Ran is the name of Ægir's wife, and the names of their nine daughters are as was written above. At this feast everything served itself, both food and ale and all the utensils that were needed for the feast. Then the Æsir discovered that Ran had a net in which she caught everyone that went to sea. So this is the story of the origin of gold being called fire or light or brightness of Ægir, Ran or Ægir's daughters, and from such kennings the practice has now developed of calling gold fire of the sea and of all terms for it, since Ægir and Ran's names are also terms for sea, and hence gold is now called fire of lakes or rivers and of all river-names. But it has happened with these terms and kennings as with others, that the more recent poets have composed in imitation of the ancient poets, as things were in their poems, and then extended into areas that they thought similar to what had earlier been included in poetry, as lake is to sea, and river to lake, and stream to river. This is therefore called allegory when terminology is extended further in meaning than there are earlier examples of, and this is all considered acceptable when it is in accordance with probability and the nature of things. Thus the poet Bragi said:

> I got from the prince fire of mackerel's seat [sea] for mountain-Fiolnir's [giant's] drink [mead of poetry]; the ruler gave it me with a cup.

Why is gold called Glasir's foliage or leaves? In Asgard in front of the doors of Val-hall there stands a tree called Glasir, and all its foliage is red gold, as in this verse where it says that

Glasir stands with golden leaf before Sigtyr's [Odin's] halls.

That is the most beautiful tree among gods and men.

Why is gold called Sif's hair? Loki Laufeyiarson had done this for love of mischief: he had cut off all Sif's hair. And when Thor found out, he caught Loki and was going to break every one of his bones until he swore that he would get black-elves to make Sif a head of hair out of gold that would grow like any other hair. After this Loki went to some dwarfs called Ivaldi's sons, and they made the head of hair and Skidbladnir and the spear belonging to Odin called Gungnir. Then Loki wagered his head with a dwarf called Brokk on whether his brother Eitri would succeed in making three precious things as good as these were. And when they got to the workshop, Eitri put a pig's hide in the forge and told Brokk to blow and not stop until he took out of the forge what he had put in. And as soon as he left the workshop and the other was blowing, a fly settled on the latter's arm and nibbled, but he went on blowing as before until the smith took his work out of the forge, and it was a boar and its bristles were of gold. Next he put gold into the forge and told Brokk to blow and not stop the blowing before he came back; he went out. And then the fly came and settled on his neck and nibbled twice as hard, but he went on blowing until the smith took from the forge a gold ring called Draupnir. Then he put iron in the forge and told him to blow and said it would turn out no good if there was any pause in the blowing. Then the fly settled between his eyes and nibbled his eyelids, and when the blood dripped in his eyes so that he could not see, he snatched at it with his hand as quick as he could while the bellows was on its way down and swept the fly away. And then the smith came back, saying it had come close to everything in the forge being ruined. Then he took from the forge a hammer, then handed over all the precious things to his brother Brokk and told him to take them to Asgard and fulfil the wager. And when he and Loki produced the precious things, the Æsir took their places on their judgment seats and the decision uttered by Odin, Thor,

Freyr was to be final. Then Loki gave the spear Gungnir to Odin, the head of hair which was to be Sif's to Thor, and Skidbladnir to Freyr, and announced the features of all the precious things, that the spear never stopped in its thrust, the hair was rooted in the flesh as soon as it came on to Sif's head, and Skidbladnir had a fair wind as soon as its sail was hoisted, wherever it was intended to go, and could be folded up like a cloth and put in one's pocket if desired. Then Brokk brought out his precious things. He gave the ring to Odin and said that every ninth night there would drip from it eight rings equal to it in weight. To Freyr he gave the boar and said that it could run across sky and sea by night and day faster than any horse, and it never got so dark from night or in worlds of darkness that it was not bright enough wherever it went, there was so much light shed from its bristles. Then he gave Thor the hammer and said he would be able to strike as heavily as he liked, whatever the target, and the hammer would not fail, and if he threw it at something, it would never miss, and never fly so far that it would not find its way back to his hand, and if he liked, it was so small that it could be kept inside his shirt. But there was this defect in it that the end of the handle was rather short. Their decision was that the hammer was the best out of all the precious things and provided the greatest defence against frost-giants, and they decreed that the dwarf had won the stake. Then Loki offered to redeem his head; the dwarf said there was no chance of that.

'Catch me, then,' said Loki.

But when Brokk tried to catch him, he was far out of reach. Loki had some shoes with which he could run across sky and sea. Then the dwarf told Thor to catch him, and he did so. Then the dwarf was going to cut off Loki's head, but Loki said that the head was his but not the neck. Then the dwarf got a thong and a knife and tried to pierce holes in Loki's lips and was going to stitch up his mouth, but the knife would not cut. Then he said it would be better if his brother Awl was there, and as soon as he spoke his name the awl was there, and it pierced the lips. He stitched the lips together, and it tore the edges off. The thong that Loki's mouth was stitched up with is called Vartari.

Here you can hear how gold is referred to in terms of Fulla's snood, in this poem by Eyvind Skaldaspillir:

The falling sun [gold] of the plain [forehead] of Fulla's eyelashes shone on the poets' Ull's boat-[shield-]fells [arms] throughout the life of Hakon.

Gold is called Freyia's weeping, as was said above. Skuli Thorsteinsson said this:

Many a death-flame-[sword-]damage-[battle-]challenger [warrior] got the more Freyia's tears in the morning where we felled each other. We were there.

And as Einar Skulason said:

With Mardoll's [Freyia's] weeping lying between the grooves [inlaid] we carry the damager [axe] of Gaut's [Odin's] mighty gate [shield], bulging with valley-trout's [serpent's] lair [gold, on which serpents lie].

And in this poem Einar has further referred to Freyia by calling her Hnoss's mother or Od's wife; thus it says here:

The strong ice [axe] of Rodi's roof [shield] is not the worse for Od's bedfellow's [Freyia's] eye-rain [tears]. With such actions [gifts] may the king reach old age.

And also:

I am able to possess Horn's [Freyia's] gold-wrapped glorious child [Hnoss; *hnoss* = treasure]. We received a valuable treasure. Ocean's fire [gold] rests on shield's damager [axe]. Freyr's niece [Hnoss] bears her mother's eyelash-rain [tears]. Battle-swan's [raven's] feeder [warrior] granted me Frodi's servants' [Fenia and Menia's] seed [gold].

Here it is also implied that Freyia can be referred to by calling her Freyr's sister. And also:

The ruler's helpful protection was all offered to me. This was close to the sea-hall. I praise highly this child of Niord's daughter [Hnoss].

Here she is called Niord's daughter. And also:

> The battle-gallant urger [warrior] of Vafud's [Odin's]
> assembly [battle] who achieves doughtiness gave me a
> mighty Van-bride's [Freyia's] daughter [Hnoss]. The
> powerful controller of sword-meetings [battles] led Gefn's
> [Freyia's] maid to the poet's [my] bed covered with Gaut-
> rek's swans' [ships'] road [sea] embers [fire, gold].

Here she is called Gefn and Van-bride. It is normal to qualify
weeping by any of the names for Freyia, and to call gold that, and
these kennings are varied in many ways, calling it hail or rain or
storm or drops or showers or cascades of her eyes or cheeks or
jowls or eyelashes or eyelids.

Here is an example of gold being called words or voice of
giants, as it was said above it could be; the poet Bragi said this:

> I had a third friend, blameless, who was hardest to the voice
> of sea-bed-globe-[rock-]Ali [giant; harshness to gold is
> generosity], but kindest to me.

He has referred to rock as sea-bed-globe, a giant as rock-Ali, and
gold as giant's voice.

What is the reason for gold being called otter-payment? It is
said that when the Æsir went to explore the whole world – Odin
and Loki and Hænir – they came to a certain river and went along
the river to a certain waterfall, and by the waterfall there was an
otter and it had caught a salmon in the waterfall and was eating it
with eyes half-closed. Then Loki picked up a stone and threw it at
the otter and hit its head. Then Loki was triumphant at his catch,
that he had got in one blow otter and salmon. Then they picked up
the salmon and the otter and took them with them, then came to a
certain farm and went in. The farmer that lived there was called
Hreidmar. He was a person of great power and was skilled in magic.
The Æsir asked if they could have a night's lodging there and said
they had plenty of provisions with them and showed the farmer
their catch. And when Hreidmar saw the otter, he called his sons
Fafnir and Regin and said their brother Otter had been killed and
also who had done it. Now the family went up to the Æsir, and
took them prisoner and bound them, and then revealed about the
otter, that he was Hreidmar's son. The Æsir offered a ransom for
their lives, as much wealth as Hreidmar himself wished to decide,

and these terms were agreed between them and confirmed with oaths. Then the otter was skinned. Hreidmar took the otter-skin and announced to them that they were to fill the skin with red gold and then cover it entirely, and these were to be the terms of their settlement. Then Odin sent Loki into the world of black-elves and he came across a dwarf called Andvari. He was a fish in a lake, and Loki captured him and imposed on him as a ransom all the gold he had in his cave. And when they came into the cave the dwarf brought out all the gold he had, and that was a substantial amount of wealth. Then the dwarf slipped under his arm one small gold ring. But Loki saw and told him to hand over the ring. The dwarf asked him not to take the ring from him, saying he could multiply wealth for himself from the ring if he kept it. Loki said the dwarf was not going to keep one penny and took the ring from him and went out, and the dwarf pronounced that this ring should be the deadly destruction of whoever possessed it. Loki said that he was happy for that to be so, and that it would have power to remain valid, this pronouncement, inasmuch as he would bring it to the ears of those who took possession of the ring. He went off back to Hreidmar's and showed Odin the gold. And when Odin saw the ring he found it beautiful and removed it from the treasure, and started paying Hreidmar the gold. The latter then filled the otter-skin as tightly as he could and stood it up when it was full. Then Odin went up to it and began covering the skin with the gold. Then he told Hreidmar to see whether the skin was now fully covered, and Hreidmar looked and examined closely and saw one whisker and said it must be covered, otherwise it was the end of any agreement between them. Then Odin took out the ring and covered the whisker and declared that they were now quit of the otter-payment. And when Odin had taken his spear and Loki his shoes and they had no need to have any more fear, then Loki pronounced that it should remain valid, what Andvari had pronounced, that the ring and the gold should be the death of him who possessed it, and this was subsequently fulfilled. Now it has been told why gold is called otter-payment or the Æsir's forced payment or strife-metal.

What more is there to tell about the gold? Hreidmar then took the gold as atonement for his son, and Fafnir and Regin demanded something of it for themselves in atonement for their brother.

Hreidmar would not let them have a single penny of the gold. The brothers then undertook this terrible course of action that they killed their father for the gold. Then Regin demanded that Fafnir should divide the gold equally between them. Fafnir replied that there was little likelihood of his sharing the gold with his brother when he had killed his father for the gold, and told Regin to be off, otherwise he would meet the same fate as Hreidmar. Fafnir had now got hold of a helmet that had belonged to Hreidmar, and put it on his head – it was known as *ægis*-helm [terror-helmet], and all creatures are afraid of it when they see it – and a sword called Hrotti. Regin had a sword called Refil. Then he fled away, but Fafnir went up on to Gnita-heath and made himself a lair there and turned into the form of a serpent and lay down on the gold.

Regin then went to King Hialprek's in Thiod and became craftsman to him. Then he took into fosterage Sigurd, son of Sigmund son of Volsung, and son of Hiordis daughter of Eylimi. Sigurd was the most splendid of all war-kings in descent and strength and courage. Regin told him about where Fafnir was lying on the gold and incited him to go and try and get the gold. Then Regin made a sword called Gram, which was so sharp that when Sigurd put it down in running water, it cut in two a tuft of wool that drifted with the current against the sword's edge. Next Sigurd split Regin's anvil down to its base with the sword. After that Sigurd and Regin went on to Gnita-heath. Then Sigurd dug a trench in Fafnir's path and got into it, and when Fafnir crawled down to the water and he passed over the trench, Sigurd thrust the sword through him, and this killed him. Then Regin came up and told him he had killed his brother, and said he was willing to accept from him in atonement that he should take Fafnir's heart and roast it on a fire, and Regin lay down and drank Fafnir's blood and lay down to sleep. But when Sigurd was roasting the heart and he thought it must be done, he tried with his finger how tough it was. And when the juice ran out of the heart on to his finger, he was scalded and put his finger in his mouth. And when the heart's blood touched his tongue, he found he knew a bird's speech, and understood what the tits sitting in the tree were saying. One of them said:

'There sits Sigurd, spattered with blood, Fafnir's heart at the

fire he roasts, wise I would consider the ring-spoiler [gener-
ous man] if he ate the shining life-steak [heart].'

'There lies Regin,' said another, 'planning with himself,
intending to trick the boy who trusts him. In his wrath he
composes crooked speeches. The maker of mischiefs in-
tends to avenge his brother.'

Then Sigurd went up to Regin and killed him, and then to his
horse, whose name was Grani, and rode it until he came to
Fafnir's lair. Then he picked up the gold and tied it in packs and
put them up on Grani's back, and climbed on himself and rode on
his way. Now the story has been told that is the origin of gold
being called lair or abode of Fafnir or metal of Gnita-heath or
burden of Grani.

Then Sigurd rode on until he came across a building on the
mountain. In it a woman was sleeping and she was wearing
helmet and mail-coat. He drew his sword and cut the mail-coat
[brynie] off her. Then she awoke and said her name was Hild. She
is known as Brynhild, and was a valkyrie. Sigurd rode on and
came to a king called Giuki. His wife's name was Grimhild.
Gunnar, Hogni, Gudrun, Gudny were their children. Gothorm
was Giuki's stepson. Sigurd stayed there a long time. Then he
married Giuki's daughter Gudrun, and Gunnar and Hogni swore
oaths of brotherhood with Sigurd. After that Sigurd and the sons
of Giuki went to Atli Budlason to ask for his sister Brynhild as
wife for Gunnar. She was living on Hindafell and around her hall
was a flickering flame, and she had made a vow to wed only that
man who dared to ride the flickering flame. Then Sigurd and the
Giukungs – they are also known as Niflungs – rode up on to the
mountain, and Gunnar then tried to ride the flickering flame. His
horse was called Goti, but this horse dared not gallop into the fire.
Then they exchanged forms, Sigurd and Gunnar, and also names,
since Grani would move under no man but Sigurd. Then Sigurd
leapt up on to Grani and rode the flickering flame. That evening
he entered into marriage with Brynhild. But when they got into
bed, he drew his sword Gram from its sheath and laid it between
them. And in the morning when he got up and dressed, he gave
Brynhild as morning gift the gold ring that Loki had taken from
Andvari, and received from her another ring as keepsake. Sigurd

then leapt on his horse and rode to his companions. He and Gunnar then changed back their forms and they returned to Giuki with Brynhild. Sigurd had two children with Gudrun: Sigmund and Svanhild.

It happened on one occasion that Brynhild and Gudrun went down to the water to bleach their hair. When they got to the river, Brynhild waded out into the river away from the bank and said she did not want to pour over her head the water that ran out of Gudrun's hair, since she had the more valiant husband. Then Gudrun followed her out into the river, saying it was her right to wash her hair in the river higher up, since she was married to a man whom neither Gunnar nor anyone else in the world was as brave as, for he had killed Fafnir and Regin and succeeded to the wealth of both. Then Brynhild replied:

'It was a greater achievement for Gunnar to have ridden the flickering flame when Sigurd did not dare.'

Then Gudrun laughed and said:

'Do you reckon it was Gunnar that rode the flickering flame? I reckon that the one that went to bed with you was the one that gave me this gold ring, and that gold ring that you are wearing and that you received as morning gift, that is known as Andvari's gift, and I reckon it was not Gunnar that won it on Gnita-heath.'

Then Brynhild was silent and went home. After this she incited Gunnar and Hogni to kill Sigurd, but because they had sworn oaths to Sigurd, they incited their brother Gothorm to kill Sigurd. He stabbed Sigurd through with a sword while he was asleep, but when Sigurd received the wound he threw his sword Gram after Gothorm so that it severed the man in two in the middle. There fell Sigurd and his three-year-old son called Sigmund, whom they killed. After this Brynhild stabbed herself with a sword and she was burned with Sigurd, while Gunnar and Hogni took over Fafnir's legacy and Andvari's gift and went on ruling their lands.

King Atli Budlason, Brynhild's brother, then married Gudrun, formerly Sigurd's wife, and they had children. King Atli invited Gunnar and Hogni to visit him, and they complied with the invitation. But before they left home they hid the gold, Fafnir's legacy, in the Rhine, and this gold has never again been found. But King Atli met them with an armed force and fought Gunnar and Hogni and they were captured. King Atli had Hogni's heart cut out while he was alive. This brought about his death. He had Gunnar thrown into a snake-pit, but he was secretly provided with a harp, and he plucked it with his toes, as his hands were tied. He played the harp in such a way that all the snakes went to sleep except for the one adder that darted at him and struck at the bottom of his breastbone, burying its head in the hollow and hanging on to his liver until he died. Gunnar and Hogni are known as Niflungs and Giukungs; hence gold is called Niflungs' treasure or inheritance.

Soon afterwards Gudrun killed her two sons and had goblets made out of their skulls with silver and gold. Then a funeral was held for the Niflungs. At this feast Gudrun had mead served to King Atli in these goblets, and it was mixed with the boys' blood, and she had their hearts cooked and given to the king to eat. And when this had been done, she told him of it to his face with many unsavoury words. There was no shortage there of strong mead, so that nearly everyone fell asleep where they sat. That night she went to the king as he slept, and with her Hogni's son, and attacked him. He died as a result. Then they set fire to the hall and the people inside were burned up. After this she went down to the sea and leapt into the sea and tried to destroy herself, but she drifted across the fiord and found herself in the land ruled over by King Ionakr. And when he saw her he took her in and married her. They had three sons called Sorli, Hamdir, Erp. They all had hair black as a raven in colour like Gunnar and Hogni and other Niflungs. Boy Sigurd's daughter Svanhild was brought up there. She was the most beautiful of all women. King Iormunrekk the Great heard of this. He sent his son Randver to ask for her hand on his behalf. And when he got to Ionakr's, Svanhild was handed over to him. He was to take her to Iormunrekk. Then Bikki said it was more suitable for Randver to marry Svanhild, since he was young, as they both were, whereas Iormunrekk was old. The young people took well to this suggestion. Next Bikki told the king about this. Then King Iormunrekk had his son taken and led to the gallows. Then Randver got his hawk and plucked off the feathers and asked for it to be sent to his father. Then he was hanged. And when King Iormunrekk saw the hawk, it struck him that just as the hawk was unable to fly and lacked feathers, so his kingdom was disabled, he being old and having no son. Then King

Iormunrekk brought this about, as he was riding from the forest after hunting with his men, and Queen Svanhild was sitting bleaching her hair: then they rode over her and trod her to death under their horses' hooves. And when Gudrun learned of this, she incited her sons to vengeance for Svanhild. And as they were preparing to set out, she provided them with mail-coats and helmets that were so strong that iron could not penetrate them. She told them what they were to do when they got to King Iormunrekk's, that they were to attack him at night while he was asleep. Sorli and Hamdir were to cut off his arms and legs, and Erp his head. But after they had started off, they asked Erp what assistance they could expect from him if they got to King Iormunrekk. He replied that he would give them the help that an arm gives a leg. They said there was no way at all that a leg could be supported by an arm. They were so angry with their mother for having sent them on their way with spiteful words, they wanted to do what would hurt her most, and they killed Erp, because she loved him most. Shortly afterwards, as Sorli was walking, he slipped with one leg and supported himself with his arm. Then he said:

'Now the arm has helped the leg. It would have been better now if Erp had remained alive.'

And when they got to King Iormunrekk's at night, while he was asleep, and cut off his arms and legs, then he awoke and called to his men, telling them to wake up. Then said Hamdir:

'The head would have been off by now, if Erp had been alive.'

Then the king's men got up and attacked them and found they could not overcome them with weapons. Then Iormunrekk shouted that they must be stoned. This was done. They fell there, Sorli and Hamdir. Thus the whole family and progeny of Giuki were now dead.

There survived boy Sigurd a daughter called Aslaug who was brought up at the home of Heimir in Hlymdales, and from her important family lines are descended.

They say that Sigmund Volsungsson was so tough that he could drink poison and not be harmed, while his son Sinfiotli and Sigurd had such hard skins that poison did not harm them if it got on to their bare flesh. Thus the poet Bragi has used the following expression in his poetry:

When on the hook of the old Lit's men's [giants'] fight-challenger [Thor] hung the coiling eel [Midgard serpent] of the Volsungs' drink [poison] coiled.

Most poets have composed poetry based on these stories and have used various elements in them. Bragi the Old composed verses about the fall of Sorli and Hamdir in the *drápa* [sequence with refrain] he composed about Ragnar Lodbrok:

And then Iormunrekk did wake with an unpleasant dream in a torrent of swords among blood-stained troops. There was uproar in Randver's chief kinsman's [Iormunrekk's] hall when Erp's raven-black brothers avenged their injuries.

Corpse-dew [blood] flowed over the benches together with the attack-elf's [warrior's, Iormunrekk's] blood on the floor where severed arms and legs could be recognized. Men's ale-giver [king] fell head-first into the pool mixed with gore. This is depicted on leaf of Leifi's lands [sea; the sea's leaf is the decorated shield].

There, so that they made a circle round the ruler's floor-horse-[house-]tub [bed], the rivet-lacking sword-sail [shield] masts [warriors] stand. Very soon Hamdir and Sorli came to be struck by everyone at once with Hergaut's [Odin's] woman-friend's [Iord's, earth's] hard shoulder-lumps [stones].

The steel-torrent-[battle-]impeller [king] caused Giuki's descendants to be hit hard when they tried to deprive Bird-hild's [Swan-hild's, Svanhild's] delight [husband] of life. And they all managed to repay Ionakr's sons for the brightly shining forehead-blows coming from dark-shirt's [mail-coat's] birch [warrior] and his sword-edge.

I can see this fall of warriors on the fair base of the shield. Ragnar gave me the Ræ's chariot [ship] moon [shield] and a multitude of stories with it.

Why is gold called Frodi's meal? The origin of that is this story, that there was a son of Odin called Skiold, from whom the Skioldungs are descended. His residence and the lands he ruled over were in what is now called Denmark, but was then known as Gotland. Skiold had a son called Fridleif who ruled the territory after him. Fridleif's son's name was Frodi. He succeeded to his father's kingdom in the period when the emperor Augustus established peace over all the world. It was then that Christ was born. But because Frodi was the greatest of all the kings in northern countries, the peace was attributed to him throughout all Scandinavia, and Scandinavians call it Frodi's peace. No one harmed anyone else, even if he came upon his father's killer or his brother's killer, whether free or bound. Also at that time there were no thieves or robbers, so that a gold ring lay for a long time on Ialangr heath. King Frodi went as a guest to Sweden to visit a king called Fiolnir. There he purchased two female slaves whose names were Fenia and Menia. They were big and strong. At that time there were discovered in Denmark two millstones so huge that there was no one strong enough to move them. But the millstones had this quality, that the mill ground out whatever the grinder prescribed. This mill's name was Grotti. Hengikiopt is the name of the person that gave King Frodi the mill. King Frodi had the slave-girls brought to the mill and told them to grind gold and peace and prosperity for Frodi. He did not give them any longer rest or sleep than while the cuckoo was silent or a song might be sung. The story goes that then they chanted the poem known as Grottasong. And by the time the poem was ended, they were grinding out an army against Frodi, so that during the night a sea-king called Mysing came there and killed Frodi, taking much plunder. Then Frodi's peace came to an end. Mysing took away with him Grotti and also Fenia and Menia and told them to grind out salt. And at midnight they asked whether Mysing was not tired of salt. He told them to go on grinding. They only went on grinding a short time before the ships sank, and there was left a whirlpool in the sea where the sea flows down into the mill-hole. It was then that the sea became salt.

'Now we are come to a king's buildings, two fore-knowing ones, Fenia and Menia.' They are at Frodi Fridleifsson's, the mighty maids, kept in thrall.

They were led to the mill-box and they demanded movement from the machine of stone. He promised neither of them rest nor pleasure until he heard the sound of the slave-girls.

They drew forth the sound of the silence-banished thing. 'Let's set up the mill-boxes, lift the stones.' He bade the maids again that they should grind.

They sang and slung the swift stone until Frodi's household mostly slept. Then said Menia — she was come to the grinding:

'Let us grind wealth for Frodi. Let us grind to the fulness of blessedness a heap of riches on the happy mill-box. Let him sit on wealth, let him sleep on down, let him awake to joy. Then the grinding will have been well done.

'Here shall no one harm another, plan him evil or work his death, or strike with keen sword, even if he found his brother's slayer bound.'

But he spoke no other word than this: 'You shall not sleep more than the cuckoos above the hall, or longer than just while I utter one song.'

'You were not, Frodi, acting entirely in your own interests, speech-friend of men, when you bought serving-maids: you chose them for their strength and for their appearance, but you did not inquire about their origins.

'Hard was Hrungnir, and his father, yet Thiassi was mightier than they, Idi and Aurnir, our kinsmen, brothers of mountain-giants, from them are we descended.

'Grotti would not have come from the gritstone fell, nor that hard rock out of the earth, nor would the mountain-giants' maid have been grinding thus, if we had known nothing about it.

'For nine winters we were play-fellows, mighty ones bred beneath the earth. The maids undertook mighty works, we ourselves moved the table-mountain from its seat.

'We rolled the boulder over the giants' dwelling-place so that because of it the ground went shaking; we slung the swift stone, the heavy rock, so that men got it.

'And we then in Sweden, two fore-knowing ones, marched into battle, we challenged bears and broke shields, we went through the grey-shirted troop.

'We cast down a ruler, supported another, provided the good Gothorm with help, there was no sitting quiet until Knui fell.

'We went on thus for those seasons so that we were renowned for heroism. There we scored with sharp spears blood from wounds, and reddened swords.

'Now we are come to a king's houses, shown no mercy and kept in thrall. Mud eats our soles and cold the rest of us. We drag war's settler [Grotti]. It is dull at Frodi's.

'Hands shall rest, stone will stand still. I have ground my turn. My spell has finished. Now no proper rest will be given to hands until Frodi thinks enough has been ground.

'Heroes' arms shall be hard shafts, weapons corpse-bloody. Awake, Frodi! Awake, Frodi, if you want to heed our songs and ancient tales.

'I see fire burning east of the city. War-tidings are awake, what is known as a beacon. An army will come hither in a moment and burn the town for the prince.

'You will not keep the throne of Lejre, red rings and mighty millstone. Let us grasp tighter, maid, the handle. We are not slaughter-maids in corpse-blood.

'My father's maid ground mightily, for she saw the doom of a multitude of men. The great supports snapped from the mill-box, enclosed in iron. Let us grind still more.

'Let us grind still more. Yrsa's son will avenge Frodi on the Half-danes. He will be called her son and brother. We both know that.'

The maids ground, exerted their strength. The young ones were in a giant fury. The shaft-poles shook, the mill-box shot down, the heavy stone burst apart in two.

And the mountain-giants' bride uttered words: 'We have ground, Frodi, so far that we must stop. The women have done their full stint at milling.'

Einar Skulason said this:

I have heard that Frodi's maids ground with great energy Grafvitnir's bed [gold]. The ruler gives gold no peace [he is generous with it]. The fair cheeks of my axe, fastened to maple, have on them this meal of Frodi [gold]. The gentle king's wealth adorns this turner of poetry.

Egil said this:

He gladdens the multitude of men with Frodi's meal.

Why is gold called Kraki's seed? There was a certain king in Denmark whose name was Hrolf Kraki. He was the most notable of ancient kings primarily for generosity and valour and humility. There is one illustration of his humility which is much celebrated in stories, that there was a little boy and a poor one whose name was Vogg. He entered King Hrolf's hall. At that time the king was young in age and slender in build. Then Vogg went before him and looked up at him. Then said the king:

'What is it you want to say, boy, since you are looking at me?'

Vogg said: 'When I was at home, I heard it said that King Hrolf at Lejre was the greatest man in the northern lands, but now there sits here on the throne a little pole (*kraki*), and they call it their king.'

Then replied the king: 'You, boy, have given me a name, that I shall be called Hrolf Kraki, and it is customary to give a gift to confirm a christening. Now I see that you have not got any gift to confirm my christening that I could accept. Now shall he give to the other who has something to give.'

He took a ring from his arm and gave it him. Then said Vogg:

'May you be blessed above all kings in your giving! And I solemnly vow to be the death of that man who becomes your slayer.'

Then said the king, laughing: 'It does not take much to please Vogg.'

There is another story told of King Hrolf that illustrates his valour, that there was a king ruling over Uppsala called Adils. He was married to Hrolf Kraki's mother Yrsa. He was at war with a king called Ali who was ruling Norway. They fixed a battle between themselves on the ice of the lake called Væni. King Adils sent a request to his stepson Hrolf Kraki for him to come to his assistance, and promised a salary to all his army while they were on the expedition, and the king himself was to get three treasures of his choice from Sweden. King Hrolf was unable to go himself because of the hostilities in which he was engaged against the Saxons, but still he sent his twelve berserks. One of these was Bodvar Biarki; there was also Hialti the Gallant, Hvitserk the Bold, Vott, Veseti, the brothers Svipdag and Beigud. In this battle King Ali and a great part of his army fell. Then King Adils took from him as he lay dead the helmet Hildisvin and his horse, Hrafn. Then Hrolf Kraki's berserks asked to be given their salary, three pounds of gold for each of them, and in addition they requested that they might take Hrolf Kraki the treasures that they were going to choose on his behalf. These were the helmet Hildigolt and the mail-coat Finnsleif which weapons could not penetrate, and a gold ring known as Sviagris which had belonged to Adils's ancestors. But the king refused all the treasures and did not pay the salary either. The berserks left, greatly displeased with their treatment, and told Hrolf Kraki how things stood. He immediately set off for Uppsala, and when he had brought his ships into the river Fyri he rode to Uppsala accompanied by his twelve berserks, none of them waiting to negotiate terms of entry. His mother Yrsa welcomed him and took him to a private room and not to the king's hall. Great fires were then lit for them and they were given ale to drink. Then King Adils's men came in and heaped wood on the fire, making it so huge that Hrolf's and his men's clothes began to be burned off them, and said:

'Is it true that Hrolf Kraki and his berserks flee neither fire nor iron?'

Then Hrolf Kraki jumped up, and so did all the rest. Then he said:

'Let us add more to the fires in Adils's buildings.'

He took his shield and threw it on the fire and leapt over the fire as the shield burned, and went on:

'He flees not fires who leaps over them.'

Each of his men in turn did the same, and took those who had been heaping up the fire and threw them on to the fire. Then Yrsa came and gave Hrolf Kraki an animal's horn full of gold and with it the ring Sviagris and bade them ride away to their troops. They leapt on their horses and rode down on to the Fyri plains. Then they saw that King Adils was riding after them with his army fully armed intending to kill them. Hrolf Kraki picked the gold out of the horn with his right hand and sowed it all over the road. And when the Swedes saw this, they leapt from their saddles and each took what he could get, but King Adils ordered them to ride on and rode himself at a furious rate. His horse's name was Slungnir, it was faster than any other horse. Hrolf Kraki saw that King Adils was riding close behind him, and took the ring Sviagris and threw it towards him and told him to take it as a gift. King Adils rode up to the ring and picked it up with the point of his spear and made it slide up on to the socket. Then Hrolf Kraki looked round and saw how he stooped down. Then he said:

'Now I have made him who is greatest among the Swedes grovel like a pig.'

So they parted. This is the reason why gold is called seed of Kraki or of Fyri plains. Eyvind Skaldaspillir said this:

> Battle-leek [sword] Ull [warrior], we used to wear on hawk-fells [arms] Fyri-plains' seed [gold] throughout Hakon's life.

As Thiodolf said:

> The prince sows his men's bright-ploughed steep acres [arms] of limb-resting rings with Yrsa's offspring's [Hrolf Kraki's] seed. The fault-shunning land-director pours Kraki's bright barley on to my own hawk's lands [arms] which provide security for flesh.

They say that a king known as Holgi, after whom Halogaland is named, was Thorgerd Holgabrud's father. Sacrifices were offered to them both, and Holgi's mound was raised with alternately a layer of gold or silver – this was the money offered in sacrifice – and a layer of earth and stone. Skuli Thorsteinsson said this:

> When I reddened Reifnir's roof-fire [shield-fire = sword] off Svold to gain wealth, I amassed warlike Holgi's mound-roof [gold] in rings.

In the old Lay of Biarki many terms for gold are listed. It says there:

The most munificent prince enriched his men with Fenia's labour, Fafnir's Midgard, Glasir's glowing foliage, Grani's fair burden, Draupnir's precious sweat, Grafvitnir's pillow.

The generous lord pushed, men received, Sif's scalp-strings, ice of bow-forcer [arm], reluctant otter-payment, Mardoll's tears, fire of Orun [a river], Idi's shining talk.

The battle-giver gladdened — we advanced beautifully adorned — with Thiassi's assembly-agenda [talk] the multitudinous hosts, with the Rhine's red metal, Niflungs' strife, the battle-bold ruler. The silent Baldr defended him.

In kennings gold is called fire of arm or joint or limb, since it is red, and silver snow or ice or frost, since it is white. In the same way gold or silver should be referred to in terms of purse or crucible or wire-drawing-plate, and either gold or silver may be meant by rocks of the arm or neck-ring of some person whose custom it was to wear a necklace. And rings mean both silver and gold if no other details are given. As Thorleik the Fair said:

The righteous prince throws the crucible's load on to thanes' adorned falcon-perches [arms]; the young ruler gives arm-cinders.

And as Einar Skalaglamm said:

The valiant prince of Lund's land does harm [gives away] joint-brands. I do not think the ruler's men will run short of Rhine's rock.

Einar Skulason said this:

Both purse snow and ocean fire lie on each side of the blood-ember's [axe's] head. I must praise the one that fights destroyers [vikings].

And as he also said:

Sea-flame rests every day on white crucible-snowdrift. He who adorns the sides of Heiti's steed [ship] with shield rules with generous heart. Never can the scales-snow be melted before the fire of the eel's surging path [the sea; the gold is a fire that gives no heat]. The feller of hosts achieves all glorious exploits.

Here gold is called fire of the eel's surging path, and silver scales-snow. Thord Mauraskald said this:

> Glad giver of hand-rock, it can be seen in the diminisher of gold wire that sword-lair [shield] Hermod [the warrior] had a good father.

Man is called the gold's breaker, as Ottar the Black said:

> I need the favour of the nobility who follow the battle-gold [sword] breaker. In here is a very active domestic troop with a wise prince.

Or gold-sender, as Einar Skalaglamm said:

> Gold-sender lets ground-getter [king] — the prince gladdens a host of men; I can receive his treasure — enjoy Ygg's [Odin's] mead [poetry].

Gold-thrower, as Thorleik said:

> With a prince's deeds the gold-thrower makes his court loyal to himself.

Gold-harmer, as Thorvald Blonduskald said:

> Gold-harmer throws arms' embers, the king gives red wealth, destroyer of evil people shifts Grani's load.

Gold-prince, as here:

> I gained a gold-prince. *Togdrapa* is made about the battle-fire-[sword-]road-[shield-]hail-[battle-]flame-[sword-]tree [warrior].

Woman is referred to in terms of gold, called dealer of gold, as Hallar-Stein said:

> The thrower of the amber [gold] of Vidblindi's boar's

[whale's] salty cool land [sea] will long remember the dealer
of reed-thong's [serpent's] league [land, i.e. gold].

Here whales are called Vidblindi's boars. He was a giant and drew
whales out from the sea like fish. The land of whales is the sea,
amber of the sea is gold. A woman is dealer (*selia*) of the gold that
she gives, and *selia* [willow] is also the name of a tree, and as was
noted above, woman is referred to by all kinds of feminine
tree-names. She is also said to be the consumer (*lóg*) of what she
gives. Log is also a word for a tree felled in a wood. Gunnlaug
Serpent-tongue said this:

> The lady was born to bring strife among the sons of men.
> The battle-bush [warrior, her father] was the cause of this. I
> was frantically eager to possess the wealth-log.

Woman is called forest. Hallar-Stein said this:

> I have smoothed with poetry's plane my refrain-ship's
> [poem's] prow [beginning], careful in my craftsmanship, for
> ale-vessel's Bil [the woman], fair bowl-forest [lady].

Rod, as Stein also said:

> You will, slender flood-fire-[gold-]keeping Sif [woman],
> strive against your good fortune like other rods of Hiad-
> ning's rocks [gold].

Prop; Orm Steinthorssen said this:

> Fiord-bone-[(precious) stone-]prop was put into exceed-
> ingly pure clothes. Spear-Freyr [warrior, man] threw tailor-
> ing over mead-Hrist [the woman].

Pillar, as Steinar said:

> All dreams of the gentle Syn [woman] of soft necklace-stand
> [neck] have deceived me. This moving current-sun-[gold-]
> pillar has put me in the lurch.

Birch, as Orm also said:

> For I have fixed the likeness of the birch of the hand's

hollow clanging fire [gold ring] in the Billing's son's [dwarf's] drink [poem] that I am performing.

Oak, as here:

The fairly-adorned coin-oak stands in the way of our pleasure.

Linden, as here:

Fiercely-attacking elm [warrior] of clashing metal-shower [battle], our heart's courage shall not lessen in the land — thus did linen-linden instruct.

Man is referred to as trees, as has been written above, called rowan (*reynir*) of weapons or battles, of expeditions and activities, of ships, and of everything he has in his power or puts to the test (*reynir*), as Ulf Uggason said:

But the sharp-looking stiff earth-rope [Midgard serpent] stared over the gunwale at country-bone-[rock-]folk's [giants'] tester/rowan [Thor] and blew poison.

Tree and beam, as Kormak said:

Beam of the killing-twig [sword] is better than many in spear-din [battle]; the sword wins land for the battle-keen earl Sigurd.

Grove; Hallfrod the troublesome poet said this:

The powerful shield-danger-[sword-] wielding grove with hair for foliage provides Ull's ash [shield] firs [warriors] in the east with great security.

Here the name fir is also used. Box; Arnor said this:

The pinnace-box bade the Rogalanders bring shields into collision at the beginning of dusk; rain [battle] of strife-clouds [shields] lasted through the autumn night.

Ash, as Ref said:

The gift-ready battle-Freyr [warrior] went into the gold-
adorned maiden's bed. The ash of Har's [Odin's] storm
[battle] achieves plenty of manliness.

Maple:

Hello! Thus greeted maple of arm-ice [sword] the mail-coat.

Spruce, as Ref said:

Since I have determined to present Thorstein with sea [a
poem] of battle-promoter's [Odin's] terror-home [breast]
— spruce of swords proposes this.

Stave, as Ottar said:

Fierce battle-stave, you held territory against two princes
where raven was not short of food [there was battle]. You
are quick to act against mankind.

Thorn, as Arnor said:

Young wealth-thorn piled up heavy heaps of slain men for
the eagles; and his men greatly assisted the erne-feeder
[warrior].

   How shall battle be referred to? By calling it weather of
weapons or shields, or of Odin or valkyrie or war-kings, or their
clash or noise. Hornklofi said this:

The prince waged storm of spears [battle] against men
where wound-goslings [arrows] clashed in Skogul's din.
Red wounds spewed blood.

Eyvind said this:

And this hero wore bush-grinner's [wolf's] grey coat [skin,
form] in Har's [Odin's] weather.

Bersi said this:

Once I seemed to bushes [warriors] of Gunn's fire [sword],

so it is said, well suited to Hlokk's snow, when we were younger.

Einar said this:

The bold monarch lets Hild's sail [shield] — sword clashes — receive most of Gondul's crashing wind [battle] where hail from strings [arrows] drives.

As Einar Skalaglamm said:

Firmly-seamed battle-birches' [warriors'] shirts [mail-coats] did not protect bow-giants [warriors] from war-Har's [warrior's] Hogni-showers [battle].

As here:

Set points' [spears'] net-band [shield-edge] against point-crash-[battle-]urger [warrior].

And also this:

The prince's enemies sank beneath eagle's claws in Gondul's din.

Weapons and armour shall be referred to in terms of battle and Odin and death-maidens and war-kings, helmet called hood or cap, and mail-coat shirt or tunic, and shield curtain; and shield-wall is called hall and roof, wall and floor. Shields are spoken of and referred to in terms of warships, as sun or moon or leaf or gleam or fence of the ship. A shield is also called Ull's ship and referred to in terms of Hrungnir's feet when he stood on his shield. On ancient shields it was customary to decorate the border which was called the circle, and shields are referred to by means of this circle. Cutting weapons, axes or swords, are called fires of blood or wounds. Swords are said to be Odin's fires, and people call axes by names of troll-wives, and refer to them in terms of blood or wound or forest or tree. Thrusting weapons it is fine to refer to as snakes or fish. Missiles are frequently referred to as hail or snowfall or storm. All these kennings are varied in many ways, for most compositions are in the form of praise poetry, where these kennings are particularly required. Viga-Glum said this:

> The host with Hanged-Tyr's [Odin's] hoods held back —
> they thought it not pleasant to venture — from going down
> the slopes.

Einar Skalaglamm said this:

> Helm-capped battle-bold Bui, who went north to Gunn's
> din, and war-keen Sigvaldi offered battle.

Rodi's shirt, as Tind said:

> When he had to discard his ring-short [damaged] Hangi's
> [Odin's] tinkling shirt; tossing horses [ships] of Rodi's
> league [sea] were cleared of mail-coat trees [warriors].

Hamdir's tunic, as Hallfrod said:

> Hard clashing-hail of Egil's weapons [bows] crashes with
> no little force on the outside of some wave-beast-[ship-]
> bushes' [warriors'] Hamdir's tunics.

Sorli's clothes, as he also said:

> As a result Sorli's bright clothes must be reddened by
> wound-fire — I learn precisely of this — in arrow-showers
> with men's blood.

As Grettir said:

> The raisers of Hlokk's curtains held their noses together,
> and Hild's wall's storm-Niords [warriors] rubbed beards
> [held a conference].

Rodi's roof, as Einar said:

> The strong ice [axe] of Rodi's roof is not the worse for Od's
> bedfellow's [Freyia's] eye-rain [tears, i.e. gold]. May this
> king reach old age.

Hild's wall, as Grettir said and was quoted above. Ship-sun, as Einar said:

> Olaf's kin reddens ship-sun-flame [sword] at sea.

Bows-moon, as Ref said:

> That was a fine day that flinger away of forearm-flame [gold rings] thrust upon my rings' hanging-road [arm] a fair bows-moon.

Ships' fence, as here:

> The righteous spears' din sweller [warrior] shot through the paint-covered vessel's fence — he was violent in battle — as through bark.

Ull's ash(-ship), as here [Thiodolf]:

> Storms of Ull's ship rage totally round the prince, where rivet-masts [swords], sheath-rigged, wave.

Hrungnir's sole-blade, as Bragi said:

> Will you hear, Hrafnketil, how I shall praise the sole-blade of the thief of Thrud [Hrungnir], which has fine colour planted on it, and the prince?

The poet Bragi composed this about the circle on the shield:

> Unless it be that the renowned son of Sigurd should desire good recompense for the resounding wheel [shield] of Hogni's maid [Hild; also the name of a valkyrie and for battle], which is circle-hubbed.

He called the shield Hild's wheel, and the circle the hub of the wheel. Land of the circle, as Hallvard said:

> The urger of the movement of points [warrior] sees red-bright circle-land fly in two, the white curved-edged disc breaks apart.

It is also said:

> A circle is most proper for a buckler, arrows for a bow.

A sword is Odin's fire, as Kormak said:

> Battle raged when the feeder of Grid's steed [wolf], he who
> waged war, advanced with ringing Gaut's [Odin's] fire.
> Weird rose from the well.

Helmet's fire, as Ulf Uggason said:

> The most powerful mountain-Hild [giantess] made the
> sea-Sleipnir [ship] lumber forward, while Hropt's [Odin's]
> helmet-fire-power-investors [berserks] felled her steed.

Mail-coat's fire, as Glum Geirason said:

> The land's defender, who defended himself against men
> mighty strongly, made the hone-scraped ringing fire of the
> mail-coat swish after that.

Shield's ice and damager of protective armour, as Einar said:

> I received red shields' ice [an axe], covered with Freyia's
> eyelid-moisture [gold], from the ruler careful of his actions.
> We carry helmet's damager in our hand.

An axe is called troll-wife of protective armour, as Einar said:

> Riders [seafarers] of Ræfil's land's [sea's] horses [ships] can
> see how beautifully engraved dragons lie just by the brow of
> the Grid of the life-protector.

A spear is called snake, as Ref said:

> My fierce dark forest-dragon [snake] of the board [shield]
> can play savagely in the man's hands where warriors meet.

Arrows are called hail of bow or string or defensive armour or
battle, as Einar Skalaglamm said:

Sword-crash-Rognir [warrior] shook bows' hail from
Hlokk's sails [shields]. The one who does not spare wolves
[criminals] saved his life bravely.

And Hallfrod:

And spear-storm gear, sewn with iron, did not protect the
hanged one's [Odin's] goslings' [ravens'] hunger-assuagers
[warriors] from bowstring's hail.

And Eyvind Skaldaspillir:

Little, they said, you let your spirits waver, defender of the
Hords' land, when mail-coat hail crashed in wounds and
bows were bent.

Battle is called the Hiadnings' weather or storm and weapons
Hiadnings' fires or rods, and there is a story that tells the origin of
this. A king whose name was Hogni had a daughter called Hild.
She was abducted in a raid by a king called Hedin Hiarrandason.
At the time King Hogni was away at a conference of kings. And
when he learned that his kingdom had been raided and his
daughter carried off, then he set out with his army to find Hedin
and got wind of him, that Hedin had sailed north along the coast.
When King Hogni got to Norway he discovered that Hedin had
sailed over the sea to the west. Then Hogni sailed after him all the
way to the Orkneys, and when he got to the place called Hoy, he
found Hedin there with his army. Then Hild went to see her father
and offered him a neck-ring as atonement on Hedin's behalf, but
in the next breath said that Hedin was ready to fight and that there
was no chance of him giving way to Hogni. Hogni's reply to his
daughter was curt, and when she got back to Hedin she told him
that Hogni was not interested in a settlement and told him to
prepare for battle. And this is what both sides did, went up on to
the island and marshalled their armies. Then Hedin called out to
his father-in-law Hogni and offered him atonement and a great
deal of gold to make amends. Then Hogni replied:
'You have offered this too late, if you want atonement, for I
have now drawn Dainsleif, which the dwarfs made, which has to
be the death of someone every time it is unsheathed, and a stroke

122

from it never fails, and no wound heals if it is inflicted by it.'

Then said Hedin: 'You can boast like this of your sword, but not of victory. In my opinion whatever serves its master well is good.'

Then they began the engagement that is known as the Hiadnings' battle, and fought all that day, and at nightfall the kings went to their ships. But during the night Hild went to the slain and woke up by magic all those that were dead. And the next day the kings went on to the battle-field and fought, and so did all those that had fallen the previous day. This battle continued day after day, with all those that fell, and all the weapons that lay on the battle-field, as well as shields, turning to stone. And when day came, all the dead men got up and fought, and all the weapons were usable. It says in poems that the Hiadnings must thus await Ragnarok. Bragi the poet composed a passage based on this story in his *drápa* for Ragnar Lodbrok:

And the Ran who wishes too great drying of veins [Hild] planned to bring this bow-storm against her father with hostile intention, when the ring(-sword) shaking Sif [Hild], filled with malice, brought a neck-ring on to the wind's horse [ship] to the battle-trunk [warrior].

This bloody-wound-curing Thrud did not offer the worthy prince the neck-ring to give him an excuse for cowardice in the meeting of metals. She always pretended to be against battle, though she was inciting the princes to join the company of the quite monstrous wolf's sister [Hel].

The land-lacking ruler of men [sea-king] does not resist the stopping of the wolf's desire [hunger, i.e. he feeds it with fallen warriors] by battle on the sand — hatred rose up in Hogni — when indefatigable edge-din-powers [warriors] attacked Hedin instead of accepting Hild's neck-rings.

This attack can be perceived on the penny [shield] of Svolnir's [Odin's] hall [Val-hall]. Ragnar gave me the Ræ's chariot [ship] moon [shield] and a multitude of stories with it.

And on the island, instead of the Vidrir [warrior] of the mail-coat's troll-wife [axe], the victory-preventing witch of

a woman had her way. The brig-elf's [sea-farer's] whole
army advanced in anger under their unwavering Hiar-
randi's [Odin's] hurdles [shields] from the swift-running
Reifnir's horse [ship].

Battle is Odin's weather, as was noted above. Viga-Glum said
this:

I used to win land for myself like earls of yore with staves of
the rod of Vidrir's [Odin's] weather. I had a reputation for
this.

Here battle is called Vidrir's weather, and the sword rod of battle,
and men staves of the sword. Here both battle and weapon are
used in a kenning for man. This is called extended when one
composes thus. A shield is land of weapons, and weapons are hail
or rain of that land if one composes allegorically.

How shall a ship be referred to? By calling it horse or wild
animal or ski of sea-kings or of the sea or of ship's tackle or of
weather. Wave's steed, as Hornklofi said:

The harsh clearer [attacker] of wave's pale steed, a child in
age, caused ships' bows to be impelled on the sea at high
time.

Geitir's horse; Erringar-Stein said this:

Even though all people tell the poet of this war in the south
— let us load Geitir's horse with stones — joyful we travel.

Sveidi's reindeer:

Battle-bold son of Svein, you have brought the long-
planked Sveidi's reindeer on the path [sea] of Solsi's bench
[ship]. Straits-animals [ships] passed from shore.

This was composed by Hallvard; here straits-animals are referred
to, and the sea as Solsi's bench. Thord Siareksson said this:

The gunwale's horse went tossing north of Sigg; a gust shot
the steed of Gylfi's league south by Aumar. And afterwards

the horse of the gull's track put both Kormt and Agdir past
the stern; the leek-horse waded past Lister.

Here a ship is called gunwale's horse and the sea Gylfi's land, the
sea the gull's track and the ship its horse, and also leek-horse; leek
is a word for mast-tree. And also as Markus said:

> The winter-survivor of the current waded fast the drifts of
> fiord-serpents [ships; their drifts are the waves]. The
> greedy-tooth of the mast-head ran over the whale's house-
> tops [waves]. The flood-bear went forward on the old
> sea-ski [ship] tracks. The shower-braving stocks-grizzly
> broke the skerry's roaring fetter [sea].

Here a ship is called bear of currents. Winter-survivor and
greedy-tooth and grizzly are names for bear, and stocks-bear is
referred to here. A ship can also be called a reindeer. Hallvard
used that expression, as was written above; and hart, as King
Harald Sigurdarson said:

> The hull cut past broad Sicily; we were splendid then, as one
> might expect. The poop-hart glided swiftly beneath men.

And elk, as Einar said:

> A man cannot stay long with you, kind chaser of rings'
> peace [giver of rings], unless something is given for it; let us
> get the flood-elk ready.

Otter, as Mani said:

> What will you, slouching, grey-cheeked old man, be able to
> do with the fellows on the ocean-otter? For your strength is
> fading.

Wolf, as Ref said:

> But the hoard-diminisher [generous man] was obedient to
> Thorstein. I stand by the bush [man] of the slipway-wolf in
> angry hone-rod [sword] conference [battle].

And ox. A ship is also called ski or waggon or carriage. Eyiolf
Dadaskald said this:

Young, he went very late in the day on ski of Meiti's fishing-station [sea] with the same sized troop against the bold lord.

Styrkar Oddason said this:

And Hogni's troop drove slipway-wagons over Heidi's snowdrifts [waves] in fury after the splendid flood-fire-[gold-]scatterer.

And as Thorbiorn said:

The loader of the slipway's sea-carriage was in the baptismal pool, the hoard-robber [generous man] who received White-Christ's highest grace.

How shall Christ be referred to? By calling him creator of heaven and earth, of angels and the sun, ruler of the world and the kingdom of heaven and angels, king of the heavens and the sun and angels and Jerusalem and Jordan and Greece, master of apostles and saints. Early poets have referred to Christ in terms of the well of Weird and Rome, as for instance Eilif Gudrunarson:

Thus has the powerful king of Rome increased his realm with lands of heath-land divinities [giants; i.e. heathen lands]. He is said to have his throne south at Weird's well.

Skapti Thoroddsson said this:

The might of the lord of monks is greatest. God has power over most things. Great Christ created the whole world and built Rome's hall.

King of heavens, as Markus said:

Wind-hall's [sky's] prince created ground and heavens as well as the virtuous host. Alone the ruler of men, Christ, can control all things.

Eilif Kulnasvein said this:

The host of the world's roof [angels] and the troop of men

bow to the holy cross. The sun's king alone is finer than all other true glory.

Mary's son, as Eilif also said:

The pure court of the heavens bows to Mary's boy, the ruler of the host performs truly glorious works. He is man and god.

King of angels, as Eilif also said:

The noble might of God's son is better than men can imagine, yet the generous lord of angels is holier and worthier than everything.

King of Jordan, as Sighvat said:

Once Jordan's prince did send four angels from the sky. Falling water washed the holy locks of its lord.

King of Greeks, as Arnor said:

I lift prayers for the causer of men's falling [in battle] to the wise guardian of Greeks and Russians. Thus I repay the prince for his gift.

Eilif Kulnasvein said this:

The splendour of heaven praises the ruler of heroes, he is king of everything.

Here he has called Christ first king of men and secondly king of everything. Also Einar Skulason said:

Bright in body the embracer of the whole world who keeps watch over the men of earth made the kingdom of heaven open for the brave lord.

Here kennings become ambiguous, and the person interpreting the poetry has to distinguish from the context which king is being referred to. For it is normal to call the emperor of Constantinople king of the Greeks, and similarly the king that rules

Palestine, to call him king of Jerusalem; so also to call the Roman emperor king of Rome or him who rules England king of the English [*engla* also = angels]. And the kenning that was quoted above, calling Christ king of men, this kenning can be applied to any king. It is normal to refer to all kings in such a way as to call them land-rulers or defenders of the land or conquerors of land or commanders of the court or defence of the people of the land. Eyvind Skaldaspillir said this:

> . . . Cargo-Tyr's . . . him land-rulers deprived of life at Oglo.

And as Glum Geirason said:

> The helmeted prince reddened whetstone's hollow [sword] on Gauts. There in the din of spears was the ground's defender to be found.

As Thiodolf said:

> May the high, joyful governor of the court bequeath to his sons inheritance and his native land. That is my wish.

As Einar said:

> Brave in disposition the land-defender wears the snake's hood [helmet of terror] above his bold hair-fell [head; i.e. he rules firmly]. The poet recounts before men the glory of the king of Hords.

It is also normal for a king who has tributary kings under him to be called king of kings. An emperor is highest of kings, but after him any king who rules over a nation is indistinguishable in all kennings from any other in poetry. Next are the people that are called earls or tributary kings, and they are indistinguishable in kennings from a king, except that those that are tributary kings must not be called national kings. And this is how Arnor the earls' poet spoke of Earl Thorfinn:

> Let the court learn how the keen-spirited king of earls pursued the sea, the irresistible prince did not cease to oppose the ocean.

Next in kennings in poetry are those men called lords. They can be referred to like a king or an earl, by calling them gold-breakers and wealth-bountiful ones and standard-men and governors of the host, or by calling them leaders of the army or of battle. For every national king who rules many lands appoints tributary kings and earls for governance of the land, together with himself, to administer the laws of the land and to defend it from hostility in those lands which lie far off from the king; and these judgments and sentences are to be considered as valid as those of the king himself. And in a single land there are many districts and it is the custom of kings to appoint administrators of justice over as many of these districts as he delegates power over, and they are called *hersar* [lords] or landed men in the Scandinavian language, but *Grafen* in Saxony and barons in England. They are also supposed to be proper judges and proper defenders of the land over the realm that is delegated to them for governance. If the king is not present, then a standard should be carried before them in battles, and they are then as legitimate army commanders as kings or earls. Next to them are the men called *holdar* [heroes]. These are yeomen who have full status as regards their lineage and all their legal rights. They may be referred to by calling them payers and keepers of money, and pledges of truce among men. These kennings can also be applied to chieftains. Kings and earls have in their train men called *hirdmenn* [courtiers] and housecarls, but landed men also have men in their service who in Denmark and Sweden are known as *hirdmenn*, but in Norway housecarls, and yet they take oaths just as *hirdmenn* do to kings. *Hirdmenn* were generally referred to as kings' housecarls in ancient times. Thorvald Blonduskald said this:

> Hail, battle-keen king, and also your brave housecarls. Men have my poetry, filled with praise, in their mouths.

King Harald Sigurdarson composed this:

> Having complete power, he waits to occupy the prince's throne. I have often seen a smaller troop of housecarls surging at the heels of an earl.

Hirdmenn and housecarls of chieftains can be referred to by

calling them a domestic troop or mercenaries or stipendiaries.
Sighvat said this:

> I have heard that such a battle was fought recently on water
> by the prince's mercenaries, that I count none of the least
> point-storms [battles] second to it.

And also this:

> It was different then on the cable-steed [ship] before the
> greeting of metals [battle] from when maiden served mead
> to these prince's stipendiaries.

Stipend-money which chieftains give is known as wages and gift.
Ottar the Black said this:

> I need the favour of the nobility who follow the battle-
> ember-[sword-]breaker [warrior]. In here is a very active
> domestic troop with a wise prince.

Earls and lords and *hirdmenn* are referred to by calling them
kings' confidants or gossips or bench-mates. Hallfrod said this:

> Battle-powerful king's confidant, whom action pleases, lets,
> fury-hasty, Hogni's clothes [mail], forged by hammer,
> jangle round himself.

As Snæbiorn said:

> Gossip of royalty makes the long-hulled rudder-tie-steed
> [ship] lean resounding stem-sword [prow] on hard wave.

Arnor said this:

> My young sons begin to suffer evident heavy hurt about me
> because of the end of the killing-renowned prince's bench-
> mate.

King's crony, as Hallfrod said:

> The match was later consummated by which the wise-
> spoken king's crony married [gained possession of] the

tree-grown only daughter of Onar [Iord, earth, the country of Norway].

Men are also to be referred to by their descent; as Kormak said:

> May the son of Harald's true trier listen; I let be heard with liveliness my fen-teeth-[rock-]Syr's [giantess's] men's [giants'] yeast-Rhine [mead of poetry].

He has referred to the earl as the king's true trier, and to Earl Hakon as son of Earl Sigurd. But Thiodolf spoke thus of Harald:

> Every difficulty increases Iarnsaxa's wind [courage] in Olaf's father, so that praise is due.

And also thus:

> Iarizleif saw in what direction the prince developed. The outstanding holy king's brother came on.

And he also said:

> Dead is he who outshone all, descendant of noblemen, Harald's brother's son.

Arnor also said this in his *drápa* [formally constructed praise-poem] for Rognvald:

> Beneficial to the people, the kinsman of Heiti decided to bring about a family connection with me. As a result strong links with the earl by marriage caused glory to be built up for us.

And as he also said about Earl Thorfinn:

> Thinly made swords bit the offspring of Rognvald the Old south of Man, and a powerful host rushed beneath their shields there.

And he also said:

> God, keep the splendid glory of the family of all-powerful

Torf-Einar from harm, and I pray for true grace for the worthy prince.

And Einar Skalaglamm also said:

Never will there be a pillar of the family of the line of Hilditonn who is a more generous battle-promoter. I am under an obligation to pursue his praise.

What is the rule for poetry without periphrasis? To call everything by its own name. What non-periphrastic terms are there for **poetry**? It is called rhyme and praise, rhapsody, encomium, eulogy. Bragi the Old spoke as follows when he was driving through a certain forest late in the evening; then a troll-wife accosted him in verse and asked who was going there:

'Trolls call me moon of dwelling-Rungnir, giant's wealth-sucker, storm-sun's bale, seeress's friendly companion, guardian of corpse-fiord, swallower of heaven-wheel; what is a troll other than that?'

He replied thus:

'Poets call me Vidur's [Odin's] thought-smith, getter of Gaut's [Odin's] gift, lack-nought hero, server of Ygg's [Odin's] ale, song-making Modi, skilled smith of rhyme; what is a poet other than that?'

And as Kormak said:

I shall continue to compose more praise about the renowned son of Sigrod; I shall pay him the stipend [poetry] of the gods' atoner [Odin]. Thor sits in his chariot.

And as Thord Kolbeinsson said:

The shield-maple frequently made many cruisers, as well as freighters and cutters, thunder on the surf. The poet's rhapsody, liberal with encomium, develops.

Encomium, as Ulf Uggason said:

There the river reaches the sea, and I have again handed
over an encomium for the sword-rain-deliverer [warrior].
Thus I raise the eulogy of thanes.

Here poetry is also called eulogy.

What names are there for the **gods?** They are also called bonds,
as Eyiolf Dadaskald said:

Spear-weather-liberal [warlike] Eirik draws land under
himself to the pleasure of the bonds and organizes battle.

And fetters, as Thiodolf of Hvinir said:

Middlingly free of deceit, he was a slow provider of service
to the god. The helmet-capped educator [Odin] of the
fetters declared there was something behind it.

Powers, as Einar Skalaglamm said:

I declare the most puissant powers imbue with strength the
rule of Hakon.

Yule-beings, as Eyvind said:

Again we have produced Yule-beings' feast [mead of poet-
ry], our ruler's eulogy, like a bridge of masonry.

Deities, as Kormak said:

The land-getter, who binds the straight mast-top, honours
the provider of the deities' fiord [the mead of poetry] with a
head-band. Ygg [Odin] won Rind by spells.

The following names for the **heavens** are written down, but we
have not found all these terms in poems. But these poetical terms
like others seem to me not proper to include in poetry unless one
finds similar terms already in the work of major poets: heaven,
twin-lit, clouded-brightness, storm-Mimir, Andlang, light-bringer,
sprinkler, rich-wetter, wide-embracer, winter-Mimir, light-
ning, coverer, Vidblain. **Sun:** day-star, disc, ever-glow, all-bright
seen, fair-wheel, grace-shine, Dvalin's toy, elf-disc, doubt-disc,

ruddy. **Moon**: lune, waxer, waner, year-counter, clipped, shiner, gloam, hastener, squinter, gleamer.

What terms for **earth** are there? It is called earth, as Thiodolf said:

> The earl, point-shower-[battle-]increaser, often causes hard ring(sword)-storms [battles] to be made before he forces earth under himself.

Field, as Ottar said:

> Host-Baldr defends field, few kings have such ability. Olaf gladdens the eagle [with corpses]. The lord of the Swedes is outstanding.

Ground, as Harald said:

> Broad ground, wrapped round by deadly-cold serpent [the Midgard serpent] lies beneath spruce [man] of holm-fetter's [Midgard serpent's] path [gold]. Hone-land's [sword's] Hod [the warrior] harms hoards [is generous].

Surface, as Einar said:

> Bold, bright men strongly defend princes' surface with sword. Helmet often shatters before the furious edge-storm [battle].

Land, as Thord Kolbeinsson said:

> And after the battle, land was subjected — careful is my word about the conflict — from Veig in the north to Agdir in the south or considerably further.

Territory, as Ottar said:

> Fierce battle-stave [warrior], you held territory against two princes where raven was not short of food [there was battle]. You were quick to act against mankind.

Hlodyn, as Volu-Stein said:

I remember how the dark earth once yawned with dug-open mouth for the disposer of green Hlodyn's bones' [rocks'] Dane's [giant's] words [gold].

Country, as Ulf Uggason said:

But the sharp-looking stiff land-rope [Midgard serpent] stared over the gunwale at the country-bone-[rock-]folk's [giants'] tester/rowan [Thor] and blew poison.

Fiorgyn:

I was loyal to the eager payer of Fiorgyn's eel's [serpent's] tinkling bed [gold], and honour be to the storm [destruction, generous giver] of the river-anvil-[rock-]Eldir's [giant's] speech [gold].

There is an animal called a **warg**. It is normal to refer to it in terms of blood or corpses in such a way as to call them its food or drink. It is not normal to use such kennings with other animals. A warg is also called wolf, as Thiodolf said:

Sufficient fare was brought to Geri, and the wolf came from the north out of the forest. Sigurd's son provides wounds to entice it.

Here it is also called Geri. Freki, as Egil said:

When point-breaker [wave of points = blood] — Freki tore wounds — grated on the prow of the raven's head.

Watcher, as Einar said:

Deadly cold Elbe was reddened with hot wound-surge [blood]. The watcher's warm ale [blood] flowed with water into Kormt's necklace [sea].

She-wolf, as Arnor said:

Evil lineage of she-wolf swallowed much-harmed corpse, and green swell turned to red, mixed with blood.

Warg, as Illugi said:

> It was pleasure for the warg when my lord drove many a
> rout. The neck-ring-diminisher [generous man, Sigurd]
> stabbed with his sword the dark forest-trout [serpent,
> Fafnir].

Bear: forest-walker, cub, winter-survivor, grizzly, snarler,
greedy-tooth, hooded one, dark one, yellow-bum, shrivelled-gut,
she-bear, Iorek, scratcher, greedy one, mighty one, bustler.

Hart: moor-treader, antlered one, horned one, Dain, Dvalin,
Duneyr, Durathror.

These are also terms for **warg** in this poem by Hall:

> The heath-dweller's hunger was sated, the grey howler fed
> on wounds, the prince reddened Fenrir's chops, the wolf
> went to drink from wounds.

And also in this poem by Thord:

> Gialp's stud waded in blood, and the dusky one's troop got
> plenty of Freki's meal [carrion]. The howler enjoyed Geri's
> ales [blood].

There are these names of **horses** listed; these horse-names are in
Thorgrim's *thula* [list]:

> Hrafn and Sleipnir, splendid horses, Val and Lettfeti, Tial-
> dari was there, Gulltopp and Goti, I heard Soti mentioned,
> Mor and Lung with Mar, Vigg, and Stuf was with Skævad,
> Blakk was able to carry a thane, Silfrtopp and Sinir, also I
> heard Fak mentioned, Gullfaxi and Ior with the gods. There
> was a horse called Blodughofi and they say he bore the
> mighty Atridi. Gils and Falhofnir, Glær and Skeidbrimir.
> Gyllir was also mentioned there.

These are also listed in *Alsvinnsmal*:

> Dag rode Drosul, Dvalin Modnir, Hialmther Hod, and
> Haki Fak. The slayer of Beli rode Blodughofi and the prince
> of the Haddings Skævad, Vestein Val and Vifil Stuf, Men-
> thiof Mor and Morgin Vakr; Ali on Hrafn, they rode to the

ice, and another one east under Adils, grey, it wandered, wounded with a spear. Biorn rode Blakk and Biar Kort, Atli Glaum and Adils Slungnir, Hogni Holkvir and Harald Folkvir, Gunnar Goti and on Grani, Sigurd.

Arvak and Alsvinn draw the sun, as was written above. Hrimfaxi or Fiorsvartnir draw the night, Skinfaxi or Glad go with the day.

There are these names of **oxen** in Thorgrim's *thula*:

> Names of ancient oxen I have precisely heard, of Rufus and Hæfir [hoofed], Rekin [driven] and Kyr, Himinhriot and Apli, Arf and Arfuni.

These are names for **serpents**: dragon, Fafnir, Iormungand, adder, Nidhogg, snake, viper, Goin, Moin, Grafvitnir, Grabak, Ofnir, Svafnir, masked one.

Cattle: cow, calf, ox, heifer, yearling, steer, bull.

Sheep: ram, tup, ewe, lamb, wether.

Swine: sow, pig, boar, hog, grice.

What terms for the **sky** and the **weathers** are there? The sky is called Ginnungagap and middle-world, bird-world, weather-world. Terms for weather are storm, breeze, gale, tempest, blast, wind. Thus it says in *Alsvinnsmal*:

> It is called wind among men, but wanderer among the gods, the great powers call it the neigher, giants call it howler, but elves noisy traveller. In Hel it is called boomer.

Gust is also a term for weather.

There are two **birds** that there is no need to refer to in any other way than by calling blood or corpses their drink or food. These are the raven and the eagle. All other masculine birds can be referred to in terms of blood or corpses, and then it means eagle or raven, as Thiodolf said:

> The prince lets blood-grouse delight in eagle's barley. The Hords' king brings Gaut's [Odin's] sickle [sword] to the gore-swan's harvest. The feeder of the vulture of the eagle's corpse-sea [blood] lets his men fence every shallow he has to defend in the south with spear-points.

These are names for **raven**: crow, Hugin, Munin, secure-mood, early-flier, year-counter, flesh-marker. Einar Skalaglamm said this:

> The army-musterer gave mountain-haunting ravens their fill. The raven got full on she-wolf's prey, and spears rang.

Einar Skulason said this:

> The splendid strengthener [feeder] of hostility-gulls [ravens] does wield the splendid gleaming-sun dog [weapon]. The troubler of Hugin's food [raven] finds an end to his trouble [gets fed].

And as he also said:

> But the king's heart swells, bulging with courage in battle, where heroes sink down. Blue-black Munin drinks blood from wounds.

As Viga-Glum said:

> When we stood on the sand-bank, shielded, eager for the din [battle] of the gore-jewel-[sword-]lady [valkyrie], secure-mood got bloody food.

As Skuli Thorsteinsson said:

> Hviting-Hlokk [woman] would not have found me last in a company of a hundred where I provided sore wounds for the early-flier.

Terms for **eagle** are: erne, old one, storm-cleaver, edged one, deluder, wound-cleaver, shrill-crier. As Einar said:

> He reddened with gore the chops of the dark-looking steed of Iarnsaxa [wolf]. Eagle tore Geri's morsel. Eagle's meat was provided by irons.

As Ottar said:

> Eagle gulps drink from corpses, she-wolf gets breakfast.

Wolf often reddens his jaw, erne finds a meal there.

As Thiodolf said:

The lady-wolf [Thiassi] flew noisily to meet the commanders of the crew [the Æsir] no short time ago in an old old-one's form.

And as follows:

I will for storm-cleaver's <feeder> work noble <Odin's> mead [poetry].

And also as Skuli said:

I stay awake early and late with sorrow, since things looked good to the falcon of shrill-crier's expanse [sea, i.e. blood; falcon = raven, looking forward to carrion]. The fellow [the poet] listens now to good tidings.

What terms for **sea** are there? It is called mere, ocean (*ægir*), engulfer (*gymir*), roarer (*hler*), main, road, depth, salt, water, swell. As Arnor said and was quoted above:

Let the court learn how the keen-spirited king of earls pursued the sea, the irresistible prince did not cease to oppose the ocean.

Here are mentioned sea and also ocean. Mere, as Hornklofi said:

When the man-harmful meeter of the sacred road [mountains] of the water's teeth [rocks] drove out on the mere the splendid fore-sheets-snake [ship] and boats.

Water is also mentioned here. Einar said this:

Water washes the craft where the sea thuds on each side, and the fine weather-vanes rattle. Surf bathes the flood's horses [ships].

Here it is called flood. Ref said this, as was quoted above:

Gymir's spray-cold spae-wife [Ran] often brings the twisted-rope-bear [ship] into Ægir's [ocean's] jaws when the wave breaks.

The main, as Hallvard said:

You had the fore-stem of the tough steed [ship] of the encircling band of all lands [ocean] directed west to the main, sword-belt-ice [sword] shaker [warrior].

Road, as here:

We have passed on the road from territory skied over by Finns. From the craft's path I can see mountains in the east illuminated by a sunbeam.

Depth, as Egil said:

I go west over the depth, and I carry Vidrir's [Odin's] thought-strand-[breast-]mere [mead of poetry]; this is my way.

Mere, as Einar said:

Cold mere washes many a day the black timbers under the generous prince. Storm-twisted elm-trouble [wind] digs into Man's encircler (sea).

Salt, as Arnor said:

The valiant nation-king cut the salt from the east with frozen strakes. Sharp weathers bore surf-flame's [gold's] diminisher [generous man] to Sigtunir.

Swell, as Bolverk said:

You fitted out a fleet from the fair territory the next year. Water went over the ships. You clove the swell with splendid surge-horses [ships].

Here the sea is also called surge. Expanse, as Ref said:

The stock-nag [ship] touches with its breast the prow-cut board-world [sea], but the expanse is thrown in over the firm gunwale. Timber suffers pressure.

The dark, as Brennu-Nial said:

Together sixteen of us baled out, lady, in four stations, and the surf rose. The dark was driven on to the main-ship's strakes.

The following are also terms for sea, so that it is normal to use them in kennings for ship or gold: Ran, who, it is said, was Ægir's wife, as in this example:

The main's embers were tossed up into the sky, the sea moved with force. I think the prows cut the clouds. Ran's way hit the moon.

The daughters of Ægir and Ran are nine, and their names have already been written: Himinglæva, Dufa, Blodughadda, Hefring, Unn, Hronn [wave], Bylgia [billow], Drofn [comber], Kolga. Einar Skulason listed six of their names – Himinglæva, Unn, Dufa, Blodughadda, Kolga, Hefring – in this verse which was quoted above:

Himinglæva stirs up the roar of the sea against the brave . . .

Wave (Hronn), as Valgard said:

Froth was piled in heaps, the swollen main surged with gold, and waves washed the frightening warships' heads.

Billow (Bylgia), as Ottar the Black said:

You cut with planed rudder the engulfing-high billows. The sheet which women spun played against the mast-top on the slipway-reindeer [ship].

Comber (Drofn), as Orm said:

The spirited Thrud who keeps the mash-tub [woman]

cultivates every good quality, and the comber-flame [gold] Lofn, firm in friendship, rejects vices.

Bore, as Thorleik the Fair said:

> The grey sea roars, and the bore carries bright froth over the red timber where the slipway bison [ship] gapes with gold-adorned mouth.

Offing, as Einar said:

> The confident ones did not notice until sea fell heavily on the wake-timber [ship]. I do not think the offing gave our friends any peace.

The overflowing, as Ref said:

> Mountains of the overflowing crash down on the sheet-bear [ship] of Gusir's gifts [flags]. The winter-survivor [bear] of boards now storms forward over Glammi's course [sea].

Shoal, as here:

> The shoal broke fast around me. The emptiness [ocean] invited me to its home. I did not accept the flat one's [sea's] offer.

Breaker, as Ottar said:

> Thin board broke above the sea and breaker thundered. Tree-killer [wind] increased. Men got harsh weather.

Bay, as Bragi said:

> Breeze-sender [giant, Hymir], who cut the thin string [fishing-line] of gulls' Møre [the sea] for Thor, did not want to lift the twisted bay-menacer [Midgard serpent].

Sound, as Einar said:

> I cut through the sound with the planking to the south of Hrund. My hand has been adorned as a result of my meeting with the prince.

Fiord, as Einar said:

> Next I see a finely inscribed serpent on the splendid yeast-
> flood [ale] tunic [horn]. May the offerer note how I treat of
> the fiord-pyre [gold] maple [man] in words.

The thunderer, as Markus said:

> I will by no means slander the loquacious flinger [generous
> giver] of the thunderer's sun [gold]. That sheath-eel [sword]
> wielder is evil who misuses poetry.

What terms are there for **fire**? As in what follows:

> The fire does not burn seldom which Magnus kindles. The
> worthy prince singes dwellings. Buildings belch smoke be-
> cause of the ruler.

Flame, as Valgard said:

> Furious flame quickly shot embers from the soot, and
> columns of smoke then rose vertically over the tottering
> houses.

Pyre, as here:

> Haki was burned on a pyre where . . . <sea-animals, ships?>
> waded surf-tracks [sea].

Gleeds, as Grani said:

> I think gleeds felled . . . <horses, i.e. ships?> of Glammi's
> track [sea]. The prince so kindled . . .

Ember, as Atli said:

> Axe is reddened with blood, embers grow, very many
> houses burn, halls flame, the sparkler rages, fine people fall.

Here the fire is also called sparkler. Smoke, as here [Thord
Siareksson]:

> The all-powerful one's lodgings burned half-built by the

Nid itself. I think it was fire that felled the hall, smoke shot grime on the host.

Burning, as Arnor said:

The angry Island-Danes' injurer did not soften his treatment of the people of Romerike. The defiance of the Heinir diminished. Burning rendered them submissive.

Beacon. Blaze, as Einar said:

The blaze was kindled quickly, and the Hising host, who got the worst of it, fled in haste.

Flickering, as Valgard said:

The bright flickering caused by the strong ruler surged over the city's fortifications. The vikings destroyed rapaciously. Sorrow afflicted the maiden.

Lowe, as Halldor Skvaldri said:

There you were able to divide their treasures. Shield's lowe [swords] thundered through homes. You were never bereft of victory.

These are words for **times**: age, formerly, period, long ago, year, season, winter, summer, spring, autumn, month, week, day, night, morning, evening, nightfall, early, betimes, late, at once, day before yesterday, next, yesterday, tomorrow, hour, while. These are further terms for night in *Alsvinnsmal*:

Its name is night among men, but obscurity in Hel, it is known as mask among the gods, giants call it sorrow-free, elves sleep-joy, dwarfs dream-Niorun.

From the equinox it is autumn until the sun sets in the position of none. Then it is winter until the equinox. Then it is spring until the moving days. Then it is summer until the equinox. Harvest-month is the name of the last one before winter, slaughter-month is the name of the first one in winter, then it is frost-month, then ram-month, then Thorri, then Goi, then single-month, then cuckoo-month and seed-time, then egg-time and lamb-fold-time, then it is sun-month and shieling-month, then there is hay-making, then it is the month of corn-reaping.

What non-periphrastic names for **men** are there? Each one in himself is simply man. The first and highest term for man is when a man is called emperor, after that king, after that earl. These three men share all the following descriptions. All-powerful one, as it says here:

> I know all the all-powerful ones east and south of the home of clippers: Svein's son is better than any fierce one to make trial of.

Here the term fierce one is also used. He is called all-powerful because he is sole ruler of all his realm. Marshal, as Gissur said:

> The marshal gladdens giantess's steed [wolf] and Hlokk's swan [raven] in battle [by providing them with carrion]. Olaf makes Ygg's [Odin's] goslings [ravens] happy with Skogul's storms [battles].

A king is called marshal because he marshals his army into troops. Ruler, as Ottar the Black said:

> The ruler will take for certain Oski's [Odin's] loveless [lacking a ruler] wife [Iord = land] in the east. The one who is all-powerful over men leads a good battle-Freyr's [warrior's] life.

Lord or laird, as Arnor said:

> The lord of Shetland, who is highest of princes, gained victory in every thundering of brands [battle]. The poet wishes to raise up the fierce one's glory.

An earl can be called duke [*hertogi*, lit. army-leader], and a king can also be referred to thus, since he leads his army to battle. Thiodolf said this:

> And the putter-down of dukes had the eyes put out of the head of the captured mound-hastener [killer]. I bring forward his praise.

Signor or seigneur, as Sighvat said:

> Signor of Norway, let the poor just like the rich now benefit
> from your laws, and give generously. Keep your word.

Munificent one, as Markus said:

> The munificent one subjected the wicked people to fire,
> death was then the fate of seafarers. Suppressor of robbers,
> you kindled the highest brightness of burning south at Iom.

Illustrious one, as Hallvard said:

> There is not under the pole of the earth [Yggdrasil] an
> illustrious one closer to the lord of monks [God] than you.
> The breaker [generous giver] of soil-ruler's [giant's] words
> [gold] saves Danes.

Land-director, as Thiodolf said:

> Fault-shunning land-director pours out Kraki's bright bar-
> ley [gold],

as was written above. The reason he is called this is that he directs
his army through the land of other kings, or directs an army away
from his own land.

There was a king whose name was Halfdan the Old, who was
the most renowned of all kings. He held a great sacrifice at
mid-winter and offered a sacrifice in order to be granted that he
might live in his kingdom for three hundred years. But the reply he
got was that he would live no longer than one long human life,
but that there would be three hundred years during which there
would be neither female nor non-noble male in his line of descent.
He was a great warrior and went far and wide through eastern
lands. There he killed in single combat a king called Sigtrygg.
Then he married a woman called Alvig the Wise, daughter of King
Emund of Novgorod. They had eighteen sons, and nine of them
were born together. Their names were as follows: one was
Thengil, who was known as Thengil [prince] of men; second
Ræsir [impeller, ruler], third Gram [fierce one], fourth Gylfi, fifth
Hilmir [helmeter], sixth Iofur [prince], seventh Tiggi [noble],

eighth Skyli or Skuli [protector], ninth Harri or Herra [lord].
These nine brothers became so renowned in warfare that ever
since their names have been treated in all records as honorific
titles, equivalent to the name of king or the name of earl. They had
no children and all fell in battles. Ottar the Black said this:

> Imbued with might, the *thengil* was already at an early age
> vigorous in battle. I pray his life may last. I consider him a
> superman.

Markus said this:

> The *ræsir* made the Rhine's sun [gold] shine from the
> red-coloured skull [figurehead] on the mere's mountains
> [waves].

Egil said this:

> The *gram* has raised up the fence-cliffs [brows] of my
> <mask's> ground [face].

Eyvind said this:

> He was merry with the sons of the people, he had to defend
> the land, the cheerful *gylfi*, he stood beneath his golden
> helmet.

Glum said this:

> The *hilmir* under his helmet reddened whetstone's hollow
> [sword] on Gauts.

Ottar the Black said this:

> May the *iofur* hear the beginning of his rhyme. The king's
> eulogy shall be raised. May he note properly the forms of
> my praise.

As Stuf said:

> Glory-spurred *tiggi* hewed with both hands the troop of

warriors there south of the Nissan. The host went cheerful
beneath their shields.

Hallfrod said this:

I am parted from the *skyli* [protector]. The time of swords
has caused this. I look for the lord of men's return. For most
this is the greatest pious hope and delusion.

Markus said this:

I summon to attend to the highly-wrought work of praise
the hawk-spirited lord (*harri*) of Danish ground.

Halfdan and his wife had a further nine sons, whose names
were: Hildir, whom the Hildings are descended from; second
Nefir, whom the Niflungs are descended from; third Audi, whom
the Odlings are descended from; fourth Yngvi, whom the
Ynglings are descended from; fifth Dag, whom the Doglings are
descended from; sixth Bragi, whom the Bragnings are descended
from – this is the line of Halfdan the Generous; seventh Budli,
whom the Budlungs are descended from – from the Budlung line
were descended Atli and Brynhild; eighth is Lofdi, he was a great
war-king, his following was a troop known as *lofdar*, his descen-
dants are known as Lofdungs, from them is descended Eylimi,
Sigurd Fafnisbani's grandfather; ninth Sigar, from him are de-
scended the Siklings, this is the line of Siggeir, who was related by
marriage to Volsung, and the line of Sigar who hanged Hagbard.
From the Hilding line Harald the Red-whiskered, grandfather of
Halfdan the Black, was descended. From the Niflung line came
Giuki; from the Odling line came Kiar; from the Ylfing line came
Eirik the Eloquent. The following are also great kings' lines: from
Yngvi, whom the Ynglings are descended from; from Skiold in
Denmark, whom the Skioldungs are descended from; from Vol-
sung in Francia, they are called Volsungs. There was a war-king
called Skelfir, and his descendants are known as the Skilfing line.
That family is in eastern lands. These family lines that have just
been named have been used in poetry in such a way as to treat
these all as honorific titles. As Einar said:

I have heard that the *hildings* [kings] went forward to hold a spear-parliament [battle] by the grey island [Holmengraa]. The green shield was made to spring in two.

As Grani said:

The *dogling* [king] gave eagles' bairn Danish blood to drink.

As Gamli Gnævadarskald said:

The young *odling* [king] launched himself as a young man out into the mighty word-activity [conflict] between haft's tongue [sword] and sword's board [shield].

As Iorunn said:

The *bragning* [king] decided to redden weapons in the wicked people's blood. The host suffered the king's wrath. Houses often fell because of embers [fire].

Einar said this:

The *budlung's* [king's] blade bit, blood fell on darts, Hild's cloud [shield] was riven at Whitby.

Arnor said this:

The descendant of *siklings* [kings] accustoms the sea-dipping frigates to be out. He colours warships inside with blood. This is a benefit to the raven.

As Thiodolf said:

The brave *sikling's* life ended in such a way that we are all in a difficult situation. The lauded *lofdung* [king] suffered life's destruction.

King Lofdi's following was a troop known as *lofdar*. As Arnor said:

Another *skioldung* [king] more excellent than you, *gram* [fierce one], will never be born beneath the sun.

Volsung, as Thorkel Hamarskald said:

The descendant of *volsungs* [kings] decided to send me gold-decorated weapons across the cool ocean.

Yngling, as Ottar the Black said:

No battle ardent *yngling* who subjected islands in the west under himself appeared on the landscape in the east until they got you.

Yngvi; this is also a word for king, as Markus said:

This generation must hear Eirik's praise, no one knows of a more outstanding *thengil* in this world. The *yngvi* held the throne of *iofur*s with long-lasting renown.

Skilfing, as Valgard said:

Skilfing [king], you took a great force south past the broad lands where cutters [warships] quivered. Sicily was devastated in the end.

Signor, as Sighvat said:

Let the poor just like the rich now benefit from your laws, signor of Norway, and give generously. Keep your word.

Poets are called *greppar,* and it is normal in poetry to refer thus to any man if desired. The men in King Half's following were known as *rekkar,* and from their name warriors are known as *rekkar,* and it is normal to refer to all men thus. Men are also called *lofdar* in poetry, as was noted above. The men in the following of the king known as Skati the Generous were known as *skatnar.* From his name anyone that is generous is known as *skati.* The following of King Bragi the Old were called *bragnar.* Men who assess people's cases are called *virdar* [*virda* = to assess]. Defenders of the land are called *fyrdar* and *firar* and *verar.*

Vikings and sailors, these are a naval host. *Beimar*, this is what the following of King Beimuni were called. *Gumnar* or *gumar* are names for the leaders of a troop, just as there is what is called a *gumi* [groom] in a bridal party. The term *gotnar* comes from the name of a king called Goti, whom Gotland is named after. He was called after one of Odin's names, it was derived from the name Gaut, for Gautland or Gotland was called after this name of Odin, while Sweden is from the name Svidur. This is also one of Odin's names. At that time all the mainland that he ruled over was known as Reidgotaland, and all the islands Eygotaland. These are now known as the Danish realm and the Swedish realm. Young men that have not settled down, while they are making their fortunes or reputation, are called *drengir*; they are called *far-drengir* who travel from land to land, king's *drengir* who are in the service of rulers, and they are also called *drengir* who are in the service of rich men or landowners. Manly and ambitious men are called *drengir*.

There are ones called *seggir* and *kniar* and troopers, these are members of a retinue; thanes and *holdar*, this is what landowners are called. Men that bring about settlement of disputes are called *lionar*. There are men that are known as champions, paladins, fighting-cocks, brave ones, valiant ones, tough ones, bravoes, heroes. These terms are contrary to them in meaning: to call a man soft, weak, insipid, milksop, wet, craven, coward, skulker, weakling, odious one, degenerate, wretch, riff-raff, scum, loafer, vagabond, poltroon, beggar, worthless one, caitiff. A generous man is called munificent one, illustrious one, *skati*, splendid-*skati*, gold-*skati*, prince of men, man of wealth, affluent one, money-bags, rich man, nobleman. The following names are contrary in meaning: niggard, close one, stingy one, tight-fisted one, churl, gift-grudger. A sage is called decision-maker, and a man without wisdom is called idiot, deranged, goose, dupe, blockhead, dolt, booby, fool, raving, frantic, bewitched. An elegant man: show-off, *dreng* [gentleman], dandy, coxcomb, gallant. Then there is what is called a rough, blatherer, scrag, hewer of wood, clown, good-for-nothing, yokel, sluggard, wastrel.

The folk of a country are called the people or community. And a slave is called captive, servant, labourer, serf.

An individual is called a man, it is a duo if there are two, a bunch if there are three, four are a company, a flock is five men, it is a troop if there are six, seven complete a crew, eight deliver an accusation-tally, nine are mates, it is a corps if there are ten, eleven make up an embassy, it is a visitation if twelve go, thirteen is a crowd, fourteen is an expedition, it is an assembly when fifteen meet, sixteen is an occupation, seventeen is a congregation, his enemies seem plenty to one who meets eighteen, he has companionship who has nineteen men, twenty men are a household. Thirty is a people, forty are a folk, fifty are a county, sixty are a muster, seventy are an army, eighty are a population, a hundred is a host.

There are also those terms that are put in place of men's names. We call these *vidkenningar* [circumlocutions] or *sannkenningar* [(true) descriptions] or *fornofn* [substitutions]. They are circumlocutions when one names something else by its normal name, and one calls the person that one wants to refer to its possessor; or when one calls the person the father or grandfather of the one that has been named. The third relationship is great-grandfather. A son is also called heir, inheritor, child, bairn, boy, successor. A brother is also called consanguinean, german, twin, cognate. A relative is also called nephew, kindred, kin, kinsman, relation, scion, posterity, stock, issue, kin-branch, family line, descent, offspring, agnate, lineage. Relations by marriage are also called affinitives, connections. A friend is also called counsel-sharer, counsel-giver, gossip, confidant, crony, old bunkie, shipmate, bench-mate, bench-partner. A bunkie is one who shares the same berth. One who is not a friend is also called enemy, adversary, fiend, destroyer, injurer, slayer, oppressor, wrecker, antagonist. We call these terms circumlocutions, as also if a man is referred to by his dwelling or his ship, when it has a name, or by one of his possessions when it is given a proper name. We call them descriptions (*sannkenningar*) when men are called sage, thinker, rhetorician, mentor, munificent one, unsluggish, heedful man, dandy. These are substitutions.

The following are non-periphrastic terms for **women** in poetry. Women who are given to a husband are called wife and bride and matron. Dame and lady are used of women who always go around with pomp and finery. Those who are clever in speech are called *snotir*. Those who are gentle in behaviour are called *drosir*. *Svarri* and *svark*, these are arrogant women. A woman who is of independent character is called *ristil*. A woman who is very rich is called *ryg*. *Feima* is the word for one who is retiring, such as young girls or women who are timid. *Sæta* is the term for a woman whose husband has left the country. *Hæl* is what one calls a woman whose husband has been killed. *Ekkia* is the term for one whose husband has died of sickness. Each one is first of all called maiden, but *kerlingar* when they are old. There are also the terms for woman that used in a condemnatory sense, and these can be found in poems, though examples are not copied down here. The women who are married to the same man are called *eliur*. A son's wife is called *snor*. A husband's mother is called *sværa*. There are also the terms mother, grandmother, thirdly *edda* [great-grandmother]. *Eida* means mother, and a daughter is also called child, bairn. A sister is also called *dis* [lady], bairn-*dis*. A woman is also known as bedfellow, gossip, confidante of her husband, and this is circumlocution.

On a man there is what is called a **head**. This shall be referred to by calling it toil or burden of the neck, land of helmet and hat and brains, of hair and eyebrows, scalp, ears, eyes, mouth; Heimdall's sword, and it is normal to use any term for sword you like and qualify it by one or other of Heimdall's names. Without periphrasis the head is called skull, brainpan, temple, crown. Eyes are called sight and glance or look, aimers. They may be referred to by calling them sun or moon, shields and glass or jewels or stone of eyelashes or eyebrows, eyelids or forehead. Ears are called auricles and hearing. They shall be referred to by calling them land or by any of the terms for earth or mouth or channel or sight or eyes of the hearing, if allegory is being used. The mouth shall be referred to by calling it land or house of tongue or teeth, words or gums, lips or something like that, and if allegory is being used, then people call the mouth a ship, and the lips the gunwale, the tongue the oar or rudder. Teeth are sometimes called rocks or skerries of words, mouth or tongue. The tongue is often called sword of speech or mouth. Facial hair is called beard, whiskers or moustaches when it is on the lips. Hair is called locks, and in the case of women, tresses. Hair is called curls. Hair is referred to by calling it forest, or by some tree-name or other, describing it in terms of skull or brainpan or head, or the beard by referring to it in terms of chin or cheek or throat.

The **heart** is called bosom. It shall be referred to by calling it corn or stone or apple or nut or ball or the like, and referring to it in terms of breast or thought. It can also be called house or ground or mountain of the thought. The breast shall be referred to by calling it house or enclosure or ship of heart, spirit or liver, land of energy, thought and memory. Thought is called mind and tenderness (*siafni*), love, affection, desire, pleasure. Thought shall be referred to by calling it wind of troll-wives and it is normal for this purpose to use the name of whichever one you like, and also to use the names of giants, and then refer to it in terms of his wife or mother or daughter. These names form a special group. Thought is also called disposition, attitude, energy, fortitude, liking, memory, wit, temper, character, troth. A thought can also be called anger, enmity, hostility, ferocity, evil, grief, sorrow, bad temper, wrath, duplicity, insincerity, inconstancy, frivolity, brashness, impulsiveness, impetuousness.

The upper **limb** can be called hand, arm, fist, paw. On the upper limb there is what is called the elbow, forearm, wrist, joint, finger, grasp, palm, nail, finger-tip, side of the hand, quick. The upper limb can be called the ground of weapons or shields, tree of shoulder and sleeve, palm and wrist, ground of gold rings and of falcon and hawk and of all terms for it, and allegorically the leg of the shoulder, bow-forcer. Legs can be called trees of the soles, insteps, stocking-feet or the like, running-shaft of the path or of walking, of the pace. The leg can be called tree or pillar of these things. Legs are referred to in terms of skis and shoes and breeches. On the leg is what is called thigh, knee, calf, shank, shin, instep, sole, toe. One can refer to the leg in terms of all these and call it tree; and the leg is called mast and yard and referred to in terms of these things.

Speech is also called words and vocabulary and eloquence, tale, story, wrangle, dispute, song, incantation, recitation, chat, quavering, conversation, talk, prating, banter, quarrel, mocking, prattle, blather, bragging, patter, inanity, cant, triviality, twaddle. Noise is also called sound, voice, resonance, howling, clamour, din, clash, uproar, roar, crack, thud, report, clatter. By means of these expressions battle shall be referred to in terms of swords or other weapons or shields.

Wisdom is called sagacity, counsel, understanding, memory, deliberation, intellect, numeracy, far-sightedness, subtlety, eloquence, genius. Dissembling is called deception, guile, shiftiness.

Læti means two things. Noise is called *læti*, disposition (*ædi*) is called *læti*, and *ædi* also means fury. *Reidi* also has two meanings. It is called *reidi* [wrath] when a man is in a bad temper, the gear (*fargervi*) of a ship or horse is called *reidi*. *Far* also has two meanings. *Far* is anger, *far* is a ship. People frequently use such vocabulary so as to compose with concealed meaning, and this is usually called word-play (*ofliost* [obvious]). People call it *lid* [joint] on a person where the bones meet, *lid* [fleet] is a word for ships, *lid* [troop] is a word for people. It is also called *lid* [help] when someone gives another assistance (*lidsinni*). *Lid* is a word for ale. There is what is called a *hlid* [gateway] in an enclosure, and *hlid* is what people call an ox, and *hlid* is a slope. These distinctions can be made use of in poetry so as to create word-play which is difficult to understand, if it is a different distinction of meaning that has to be taken than the previous line seemed before to indicate. Similarly there are also many other such words where the same term applies to several things.

Atli, Frodi, Ali, Glammi, Beiti, Ati and Beimuni, Audmund, Gudmund, Atal and Gestil, Geitir, Gauti, Gylfi, Sveidi.

Gæir, Eynef, Gaupi and Endil, Skekkil, Ekkil, Skefil and Solvi, Half and Hemlir, Harek and Gor, Hagbard, Haki, Hraudnir, Meiti.

Hiorolf and Hraudung, Hogni, Mysing, Hunding, Hviting, Heiti, Mævil, Hialmar, Moir, Hæmir, Mævi, Rodi, Rakni, Rer and Leifi.

Randver, Rokkvi, Reifnir, Leifnir, Næfil, Ræfil, Nori, Lyngvi, Byrvil, Kilmund, Beimi, Iorek, Iosmund, Thvinnil, Yngvi, Teiti.

Virfil, Vinnil, Vandil, Solsi, Gautrek and Hun, Giuki, Budli, Homar, Hnefi, Horvi, Sorvi. I can see no more **sea-kings.**

I shall tell the names of **giants.** Ymir, Gang and Mimir, Idi and Thiassi, Hrungnir, Hrimnir, Hraudnir, Grimnir, Hvedrung, Hafli, Hripstod, Gymir.

Hardverk, Hrokkvir and Hastigi, Hræsvelg, Herkir and

Hrimgrimnir, Hymir and Hrimthurs, Hval, Thrigeitir, Thrym, Thrudgelmir, Thistilbardi.

Geirrod, Fyrnir, Galar, Thrivaldi, Fiolverk, Geitir, Flegg, Blapthvari, Forniot, Spretting, Fialar, Stigandi, Som and Svasud, Svarang, Skrati.

Surt and Storverk, Sækarlsmuli, Skærir, Skrymir, Skerkir, Salfang, Oskrud and Svart, Ondud, Stumi, Alsvart, Aurnir, Am and Skalli.

Kott, Osgrui and Alfarin, Vindsval, Vipar and Vafthrudnir, Eld and Aurgelmir, Ægir, Rangbein, Vind, Vidblindi, Vingnir, Leifi.

Beinvid, Biorgolf and Brandingi, Dumb, Bergelmir, Dofri and Midiung, Nati, Sokmimir. Now there have been listed the names of very powerful giants.

I shall list the names of **troll-wives**. Grid and Gnissa, Gryla, Bryia, Glumra, Geitla, Grima and Bakrauf, Guma, Gestilia, Grottintanna.

Gialp, Hyrrokkin, Hengikepta, Gneip and Gnepia, Geysa, Hala, Horn and Hruga, Hardgreip, Forad, Hryggda, Hvedra and Holgabrud.

Hrimgerd, Hæra, Herkia, Fala, Imd, Iarnsaxa, Ima, Fiolvor, Morn, Ividia, Amgerd, Simul, Sivor, Skrikia, Sveipinfalda.

Oflugbarda and Iarnglumra, Imgerd, Ama and Iarnvidia, Margerd, Atla, Eisurfala, Leikn, Munnharpa and Myrkrida.

Leirvor, Liota and Lodinfingra, Kraka, Vardrun and Kiallandi, Vigglod, Thurbord. We wish to name Ryg last, and Rifingafla.

Thor is called Atli and Asabrag. He is Ennilang and Eindridi, Biorn, Hlorridi and Hardveur, Vingthor, Sonnung, Veud and Rym.

Names of **Æsir**:

Odin's sons are Baldr and Meili, Vidar and Nep, Vali, Ali, Thor and Hildolf, Hermod, Sigi, Skiold, Yngvi-Freyr and Itreksiod, Heimdall, Sæming.

There still remain some names of **giants**: Eimgeitir, Ver, Im, Hringvolnir, Viddi, Vingrip, Vandil, Gyllir, Grimnir, Glaumar, Glam, Samendil.

Vornir, Hardgreip and Vagnhofdi, Kyrmir, Suttung and Kaldgrani, Iotun, Ogladnir and Aurgrimnir, Grimling, Gusir, Ofoti, Hloi, Ganglati and Helregin, Hrossthiof, Durnir, Hundalf, Baugi, Hraudung, Fenrir, Hroar and Midi.

Yet shall be listed names of **Æsir**. There is Ygg and Thor and Yngvi-Freyr, Vidar and Baldr, Vali and Heimdall. Then there is Tyr and Niord, I list Bragi next, Hod, Forseti. Here is Loki last.

Now shall all the **Asyniur** be named. Frigg and Freyia, Fulla and Snotra, Gerd and Gefiun, Gna, Lofn, Skadi, Iord and Idunn, Ilm, Bil, Niorun.

Hlin and Nanna, Hnoss, Rind and Siofn, Sol and Saga, Sigyn and Vor. Then there is Var, and Syn must be named, but Thrud and Ran reckoned next to them.

Freyia also wept gold for Od. Her names are Horn, Thrungva, Syr, Skialf and Gefn, and likewise Mardoll. Her daughters are Hnoss and Gersemi.

There are yet others, Odin's maids, Hild and Gondul, Hlokk, Mist, Skogul. Then are listed Hrund and Eir, Hrist, Skuld. They are called norns who shape necessity.

Now I shall list Nipt [sister] and Dis [**lady**]. *Snot,* bride, lady, *svarri, sprakki,* matron, dame, woman, *feima,* widow, *ryg,* wife, *dros, ristil, sæta,* maid, *svark* and *hæl,* maiden and *kerling.*

It is time to say the names for **men**. *Greppar* and *gumnar, gumar* and *drengir, gotnar, rekkar,* fighting-cocks, *seggir,* troop, brave ones and affluent ones.

Bragnar, thanes, *beimar, holdar, firar* and sailors, *fyrdar, holdar,* company, household, flock, tough ones, *kniar* and champions, paladins, mates.

Population and embassy and bravoes, troopers and *lofdar,* people and crews, community, show-offs, *lionar* and expeditions, munificent one, illustrious one, prince of men, sage.

Then there is dandy and gold-*skati*, then there are elegant men and affluent ones and money-bags and show-offs, host and *helming* [troop] and chieftains.

Folk and county, assembly, public. Now there is press and crowd, bunch, wealth-*skatar*, household guard and army, corps, gallants, crew and muster, occupation, coxcombs, being and *brionar*.

Still there are left some names of people: court and guests and housecarls, domestic troop and household. If I mention everything, confidant and bunkie and mentor.

Domestics, old bunkies, bench-mate and gossip, armoured ones and retinues. Then there are fellows and relations together, friend, shipmate, mercenaries, heroes.

Great-grandfather and kindred, grandfather, son, father, brother, german, consanguinean and cognate, bairn, lad, nephew and inheritor. Then there are twins and agnates.

Relative, connection, posterity and child, kin and kin-branch, kinsman, family line, boy, speech-mate, in-law and crony, issue, genealogy, lineage and youth.

Bench-partners and affinitives, offspring is next and stock. Then there is counsel-sharer. Servants, slaves, serf, labourers, workmen, captives.

These are terms [for **battle**]: row and tumult, clangor, spear-fight and spear-grab, strife and clamour, shield-violence and stir, unrest and onslaught, victory, campaign, fray.

Scrap, murder and slaying, attack and action, enmity, threat, tussle, broil and affray. Then there is battle and doom, storm and pugnacity, host-taker, thunder.

I shall say the words for **swords**: glaive and Hrotti, useful, Dragvandil [draw-wand], Groa [grower], Gram [angry], screamer, clamourer and end-scored, scythe and polisher, honour, glinter.

Servant, clanger, cutlass, Skrymir, Laufi, ale-tarry, long-beard and worm-borer, legbiter and quiet and Leifnir's hurt, host-striker, Hneitir [wounder] and *hafrakan*.

Lotti, shover, thruster, *mækir*, aimed, hand-waver and Mistletoe, metal, thriver and striker and mid-decorated, Fetbreid [broad-track], gate-flame and life-quencher.

Wavy, threaded, corpse-pain and brand, werwolf, corpse-maker, wind-bright and torment, ash, pain-wader, edge-sharp, flitter and ugly-flitting, hall-fence, grip.

Keen, head-sharp, skull-crusher, corpse-Gaut, host-shining and flesh-Mimir, wound-strip, deceiver, flickerer, rivet-failer, burnished, heaper, notched, gate-flame.

Mimung and feller and symbol-wolf, ringed, corpse-enclosed, crane, twist-borer, crooked, millstone-biter, light, hardened, wolf, overcomer, wall-damager.

Terrifier, pale-maker, router, notcher, shooter, trembler, polished, tearer, breaker, white one, Bæsing, Tyrfing [tarry], hooked and ring. One will come across night-bringer.

Flame and hand-ringer, long-keen and fire, eagle and frightener and rivetted, failer, jabber, ram and diminisher, blaze and long-neck, exciter, inciter.

Feller, blancher, Fafnir [embracer], piercer, battler, flamer, offspring, flexible, scyther, polisher, swallower, cutter and corpse, Goin, guest-Moin [moor-guest] and mockery, crasher, Nidhogg [mean-striker].

Point, blood-band, wound-knuckles, blood-strip, blood-warp and bloody-eddy, blood-waker, lying striker, blood-grip, eddy-warp and brand, edge-strips, folk.

Cries, cutters and Olrod's gift, mark, battle-rim and mis-hit, fringe and burnished, under-drawer, wolf and Kaldhamar's gift, corpse-bast and shoulder.

Sword and clamourer and link-rivet, clench-plate, victory-knob, hilt and tang, hand-grip, blow-polished and mid-stick.

Axe and iron-sparth, horny, scraper and bearded, cutter and gaper, power-span, Gnepia [towering], giantess and Fala [frightener], spiked and bulging, whiskered and Vigglod [battle-bright], hewer and stretched. Then there is soft-horned: this is considered the highest of names for axe.

Dart, **spear** and sting, *dof*, lance and rod, spike, shaft and wearier, singed, corpse-sword, pike, javelin, stinger, glaive, halberd, gavelock, Frankish, Gungnir, Poitou lance.

Arrow is also *akka,* point, white-mouth, Fenia and drift, flight, noisy mover, *bosl,* bale, lancet, spike and Hremsa [claw], gain-flying and stormer, gain and shaft-quick.

Flight-bright, flight-swift, Fifa [lion's tooth] and shot, we shall mention finder and Gusir's work. There is Iolf's work but highest is whizzer.

Elm, curve, **bow**, yew and double-wood, bend, bright and noisy, seemly, noisy clanger. But I declare that all weapons together are called irons, arrow and strikers, isen and spears.

Shield, narrow-hall, cover, hall-binder, bender, lee-edge and buckler, fight-bend, targe, storm-bright and protection, wide, pale, engraved, battle-bright and linden.

Clamourer, dew-scraper and jewel-shelterer, war-light, stony and war-shelterer, cooled and edged, soiled, boarded, protector, bordered, pure, double-boarded.

Battler and roarer, ever-protector, brilliant, circle, fair-dark, carried, mid-life-protector.

I shall say the names of Hropt's hood [**helmet**]: helm, gold-coloured, coverer, slaughter-rimy, stone-rimy, hollowed and protection, life-protector, fine-looker and eager-brown.

Battle boar (Hildigolt), top, army-crest and warmer, mask, terrifier, gleamer, dome.

Byrnie, arriver, helm-ringer, coat and close, cold, Finn's legacy (Finnsleif), battle-goer, pliable, hindrance and blood-played.

Sea, ever-lying, salt, ocean (Ægir), main, wetness, swim, flat one, dead calm and bay, resounding, overhang, emptiness, brawler, rocker and mere, sucker, suck, same, swallower, maelstrom and fiord.

Sound, creek, good passage, fluid and expanse, tempest,

depth, breaker, dark, flood and surf, swell, sparkler, engulfer (Gymir) and flower, rumbler and unquiet, surge, fen, snatcher.

Crashing, wake, league, fishing-ground, inlet and fishing-bank, water, deep and submersion, cove, tarn and canal, storm, ditch, pool, current, stream and brook, channel, spring, fount, eddy, waterfall and firth.

Hefring [lifting], roller, white one and offing, Hronn [wave], Ran [plunderer], Kolga [cold one] and Himinglæva [heaven-bright], Drofn [comber], Unn [wave] and sweller, Dufa [dip], Bylgia [billow], shoal and bore, Blodughadda [bloody-haired].

[**Rivers**] Gioll [noisy], Glit [shining], Gera [greedy], Glod [glowing]and Valskialf,Van [hope], Vid [wide],Vimur, Ving and Ysa [Ouse], Sid [low], Sudr [south], Freka [demanding], Sekin [pushing], Einstika [lone-progressing], Elbe, Ro [peace], Ekla [want], Ekin [driven], Rennandi [running].

Tyne [stormer], Rhine, Nid, Tholl, Rim, Ysia [hastener], Don, Ogn [water], Dyna, Dyn [thunderer], Hollfara [sloping course], Orun and Bro, Audskialg, Lud, Mun, Merkrida, Mein and Sax-elbe.

Tiber, Durn, Dvina, Thames, Vond [difficult] and Strand, Marne and Göta älv, Alin, Unn [wave], Olga and Euphrates, Ogn, Eidrennir [isthmus-runner] and Aberdeen.

Rogn, Hronn [wave] and Raun [test], Raumelf [Glomma], Hnipul, Hnopul, Hialmunla, Humber, Dvina, Vil [trouble], Vin [drier up], Vella [welling], Valin, Semd, Salin, Dnieper, Drammen, Strauma [torrent], Nissan, Mynt [mouthed], Gnapa [leaning].

Gilling [resounding] and Nile, Ganges, Tweed, Luma, Vervada, Loire and Gunnthro [battle-trough], Vidsvol [wide-cool], Vegsvinn [way-swift], Yn, Thiodnuma [great container], Fiorm [hurrying], Strand and Spey and Fimbulthul [mighty mumbler].

Nyt [profitable], Hronn [wave] and Naud [need], Not [wet], Slidr [terrible] and Hrid [storm], Kormt, Leiptr [lightning] and Ormt [armed], two Kerlaugs [baths], Gomul

[old], Sylg [swallower] and Yn and Geirvimul [spear-swarming], Ylg [she-wolf], Vod [ford] and Flod [flood]. Jordan is last.

[**Fish**] Salmon and ling, whiting, cusk, sea-trout, milter salmon, perch and kelt, lobster, lumpsucker, milter, fluke, mackerel, trout and Andvari [watcher; pike].

Herring, saithe, skate, launce, brown trout and redfish, codfish and houting, roach, flounder, *fylding*, sturgeon and sea-scorpion, mackerel-shark, catfish and Greenland shark.

Weever, miller's thumb and prawn, trout, shell-fish, sword-fish and pollack, porbeagle, turbot and hornfish, bullhead, gurnard and *fengrani*.

Codling, coal-fish, cod, *vartari*, shallow-haunter, pike, gilled, torsk, eel and carp, crab, garfish, shark and moonfish, stickleback, sea-urchin.

Buck-whale, pike-whale and sea-steamer, dolphin, *haf-stramb* and porpoises, rorqual, rorqual-calf and red-crest, sperm whale, walrus, nordcaper.

Greenland whale, cow-whale, narwhal and pilot whale, humpback, fin whale and *skuta*-whale, right whale, killer whale and sei whale, horse-whale, bottle-nosed whale, lesser rorqual and grampus.

Now I shall expound the names of **ships**. Ark, oar-claw, ash, Sessrumnir, cutter, scout, ship and Skidbladnir, nave, Naglfari, row-boat, snack.

Freighter, buss, bow-cold and reindeer, bac, thole-strap-fixed, rimy-bowed, cruiser, boat and pinnace, brig, Hringhornir, long-boat, keel, longship, Leifnir, carvel.

Ring, Gnod, greedy, fast, Modroi, thole-strapped, prowed and pool-beater, owl, lighter and Askvitul, dinghy, cat-boat, cat, vessel and Skalp [cockle].

Merchantman, cog, knuckle, coble, dug-out, drake, Ellidi, dromond and pram, fir, steed, galley, ferry, scow, bark, craft and delight, frequent-traveller and *lid* [fleet].

Sail, lap, mast, holdfast, steering-oar, planking, rivet-row, seam and sheet-rope, stay, stem, steering-tie, studdle and buntline, pennant and black-strakes, bench, stern and cable.

Bow-rails, shrouds, reef-points and sheet, spike, mast-tree, nails, poop-supports, leek [mast], mast-top, line, ears, flag, flag-beard and plug.

Hound, mast-head-sheave and tiller, strake, bow, fifth strake and hawse-stem, clew-line, hawse, hank and back-stays, tholes, heel, hammer, help-rope and leech.

Yard, parrel, reef, rib and thole-straps, windlass, poop, wand, thole-pins, winch, tacking-boom, prow-carving, brands [bow-decorations], transoms, bowline, bulkheads.

Prow, knee, boarding, belt and bows, keel, board (mast-) wedge and garboard, bollards, carling, claws and thwarts, tack, gunwales, cleats and decking.

Guys, halyard, dale, oars, braces, clinch-plates, bridge and pins, sand-strake, keel-heel and anchor, buoy-rope, bailer and crow's-nest.

Earth, landscape, glebe, marl and Hlodyn, humus, Sif, Fior-gyn, ground, surface and orb, field, meadow and Fife, coun-try, loam and coast, land, soil, march, territory and marsh.

Holt, ridge and fells, hillside and rise, knoll, heath and hollow, hillock and slope, crust, dale and wold, coomb and tongue, mould, flag, hogback, moor, depression and sand.

In addition shall be said names of **oxen:** Arvak [early wakener], bellower and Iormunrek, neat, Freyr, Regin, smith, island-driller, Rufus and driven and dark-sided, fighter, gorer, Vingnir, guide.

Himinhriot, cattle and hard-goer, Hæfir [hoofed], stout one, roarer, stot, Hlid, Stuf and Lit, Hrid [storm], draught-ox, Arf [inheritance], Iormuni and mighty smith.

Spark, Apli [dapple] and goldenhorn, wealth, bullock, elder and Arfuni, steer, stormer, yeller, noise and membered, yearling, bull, tarb, dirty.

A **cow** is called heifer, quey and lower and Audhumla; she is the noblest of cows.

Ram, mighty-horn, horn-squealer, *gumar*, glowing-horn and shining-horn, teg, Hallinskidi, berry, wretched-horn and Heimdali, tup, middler, bleater, Mord and wether.

A **goat** is called Grimnir and Geirolnir, Tanngniost, *kiappi* and Tanngrisnir, squinter and rusher; a buck is Grim counted.

There is also one called Heidrun; nanny-goat and kidling. Coal-muzzle is a kid as well.

Bear, grizzly, mighty one, she-bear, *elgvidnir,* dark-tooth, ice-wolf and broadway, haltered, *bassi*, growler, leopard, rough, greedy one, robber, Iorek, *mosni*, forest-walker, cub, snarler, winter-survivor, greedy-tooth, yellow-bum, hooded one, shrivelled-gut.

Hart, Durathror, *hlid*, Eikthyrnir, Duneyr, Dain, Dvalar, moor-treader.

Hog, slaughter-shiner, grice, Hrimnir, swine-*tar*, boar, Sæhrimnir, barrow, shoat, slaughter-bear, dirt-treader, thriver, warlike, *skunp*, Thrond [thriving], Van-child.

Warg, **wolf,** Geri, watcher and grey beast, Hati, Hrodvitnir and heath-dweller, Freki and forest-dweller, Fenrir, leopard, Goti, worthy, noisy, howler, fighter, dusky, dreadful and dark-cheeked.

And moreover the names of the **she-wolf** are: wargin, barker and dusky, faintness.

There are nine **heavens** on high that are listed. I know the nethermost, it is Vindblain [wind-dark], it is Heidthornir [clouded-brightness] and Hregg-Mimir [storm-Mimir]. The second heaven is Andlang [extended] — this you can understand — the third Vidblain [wide-dark]. I declare that Vidfedmir [wide-embracer] is the fourth, Hriod [coverer], and Hlyrnir [twin-lit] I think is the sixth; Gimir [fiery or jewelled], Vet-Mimir [winter-Mimir]. I guess now that eight heavens have been enumerated. Skatyrnir [rich-wetter] stands higher than the clouds, it is beyond all worlds.

Sun and day-star, sight, fair-wheel, lightning, coverer, toy, grace-shine, disc, lightning, doubt-disc and light-bringer, sprinkler, elf-disc and Dvalin's toy.

Hattatal
[list of verse-forms]

which Snorri Sturluson composed about
King Hakon and Duke Skuli

What kinds of verse-form are there in poetry?

They are of three kinds.

What are they?

Those that are in accordance with rule, or licence, or prohibition.

What kinds of rule for verse-forms are there?

Two.

What are they?

Normal and varied.

In what does the normal rule for verse-forms consist?

In two things.

What are they?

Number and distinction.

What kinds of number are there in the rule for verse-forms?

Three.

What are they?

One kind of number is how many verse-forms are found in the poetry of major poets. The second is how many lines there are in one stanza in each verse-form. The third is how many syllables are put in each line in each verse-form.

What kinds of distinction are there in the rule for verse-forms?

Two.

What are they?

Distinction of meaning and distinction of sound.

What is distinction of meaning?

All meaning is distinguished by spelling, but sound is distinguished by having syllables long or short, hard or soft, and there is a rule of distinctions of sound that we call rhymes, as in this verse:

> Lætr sár [= sá er] Hákun heitir
> (hann rekkir lid) bannat
> (iörd kann frelsa) fyrdum
> fridrofs (konungr) ofsa.

> Siálfr rædr allt ok Elfar
> ungr stillir sá milli
> (gramr á gipt at fremri)
> Gandvíkr iöfurr landi.

He causes, whose name is Hakon — he emboldens troops — peace-breaking arrogance — the king knows how to free the land — to be banned to men. Himself he rules the land from Gandvik, this young ruler — the king's grace is the greater — all the way to the Elbe, the prince.

Here there is one aspect of spelling that determines the verse-form and creates the poetical effect, that there are twelve staves [alliterating sounds] in the stanza, and three are put in each quarter-stanza. In each quarter-stanza there are two lines. Each line contains six syllables. In the second line there is put first in the line the stave which we call the chief stave. This stave determines the alliteration. But in the first line this stave will appear twice at the beginnings of syllables. We call these staves props. If the chief stave is a consonant, the props must be the same letter, as here:

> Lætr sá er *H*ákun *h*eitir
> *h*ann rekkir lid bannat

But it is wrong if these staves come at the beginning of syllables more often or less often than this in a quarter-stanza. And if the chief stave is a vowel, the props must also be vowels, and it is more elegant that each of them should be a different vowel. It is then also acceptable for initial vowels to come more frequently in the quarter-stanza in pronouns or in particles of the following kinds: *ek* [I], or: *en, er, at, í, à, of, af, um* [but, when, that, in, on, about, by, around], and this is licence and not the normal rule.

There is a second aspect of the spelling that is involved in the rule of the sound which constitutes the verse-form and poetical effect. This distinction in the *dróttkvætt* [court-metre] form requires that the quarter-stanzas have the same arrangement of letters and sounds. In the odd lines this rule is analysed thus:

> iörd kann frelsa fyrdum

Here there is: *iörd . . . fyrd-*. There is one syllable in each position and each has a different vowel and also initial consonant, but there are the same letters after the vowel in both words. This rule of assonance we call *skothending* [half-rhyme]. But in the even lines it is thus:

> fridrofs konungr ofsa

Here there is: *-rofs . . .ofs-*. There is the same vowel and all the same sounds following it in both words, but the words are distinguished by their initial letters. This is called *adalhendingar* [full rhymes]. The rhymes in *dróttkvætt* form must be so arranged that the second rhyme in each line, which is called *vidrhending*, this must be in the last syllable but one. But the rhyme which is called *frumhending* [first rhyme] appears sometimes at the beginning of the line – then we call it *oddhending;* sometimes in the middle of the line – then we call it *hluthending*. This is *dróttkvætt* form. This is the form most often used for elaborate poetry. This is the foundation of all verse-forms just as speech-runes are the principal sort of runes.

How is the rule for verse-forms varied?

In two ways.

How?

In meaning and in sound.

How may it be changed in meaning?

In two ways.

How?

By keeping or changing the forms.

How may the verse-forms be varied and the same form be kept?

By using kennings [periphrastic descriptions] or *studning* [support] or extended kennings or literal kennings or by composing with allegory.

What are the forms using kennings?

As follows:

> Fellr of fúra stilli
> fleinbraks limu axla
> Hamdis fang thar er hringum
> hylr ættstudill skylia.
> Holt felr hildigelti
> heila bæs ok deilir
> gulls í gelmis stalli
> gunnseid skörungr reidir.

Hamdir's tunic [a coat of mail] falls around the operator of the fire of the spear-clash [user of the sword, warrior] where the upholder of the king's dynasty protects the limbs of his shoulders with rings [mail]. The outstanding one covers the hill of the dwelling of the brain [his cranium] with a battle-boar [helmet] and the distributor of gold brandishes the battle-fish [sword] in the hawk's perch [hand].

Here in this verse all the concepts are expressed by kennings, though the rhymes and length of lines and distribution of staves [alliteration] go as was prescribed above. Kennings are distinguished by three kinds of usage: first there are simple kennings, second double, third extended. It is a kenning to call battle 'spear-clash', and it is a double kenning to call a sword 'fire of the spear-clash', and it is extended if there are more elements:

> Úlfs bága verr ægis
> ítr báls hati málu;
> sett eru börd fyrir bratta
> brún Míms vinar rúnu.
> Orms váða kann eidu
> allvaldr göfugr halda;
> menstrídir nót módur
> mellu dólgs til elli.

The splendid hater of the fire of the sea [he who likes to rid himself of gold, the generous prince] defends the beloved of the enemy of the wolf [Odin's wife Iord, earth, i.e. land]; ships' prows are set before the steep brows [cliffs] of Mim's friend's [Odin's] wife [Iord, land]. The noble mighty-ruler knows how to hold the serpent's attacker's [Thor's] mother [Iord, land]. You who torment necklaces [by giving them away generously], enjoy the troll-wife's enemy [Thor's] mother until old age.

What are literal kennings [descriptions]?
As follows:

> Stinn sár thróask stórum,
> sterk egg frömum seggium
> hvast skerr hlífar traustar.
> Hár gramr lifir framla.

Hrein sverd litar harda
hverr drengr. Göfugr thengill
(ítr rönd furask undrum)
unir biartr snöru hiarta.

Severe wounds increase greatly, strong edge cuts sharply
trusty shields for bold men. The high prince lives honour-
ably. Each warrior dyes clean swords mightily. The noble
ruler, bright, rejoices in a bold heart. The fine shield is
furrowed amazingly.

It is a literal description when the word is supported with a literal
epithet like this, for instance to call wounds severe, because great
wounds are heavy; and it is normal to say that they increase. A
second literal description is when the wounds increase greatly.
Here we have one line and two literal descriptions. In the second
line the edge is said to be strong and men bold. In the third, we
have cuts sharply, and the shield is trusty, and in the fourth line
the description of the king as great, and his life as honourable, and
then the description of the sword as clean and mightily reddened,
and a certain one of the troops, and it would be normal language if
the man were named. The king is said to be noble, the shield was
splendid and was furrowed wonderfully quickly, the king re-
joiced, happy with valiant heart. Now there are here exemplified
sixteen literal descriptions in eight lines, but they add greatly to
the poetical effect even if this scheme is not imitated precisely.

There are three kinds of literal description: one is called ordin-
ary literal description, the second support, the third doubly
strengthened.

Ódharda spyr ek eyda
egg fullhvötum seggium.
Dádrökkum veldr dauda
dreng ofrhugadr thengill.
Hamdökkum fær Hlakkar
hauk munnroda aukinn.
Veghræsinn spyr ek vísa
valdr ógnthorinn skialdar.

I hear that the mighty hard edge destroys very brave men.
The most valiant prince causes the death of the deed-bold
warrior. The battle-daring shield-wielder brings increase to

the mouth-reddening of Hlokk's dark-coated hawk [the raven, whose mouth is reddened by carrion]. I hear that the ruler has glory to boast of.

Here a support accompanies each literal description, as for instance when the edge is said to be mighty hard, and the men very brave. This is a literal description: hard edge, brave men. It is a support when another confirmatory word accompanies the literal description.

What is allegory?

As follows:

> Svidr lætr sóknar nadra
> slídrbraut iöfurr skrída.
> Ótt ferr rógs ór réttum
> ramsnákr fetilhamsi.
> Linnr kná sverda sennu
> sveita bekks at lcita.
> Ormr thyrr vals at varmri
> víggiöll sefa stígu.

The wise prince makes the adders of battle [swords] creep the scabbard-path [be drawn]. The mighty war-snake goes swiftly from the straight strap-slough [scabbard]. The sword-quarrel serpent can seek the stream of blood. The worm of the slain rushes along the mind's path to the warm war-river.

This is allegory to call a sword a worm and use an appropriate determinant, and call the scabbard its path and the straps and fittings its slough. It is in accordance with a worm's nature that it glides out of its slough and then often glides to water. Here the allegory is so constructed that the worm goes to find the stream of blood where it glides along the path of thought, i.e. men's breasts. Allegory is held to be well composed if the idea that is taken up is maintained throughout the stanza. But if a sword is called a worm, and then a fish or a wand or varied in some other way, this is called a monstrosity, and it is considered a defect.

Now the *dróttkvætt* form has been presented with five distinct variants, and yet it has been the same verse-form, normal and without departure from it. And frequently some or all of these variant features are found in a single stanza, and that is normal, because kennings enlarge the vocabulary resources, literal descriptions enhance and expand the sense, allegory displays art and verbal skill.

It is a licence in verse-forms to have slow or quick syllables so that there is a drawing on or back from the normal number of the rule, and they can be found so slow that there are five syllables in the second and fourth line, as here:

> Hiálms fylli spekr hilmir
> hvatr Vindhlés skatna.
> Hann kná hiörvi thunnum
> hræs thiódár ræsa.
> Ýgr hilmir lætr eiga
> öld dreyrfá skiöldu.
> Styrs rýdr stillir hersum
> sterkr iárngrá serki.

The bold king quietens men with Vindhler's helmet-filler [Heimdall's head, i.e. a sword]. He does make flow the mighty corpse-rivers with slender sword. The terrible prince makes men have gore-stained shields. The strong ruler reddens lords' iron-grey battle-shirts.

In this verse the first rhymes in each line are all *oddhendingar* [first-syllable rhymes], and yet this verse-form is *dróttkvætt* in form.

Now we shall demonstrate syllables that are so quick and placed so close to each other, that as a result the length of the line is increased:

> Klofinn spyr ek hiálm fyrir hilmis
> hiarar egg. Duga seggir.
> Thví eru heldr thar er skekr skiöldu
> skafin sverd litud ferdar.
> Bila muna gramr thó at gumna
> gular rítr nái líta.
> Draga thorir hann yfir hreina
> hvatan brand thrumu randa.

I hear that helmet is cloven before the prince's sword-edge. Men act well. So where shields are shaken troop's burnished

swords are quite coloured. The king will not give way
though he gets to see men's yellow shields. He dares to draw
keen sword over pure noise of shields.

Here there are nine syllables in the first and third lines, and seven
in the second and fourth. This is an example of the maximum
number of syllables that can be in a line in the *dróttkvætt* form,
and from this it can be seen that it is easily acceptable to have
seven or eight in the first and third lines. In this stanza the first
rhymes in each line are *hluthendingar* [middle of the line rhymes]
and this makes it possible to lengthen the line by putting as many
syllables as possible before the rhymes.

The second licence in verse-forms is to have in the *dróttkvætt*
form one or two lines in the stanza with *álög* [extensions] or
detthent [falling rhyme] or *dunhent* [echoing rhyme] or *skiálfhent*
[shivering] or with some variation that does not spoil the poetic
form. A third licence is having *adalhendingar* [full rhymes] in the
first and third lines. A fourth licence is shortening syllables so as to
make one out of two and take away the vowel from one of them.
We call this *bragarmál* [poetical speech], as in this composition of
Thorarin Mahliding:

> Vardak mik thars myrdir
> mordfárs vega thordi.

[*Vardak* for *varda ek; thars* for *thar es*]
I defended myself <from women's reproach> where the
battle-danger's [sword's] destroyer [warrior, here the poet]
dared to fight.

This category extends much further. It is the fifth licence to vary
tenses within the half-stanza. The sixth licence is having *samhend-
ingar* [coincident rhymes] or *lidhendingar* [helping rhymes] in
dróttkvætt. It is the seventh to have the same word in both
half-stanzas, and this is considered a defect in single-stanza
poems. The eighth is effective repetition of what has been uttered
earlier, either a whole line or less. The ninth is extending a
kenning to a fifth determinant, but it is out of proportion if it is
extended further. Even if it can be found in the works of ancient
poets, we no longer tolerate it. The tenth is when the stanza has a

drag [appendage] or a *studill* [buttress, additional line at the end].
The eleventh is that *er* [is, who] or *en* [but] or *at* [that] may be put
more often than once in a half-stanza, as in Ref's verse:

> Sæll er hinn er hranna
> hádýra vel stýrir
> (tíd erumk vitnis váda
> víngerd) unir sínu.

Happy is that steerer of the tall animal of the waves [ship]
who is well content with his lot. I am practised in the wolf's
danger's [Odin's] wine-making [poetry-composing].

And this also applies [i.e. it is a licence, a repetition] if it happens
in the second half-stanza, when a person has been named or has
been referred to by a kenning in the first half, even if he is then
referred to in no other way than 'he', or 'the other', or 'this
person', or 'that person'. The twelfth is *atridsklauf* [tmesis?].
   What is variation of tense?
   Of three kinds.
   How?
   That which was, that which is, that which shall be.
   What is the rule for varying verse-forms by meaning only?
   This may be done by giving a name to the variant forms and
thus making a distinction in the first kind of number that relates to
verse-forms, but keeping the second and the third numbers in the
rule. This means, in accordance with what was set down above,
having eight lines in the stanza, and the third kind of number is
having six syllables in the line, with the same rule as before for the
rhymes. The verse-forms are altered by various turns of phrase,
and this is one form which is called *sextánmæltr* [sixteen-
sentenced]:

> Vex idn. Vellir rodna.
> Verpr lind. Thrimu snerpir,
> Fæsk gagn. Fylkir eignask.
> Falr hitnar. Sedsk vitnir.
> Skekr rönd. Skildir bendask.
> Skelfr askr. Gridum raskar.
> Brandr gellr. Bryniur sundrask.
> Braka spiör. Litask örvar.

Labour grows. Field goes red. Shield is thrown. Battle grows harsh. Victory is won. The prince gains. Dart grows hot. Wolf is sated. Targe is shaken. Bucklers are bent. Ash [-spear] shivers. Peace is disturbed. Brand rings. Mail-coats are split. Spears crack. Arrows are dyed.

Here there are two complete sentences in each line, but the length of lines and the syllables and alliteration as in *dróttkvætt*.

Next *dróttkvætt* form is varied in another way, and again in meaning only. This verse-form is called *áttmælt* [eight-sentenced]:

> Iörd verr siklingr sverdum.
> Sundr riúfa spiör undir.
> Lind skerr í styr steinda.
> Stökkr hauss af bol lausum.
> Falla fólk á velli.
> Fremr mildr iöfurr hildi.
> Egg bítr á lim lýti.
> Liggr skör snidin hiörvi.

The king defends the land with swords. Spears tear wounds open. The coloured shield is cut in battle. The head flies from the separated body. Hosts fall on the field. The generous prince wages war. The edge bites blemishes on limbs. The scalp lies cut by sword.

Here a sentence is completed in each line. This is the third:

> Ýskelfir kann úlfum
> audmildr búa gildi.
> Lætr gyldis kyn gáti
> gunnsnarr una harri.
> Fær gotna vinr vitni
> valbiór afar stóran.
> Vargr tér ór ben bergia
> blóddrykk ok grön rióda.

The bow-shaker [warrior] generous with wealth knows how to prepare the wolves a feast [make war]. The battle-keen lord lets the wolf's kin rejoice in prey. The friend of men gives the wolf a very great deal of corpse-beer [blood].

The warg does taste blood-drink from the wound and redden its lips.

Here the sentence ends in two lines. The verse form that will be written next is the fourth of those that have variation, but the fifth in the number of verse-types. It is called *stælt* [inlaid]:

> Hákun veldr ok höldum
> (hardrádum gud iardar
> tiggia lér med tíri)
> teitr thiódkonungs heiti.
> Vald á vídrar foldar
> (vindræfurs iöfurr gæfu
> ödlingi skóp ungum)
> örlyndr skati giörla.

Hakon possesses as well as subjects — God grants the firm-ruling prince land with glory — happy, the name of great king. Power over a wide realm — the lord of the winds' roof [heaven] has bestowed grace on the young nobleman — the generous prince has completely.

Here we have:

> Hákun veldr ok höldum
> teitr thiódkonungs heiti,

Hakon possesses as well as subjects, happy, the name of great king,

but the second and third lines belong together in sense, and this is called a *stál* [inlay]. This is the fifth:

> Manndyrdir fá mærdar
> mæt öld fira gæti
> lýtr audgiafa ítrum
> öll. Stód sær of fiöllum.
> Riódvendils gat randa
> ræki-Niord at sækia
> hæf ferd var sú harda
> heim. Skaut iörd or geima.

His virtues bring glory to the protector of men, all noble
mankind bows to the splendid wealth-giver. The sea lay
over the mountains. I was able to visit at home the Niord
[king] who cultivates the reddening rod of shields [sword],
that journey was very fitting. The earth sprang out of the sea.

This we call *hiástælt* [abutted]. Here the first, second and third
lines belong together in sense, and yet this sentence includes one
syllable comprising a complete word from the fourth line, and the
five syllables that follow complete a full sentence and the express-
ion has to be proverbial statements.

This is the seventh, *langlokur* [late conclusions]:

> Hákun rædr med heidan—
> Hefir drengia vinr fengit
> (lönd verr budlungr brandi
> breidfeld) mikit veldi.
> Rógleiks náir ríki
> remmi-Týr at stýra
> (öld fagnar thví) eignu
> —ordróm konungdómi.

Hakon rules with bright ... The friend of warriors has
gained great power, the prince defends his extensive lands
with the brand. The Tyr who encourages the play of hostil-
ity [war, i.e. the king] is able to rule his own kingdom. Men
welcome this. ... glory the kingdom.

Here a sentence begins in the first line and is completed in the last,
and they make up a separate statement. This is the eighth verse-
form, *tiltekit* [linked]:

> Theim er, grundar grímu
> gialdseids ok var faldinn,
> (drótt man enn thann) átti
> ádr hans fadir ráda.
> Gunnhættir kná grýttu
> (gramr býr of threk) stýra
> (stórt rædr hann en hiarta
> hvetr) budlunga setri.

... which his father had to rule before, being crowned with
the ground-gold-fish's helmet [helmet of terror]; the court

still remembers him. He who risks battle is able to rule the prince's bouldered seat [Norway]. The king has great endurance. He rules mightily and his valour urges him.

Here the first half-stanza is dependent on the preceding stanza, and the word that is known as *afleiding* [antecedent], which was the last in the previous stanza, links with this half-stanza, and this half-stanza is otherwise not correct in expression.

This is the ninth verse-form, *drögur* [drawings]:

> Setr of vísa vitran
> vígdrótt—en thar hníga—
> (ýr dregsk) vid skotskúrum
> skialdborg—í gras aldir.
> Vápnriódr stikar vída
> (vellbriótr á lög) spiótum
> (thryngr at sverda söngvi)
> sóknhardr thrömu iardar.

The war-band sets a shield wall around the wise ruler against missile-showers and men sink there into the grass; bow is drawn. The battle-hard weapon-reddener fences widely the borders of the land with spears; the gold-breaker [generous king] presses over the sea to the song of swords [battle].

The word that is first in this stanza is the last in the preceding one, and thus the second is 'drawn' from the first. Hence it is called 'drawings'.

Next is the tenth verse-form, which we call *refhvörf* ('fox-turns', antithesis). In this verse-form those words are chosen to be placed next to each other that have most dissimilar meanings, and yet both words should have the same cadence if it is to be most effective. But for this form it is difficult to find all words of opposite meanings, and so in it for this reason some words are stretched [in meaning] for convenience. But it is demonstrated in this next stanza how words will be found if they are sought carefully, and it will be apparent in it too that most first attempts can bear improvement. The verse is as follows:

> Síks glódar verr sækir
> slétt skard hafi iardar.

177

Hlífgranda rekr hendir
heit köld loga öldu.
Fliótt válkat skilr fylkir
fridlæ; röduls sævar
ránsid ræsir stödvar
reidr—gladr—frömum meidum.

The ditch-glede's [gold's] attacker [generous king] defends
the sea-smoothed land-cleft [fiords, Firdir in Norway]. The
wave-flame [gold] thrower [generous king] drives away
cold threats with shield-harmer [sword]. The happy leader
perceives hastily-weighed peace-destruction [warfare]; the
angry ruler puts a stop to the plundering habits of bold
sea-sun [gold] trees [warriors].

Here in the first line are the words: *síks glódar*. *Sík* [ditch] is
water, *glód* [glede] is fire, and fire and water are contrary to each
other. *Verr* [defends] *sækir* [attacker/attacks]: it is different to
defend and to attack. The second line is: *slétt skard hafi iardar*.
Slétt [smooth], that is even, *skard* [cleft], that is unsmooth, and
similarly: *hafi iardar*. *Haf* is sea, *iörd* is land. And so it says in the
one phrase that one goes from sea to land. The third line is thus:
hlífgranda [shield-harmer]. This is an obvious case of *refhvörf*,
and similarly *rekr* [drives] *hendir* [thrower/catches]. He who *rekr*
moves something away, while he who *hendir* stops something.
Similarly the fourth: *heit* [threat/hot] *köld* [cold], these words are
obvious and similarly: *loga* [flame] *öldu* [wave]. *Logi* is fire, *alda*
is sea. The fifth line is: *fliótt válkat*. *Fliótt* [hastily] is what is quick,
válkat [weighed/hovered] what is slow, and then: *skilr fylkir*. He
who *skilr* [perceives/divides] scatters, but he who *fylkir* [leader/
musters] gathers. The sixth line is: *fridlæ*. *Fridr* [peace] is recon-
ciliation, *læ* [destruction/fraud] is machination, and again: *rödull*
sævar. *Rödull* is the sun, and it is used for fire in all kennings. *Sær*
[the sea] is as before contrary to fire. The seventh line is: *ránsid*
[plundering habit/morality]. *Rán* is immorality. And then *ræsir*
stödvar. He moves something who *ræsir* [ruler/impels] and holds
something back who *stödvar* [puts a stop to]. The eighth line is:
reidr gladr [angry happy]. The meaning is obvious, and then:
frömum [bold/advance] *meidum* [trees/injure]. It is quite different
to cause someone advancement or injury. Here are demonstrated
in this stanza sixteen phrases of contrary meanings, and most of

them have to be turned to their proper meaning by means of word-play, and this is how it is to be understood: ditch-glede, i.e. gold; attacker of gold, that is a man; he defends the cleft of land smoothed by the sea, i.e. Firdir, this is the name of a district in Norway; with shield-harmer, i.e. a weapon; thrower of wave-flame is a man, who drives away cold threats with the sword, that is to punish wickedness; hastily-weighed may be said of what is unpremeditated, he perceives this from the hostility; a king is called *fylkir* [leader]; the ruler puts a stop to the plundering habits of bold sea-sun-trees. This is called the greatest *refhvörf*.

This is another *refhvörf*, and here there are only half as many lines that are composed with *refhvörf*, and there are two of them in alternate lines, and so it is known as the greatest also:

> Blód fremr (hlökk at hádisk
> heldr slitnar dul) vitni.
> Skiöldr, en skatnar foldir,
> skelfr hardr, taka varda.
> Fal lætr of her hvítan
> hollr gramr rekinn framdan,
> en tiggia sonr (seggium
> svalr brandr) dugir (grandar).

Blood benefits wolf, it rather breaks concealment that battle is waged. Hard shield shakes and men begin to defend lands. The true prince makes the white inlaid spear be advanced over the host and the king's son acts well; cool sword harms men.

Here there are these *refhvörf* in every other line: *heldr* [rather/holds] and *slitnar* [breaks], and *dul* [concealment] and *vitni* [wolf/witness]. *Dul* is hiding, but *vitni* is demonstration. In the fourth line are these: *skelfr* [shakes/trembling) *hardr* [hard/firm], *taka* [begin/seize] *varda* [defend]. In the sixth line is: *hollr* [true/gracious] *gramr* [prince/angry], *rekinn* [inlaid/driven back] *framdan* [advanced]. In the eighth line is *svalr* [cool] *brandr* [sword/brand]; brand is a word for fire; *dugir* [acts well/helps] *grandar* [harms]. This is composed using word-play. Here also it is another signification of the words that must be taken for the sense as follows, saying that blood benefits *vitni*, i.e. the wolf, and concealment or secrecy is broken or breached in that *hlökk*, i.e.

battle, is waged. And in the second couplet we have that hard
shield shakes and men begin to defend the kingdom. And in the
third couplet we find that the true prince makes the white inlaid
spear be advanced over the host; that which is moved forward is
advanced. In the fourth couplet we find that the cool sword harms
men, but the king's son acts well.

This is the third *refhvörf* form:

> Segl skekr of hlyn—Huglar—
> (hvast drífa skip) rasta,
> en föll—of gram—Gylli
> grunn (diúp) hata unna.
> Né Rán vidr hafhreinum
> háraust—skapar flaustum—
> (hrönn fyrir húfi thunnum
> heil klofnar) frid—deilu.

Sail shakes above the prince on the current-maple [ship];
tall ships drive keenly; the shallows near Hugl are danger-
ous to the waves' horse [ship]. Noisy Ran does not create
peace for the sea-deer [ships]; she causes conflict for cruis-
ers, the entire wave breaks before the slender bow.

This counts as the greatest *refhvörf*. Here there is one line in each
half-stanza that is composed with *refhvörf*, and there are two in
each, as follows: *grunn* [shallow] *diúp* [tall/deep], *hata* [are
dangerous to/hate] *unna* [waves'/love]. And in the second half-
stanza we have: *heil* [entire] *klofnar* [breaks], *frid* [peace] *deilu*
[conflict]. This counts as one of the greatest *refhvörf* and is the
least of the type.

Now we begin the lesser *refhvörf*. Here there is one *refhvörf* in
the line.

> Hélir hlýr at stáli,
> hafit fellr, en svífr thelli
> (ferd dvöl firrisk) harda
> fram mót lagar glammi.
> Vindr réttr vádir bendir;
> vefr rekr á haf snekkiur;
> vedr thyrr; vísa idiur
> (varar fýsir skip) lýsa.

180

The bow [/warms] freezes at the prow, the sea [/lifted] falls but the timber glides hard forwards against [/back] the water's uproar; the crew [/movement] is deprived of rest. The direct [/straightens] wind [/twists] bends the sails; the cloth [/folds] drives [/unfolds] the warships over the sea; the weather [/paces] whistles [rushes]; the ship is eager for [/exhorts] harbour [/warns]; the labours reflect glory on the ruler.

Here there is one *refhvarf* in each line and most involve word-play. This is the second of the lesser:

> Lung frá ek lýda thengils
> (lá reis of skut) geisa,
> en svörd of her herda.
> Hlióp stód und gram Róda.
> Thiód fær thungra skeida
> thröng rúm skipat löngum;
> stál lætr styriar deilir
> stinn klökk í mar sökkva.

I have heard that the troops' king's ship rushed, the water [/lay down] rose up above the stern, and that the thongs stiffened above the host. Rodi's stallion [the ship/stood still] galloped beneath the prince. People are able for a long time to man the narrow benches [/spacious] of the heavy warships; the battle-dealer makes prow which is stiff softly sink into the sea.

Here there is *refhvörf* in every other line. This is the third:

> Himinglæva strýkr hávar
> (hrönn skilia sog) thiliur.
> Lögstíga vill lægir
> liótr fagrdrasil brióta.
> Lýsheims náir lióma
> (lídr ár) of gram blídum
> (udr rekkir kiöl klökkvan
> köld) eisa; far geisar.

Himinglæva strokes the high planks, the keel parts the wave. The ocean tries to break, ugly, the fair horse of the sea-paths. There manages to shine around the happy prince

the fish-home's [sea's] fire [gold], cold wave encourages
pliant keel; oar moves; vessel speeds.

Here there is *refhvörf* in each half-stanza. This is the least
refhvörf.

There is also the verse-form that we call *refhvörf*'s brother:

> Firrisk hönd med harra
> hlumr. Lídr vetr af sumri,
> en flaust vid lög Lista
> löng taka hvíld at göngu.
> Öl mædir lid lýda
> (létt skipask höll) it rétta,
> en skál at giöf góla
> gulls svífr (tóm) in fulla.

The oar-handle is separated from the hand among the lord's
men. After summer comes winter, the long ships have a rest
from travelling over the sea near Lister. The company of
men is made sleepy by the ale, so proper [/straight], the hall
[/askew] soon gets crowded when empty, and the full gold
cup glides readily as a gift.

Here in the second and fourth lines there are words of contrary
meaning like *refhvörf*, but they are not adjacent to each other and
there is a syllable between them and they do not have the same
rhythm. These verse-forms that have just been written are *drótt-
kvætt* in rhymes and length of line: they have six syllables in each
line and full rhymes in the second and fourth but half-rhymes in
the first and third.

What variations of *dróttkvætt* affect rhymes and line-length?
As in this example, *dunhenda* [echoing rhyme]:

> Hreintiörnum gledr horna
> (horn náir lítt at thorna,
> miödr hegnir böl bragna)
> bragningr skipa sagnir.
> Fólkhömlu gefr framla
> framlyndr vidum gamlar,
> hinn er heldr fyrir skot skiöldum,
> skiöldungr hunangs öldur.

The prince gladdens the ships' crews with pure lakes of horns [drink]. The horn does not get to dry out too much. Mead keeps back men's miseries. The bold-hearted king who holds shields in front of missiles gives generously old honey-waves [mead] to army-rod-[sword-]trees [warriors].

Here there are the same words at the beginning of the second and fourth lines as are at the end of the first and third. This is *tilsagt* [annotated]:

> Röst gefr ödlingr iastar
> —öl virdi ek svá—fyrdum.
> Thögn fellir brim bragna
> —biór forn er that—horna.
> Máls kann mildingr heilsu
> —miödr heitir svá—veita.
> Strúgs kemr í val veiga
> —vín kallak that—galli.

The king gives currents of yeast—that is what I adjudge ale to be—to men. Men's silence is dispelled by surf—that is old beer—of horns. The prince knows how speech's salvation—that is what mead is called—is to be given. In the choicest of cups comes—this is what I call wine—dignity's destruction.

Now we have *ordskviduháttr* [proverb-form]:

> Fúss brýtr fylkir eisu
> fens—bregdr hönd á veniu.
> Ránhegnir gefr Rínar
> röf—spyrr ætt at iöfrum.
> Miök trúir ræsir rekka
> raun—sér giöf til launa.
> Rád á lofdungr lýda
> lengr—vex hverr af gengi.

The leader is eager to distribute fen's fire [gold] — the hand tends to act in accordance with custom. The punisher of plundering gives Rhine's amber [gold] — princes become famous among men. The ruler greatly trusts his men's experience — a gift looks to its recompense. The king has power over men for the future — each man gains from companionship.

Iskalda skar ek öldu
eik—var súd in bleika
reynd—til ræsis fundar
ríks—emk kudr at slíku.
Briótr thá hersirs heiti
hátt—dugir sæmd at vátta—
auds af iarla prýdi
ítrs—vara siglt til lítils.

I cut the ice-cold wave with oak — the pale planking was put to the test — to meet the powerful ruler — I am renowned for such. The breaker of splendid wealth [man, the poet] received the noble name of *hersir* [lord] — it is worth reporting the honour — from the ornament of earls — the sailing was not for nothing.

This is *álagsháttr* [extension-form]. Here the second and fourth lines begin with a complete word of one syllable and this word belongs in sense with the previous line, but the five syllables that follow are a separate statement.

Next is the first verse-form to be written which is varied from *dróttkvætt* form by a complete change of form, and from now on we shall exemplify the distinctions by which *dróttkvætt* form is varied when it is changed in alliteration or rhyme or length of line, which is sometimes increased and sometimes shortened. This is *tvískelft* [double-shaken]:

Vandbaugs veitti sendir
vígrakkr—en giöf thakkak
skialdbrags skylia mildum—
skipreidu mér—heida.
Fann næst fylkir unna
föl dýr at giöf stýri
stálhreins. Styriar deilis
stórlæti sá ek mæta.

The war-bold shield-wand [sword] provider [warrior] gave me a ship-levy estate, and I thank the prince generous with shield-crash [battle] for the fine gift. The ruler next found available as a gift wave-animals [ships] for the stem-deer [ship] steersman [the poet]. I saw the splendid munificence of the hostility-controller [king].

Here the variation in the form is in the first and third lines: here the alliterating syllables come so close to each other that there is just one syllable between them. These *studlar* [props] constitute *skiálfhendur* [shiverings], and the first one is the beginning of the line, and the rhymes are placed as early as possible. But if the *frumhending* [first rhyme] comes in the syllable next to the first, it is still *skiálfhenda*.

This is the *detthendr* [falling rhyme] form:

> Tvær man ek hilmi hýrum
> heimsvistir ótvistar,
> hlaut ek ásamt at sitia
> seimgildi fémildum.
> Fúss gaf fylkir hnossir
> fleinstýri margdýrar,
> hollr var hersa stilli
> hoddspennir fiölmennum.

I remember two not unenjoyable visits to the cheerful prince, I got to sit in company with the generous gold-payer. The ruler gave eagerly most valuable treasures to the spear-guider [the poet], the hoard-spender [the poet] was loyal to the controller of lords with his great company.

Here the form is varied in the second and fourth lines, and it is the fourth syllable [which is long and stressed] that is significant for the form.

This is *draugsháttr* [ghost-form]:

> Tholl bid ek hilmis hylli
> halda grænna skialda.
> Askr beid af thví throska
> thiliu Hrungnis ilia.
> Vígfoldar niót valdi
> vandar margra landa—
> nýtr vartu oss—til ítrar
> elli—dólga fellir.

I pray that the green shields' fir [the poet] may keep the prince's favour. Hrungnir's sole-plank [shield] ash [the poet] has gained advancement from this. Battle-land-[shield-]wand [sword] wielder [warrior], enjoy many lands

until splendid old age. You have been beneficial to us, feller
of enemies.

Here again the variation in form is in the fourth and second lines,
and here it is the third syllable [which is long and stressed] that is
significant.

Here begins the second poem.

> Stáls dynblakka stökkvi
> stinngeds samir minnask
> (álms bifsæki aukum
> Yggs feng) á lof thengils.
> Odds bláferla iarli
> örbriót né skal thrióta
> (Hárs saltunnu hrannir
> hrærum) ód at stæra.

It befits the impeller [sailor, the poet] of the noisy stem-
horses [ships] to recall the glory of the firm-minded prince.
We activate Ygg's [Odin's] gain [poetry] for him who seeks
to make the bow quiver [the warrior]. The eager breaker
[warrior, the poet] of the point's [arrow's] dark paths
[shields] shall not cease to increase eulogy for the earl. We
stir the waves of Har's [Odin's] hall-vat.

This is called *bragarbót* [poem's improvement]. Here the form is
varied in the first and third lines. Here the props are placed as far
apart as possible, but the rhymes so that they are separated by
only one syllable. This distinguishes the form.

This form is called *ridhendur* [rocking rhymes]:

> Él threifsk skarpt of Skúla
> skýs snarvinda lindar,
> egg vard hvöss í höggum
> hræs dynbrunnum runnin.
> Sveimthreytir bió sveita
> sniallr ilstafna hrafni.
> Páll vard und fet falla
> fram thrábarni arnar.

The sharp storm [battle] of the keen spear-wind cloud
[shield] raged around Skuli, the sharp edge was flooded with

rushing corpse-streams amid the blows. The brave turmoil-
performer [warrior] covered the raven's sole-stems [claws]
with blood. Paul had to fall down beneath the tread of the
eagle's beloved offspring.

Here the form is varied in the second and fourth lines. There the
rhymes come both together near the end and they both have the
same sound in the ending and it is better that one of them is
followed by a consonant.

This form is called *veggiat* [wedged]:

> Lífs vard rán at raunum
> (réd sverd) skapat miög ferdum.
> Stöng ód thrátt á thingi
> thiódsterk, lidu fram merki.
> Hraud of hilmis bródur
> hvöss egg fridar ván seggium.
> Spiót nádu blá bíta.
> Búandmenn hlutu thar renna.

Robbing of life came to be made very much a reality for
soldiers, sword was the cause. Mighty strong standard
advanced irresistibly at the assembly [battle], banners went
forward. Sharp edges deprived men of hope of peace around
the king's brother. Dark spears got to bite. Peasants there
had to flee.

Here there is variation of form in the second and fourth lines and
there one syllable is added just before the last two and thus the
length of the line is increased.

Now we have *flagdaháttr* [monster form]:

> Flaust bió fólka treystir
> fagrskiöldudustum öldum.
> Leid skar bragnings bródir
> biartveggiudustu reggi.
> Hest rak hilmir rasta
> hardsveipadastan reipum.
> Siár hlaut vid thröm thióta
> thunghúfudustu lungi.

The tester of armies provided a craft with the most beautifully shielded men. The king's brother cut the sea with the most brightly sailed pinnace. The prince drove the current-horse with most tightly-twisted ropes. The sea had to resound against the side of the most heavily planked long-boat.

Here the form is varied in the second and fourth lines: here there is both a syllable added and the word is extended to the superlative degree, and three syllables come after this extra syllable and it is normal *dróttkvætt* if it is taken out.

This form is the old *skiálfhenda* [shivering]:

> Reist at Vágsbrú vestan
> (varrsíma bar fiarri)
> heitfastr hávar rastir
> hiálm-Týr svölu stýri.
> Stökr óx er bar blakka
> brims fyrir iörd it grimma
> herfiöld (húfar svöldu)
> hrannlád búandmanna.

The helmet-Tyr [warrior], true to his word, cut deep currents with cold steering-oar from the west to Vagsbru. The line of the wake stretched far. The peasants' flight increased when the grim wave-land [sea] bore a great multitude of horses of the sea [ships] past the coast. The planks were made cold.

Here there is *skiálfhent* [shivering, i.e. alliteration separated by only one syllable] with full rhyme in the third line in each half-stanza, but in other respects as *dróttkvætt*. This form was invented by Veili. He was at the time lying on an outlying skerry, having escaped from a shipwreck, and they were badly off for clothes and the weather was cold. Then he composed a poem called the shivering poem or the refrainless *drápa* [formally constructed poem], and it was based on the story of Sigurd.

This is called *thríhent* [triple-rhymed]:

> Hristi hvatt thá er reistisk
> herföng miök löng véstöng.
> Samdi fólk en frömdusk
> fullsterk hringserk grams verk.

> Hönd lék—herium reyndisk—
> hiörr kaldr—allvaldr mannbaldr.
> Egg- (frá ek breida bioggiu
> bragning fylking) stód -thing.

Armour was shaken violently when the very long standard
was raised. The army donned the mail-shirt and the prince's
most mighty deeds were achieved. Cold sword waved in
hand, the ruler proved outstanding to the hosts. I heard that
the leader drew up the broad battle-line, the parliament of
edges [battle] took place.

There are here three full rhymes in the second and fourth lines and
they all have the same endings, and there is a syllable in front of
each of them.

Now we have the precious [ornate] form:

> Vann—kann virdum banna
> vald—giald—höfundr aldar—
> ferd verd fólka herdi
> fest mest—sá er bil lestir.
> Hátt thrátt hölda áttar—
> hraud aud iöfurr raudum—
> (that) gat thengill skatna
> thiód (stód af gram) bióda.

Deserving men caused to be made very great payment to the
increaser of battles. The judge of men who destroys hesita-
tion knows how to stop men's arrogance. The prince of men
was able to show the group of the clan of *höldar* [land-
owners] powerfully how to behave. This arose from the
ruler. The chieftain gets rid of red wealth.

Here there are in the first and third line two full rhymes together,
and the third as usual at the end.

> Farar snarar fylkir byriar,
> freka breka lemr á snekkium,
> vaka taka vísa rekkar,
> vidar skridar at that bidia.
> Svipa skipa sýiur heppnar
> sömum thrömum í byr römum.

Haka skaka hrannir blökkum
hlidar, midar und kiöl nidri.

The ruler undertakes swift journeys, strong waves lash the
warships, the chieftain's men begin to stay awake and then
urge on the timber's movement. The fortunate planks flex
the fine ships' gunwales in the powerful wind. The waves
shake the sides of Haki's horses [ships], there is movement
down under the keel.

Here there are three rhymes in the line, with half-rhyme in the first
and third lines, and the third rhyme <as usual at the end>, and
there is a syllable next to each rhyme.
This verse-form is called *tiltekit* [linked]:

Ok hialdreifan hófu
hoddstiklanda miklir
(mordflýtir kná mæta
málmskúrar dyn) hiálmar
hialdrs thá er hilmir foldar
hugdýrum gaf stýri—
ógnsvellir fær allan—
iarldóm—göfugr sóma.

And great helmets enhanced the battle-happy treasure-
thrower [generous lord]. The urger of killing [war-leader]
can meet the metal-storm-clash [battle] when the king of the
land gave the noble-hearted battle-controller an earldom.
The honourable war-sweller receives all glory.

Here it is the fifth line that varies the form and in this line the
language is dependent on the first half-stanza, and in the incidence
of alliteration this line becomes very similar to the new *skiálf-
henda* [shivering].
This verse-form is called *greppaminni* [poets' reminder]:

Hverr fremr hildi barra?
Hverr er mælingum ferri?
Hverr gerir höpp at stærri?
Hverr kann aud at thverra?
Veldr hertogi hialdri,
hann er first blikurmanni,

hann á höpp at sýnni,
hann vélir blik spannar.

Who wages harsh war? Who is far from niggardly? Who achieves greater success? Who knows how to diminish wealth [be generous with gold]? The duke brings about war, he is furthest from being a miser, he has clearer success, he cheats the light of the palm [gives away gold].

This verse-form is a verbal variation of *dróttkvætt* form.
   Now we have the form that we call *lidhendur* [helping rhymes]:

Velr ítrhugadr ýtum
otrgiöld iöfurr snotrum.
Opt hefr things fyrir þröngvi
thungfarmr Grana sprungit.
Hiörs vill riódr at rídi
reidmálmr Gnitaheidar.
Vígs er hreytt at hættis
hvatt Niflunga skatti.

The splendid-minded prince selects otter's payment [gold] for wise men. Often has the heavy burden of Grani [gold] broken [been distributed] because of the assembly-compeller [ruler]. The sword-reddener [warrior] desires the loaded metal of Gnita-heath [gold] to be scattered. The Niflungs' treasure is flung energetically with the battle-darer.

It is *lidhendur* when there is the same sound in front of the rhymes, and it is correctly composed *lidhendr* form when in the second and fourth lines there is *oddhending* [rhyme in the first syllable of the line] and half-rhyme with the rhymes that are in the preceding line, and then there is the same initial sound for all these three rhyming syllables.
   Next is the verse-form that we call *rétthent* [consistently rhymed]:

Alraudum drífr audi,
ógnrakkr firum hlakkar,
veit ek, hvar vals á reitu
verpr hringdropa snerpir.

191

> Sniallr lætr á fit falla
> fagrregn iöfurr thegnum
> (ógnflýtir verr ýtum
> arm) Mardallar hvarma.

There is scattering of the all-red wealth [gold], I know, where the attack-bold battle-sharpener [warrior] throws ring-droplets [gold] on men's hawk-lands [arms]. The bold prince makes the fair rain of Mardoll's lids [gold] fall on subject's limbs, the attack-hastener [warrior] covers men's arms.

Here there are full rhymes in the first and third lines, but care has been taken to leave out the half-rhymes.

Now comes *alhent* [fully rhymed]:

> Frama skotnar gram. Gotnum
> (giöf sannask) röf spannar—
> menstiklir—vensk mikla—
> manndýrdir vann skýrdar.
> Herfiöld—bera höldar—
> hagbáls lagar stála
> fridask sialdan vid valdi—
> vallands svala branda.

Glory befalls the prince. The necklace-thrower [generous ruler] makes virtues evident, palm's amber [gold] becomes quite normal to men, the gift is made real. The multitude of finely-made sea-pyres [gold ornaments] is seldom left in peace with the steel-wielder [warrior], yeomen wear cool hawk-land brands [gold ornaments].

Here there are two pairs of full rhyme in each line. This is considered to be the most beautiful and choicest, if it is composed well, of the verse-forms that poems are composed in, and it is proper *alhending* if there is not found in it *at* [that], *ek* [I], *en* [but] or other particles of that kind, unless they form part of the rhyme-scheme, but everyone has not avoided this, and so it is not wrong, as for instance in Bishop Klæng's verse:

> Bad ek sveit á glad Geitis,
> gör er íd at för tídum,

> drögum hest á lög lesta,
> lid flýtr en skrid nýtum.

I ordered the troop on to Geitir's steed [ship], labour is performed repeatedly in the journey, we drag the cargo-horse on to the sea, the vessel floats and we make use of motion.

Next is the verse-form that we call the lesser *alhenda*, it has half-rhymes in the first lines [of the couplets] in each half-stanza, as follows:

> Samthykkiar fremr sökkvi
> snarr Baldr hiarar aldir.
> Gunnhættir kann Grotta
> gladdript hrada skipta.
> Féstrídir kná Fróda
> fridbygg lidi tryggva.
> Fiölviniadr hylr Feniu
> falr meldr alinveldi.

The swift sword-Baldr [warrior] benefits men with the destroyer of unity [gold]. The battle-darer knows how to quickly share out Grotti's bright snow [gold]. Money's enemy does entrust men with Frodi's peace-barley [gold]. Fenia's meal [gold], which has many resting-places, being offered, covers the realm of the forearm.

The lesser *alhenda* is correctly composed if the pattern is maintained throughout the stanza, but if it is mixed with full *alhenda* so that in it some or all of the rhymes in a line are half-rhymes, then it is not correct.

This is *stamhendr* [stammering rhyme] form:

> Lætr undin brot brotna
> bragningr fyrir sér hringa.
> Sá tekr fyrir men menia
> mætt ord of sik fættir.
> Armr kná vid blik blikna
> brimlands vidum randa
> thar er hönd at lid lidnar
> lýslódar berr glódir.

The chieftain makes twisted ring-fragments fragment before him [distributes gold]. Because of the necklaces this necklace-diminisher receives fitting renown about himself. The shield-trees' limb does gleam with the gleam of the surf-land [gold] where the hand wears fish-path-embers [gold] with which the arm is armed.

Here in the first and third lines one syllable is repeated and this forms the rhyme, and thus we call this *stamhent* [stammer-rhymed] because the rhyme is produced by stuttering, and the rhymes are positioned in the line like *ridhendur* [rocking rhymes].

Now we have the verse-form that is called *samhent* [coincidentally rhymed]:

> Virdandi gefr virdum
> verbál lidar skeria.
> Gledr vellbrióti vellum
> verdung afar thungum.
> Ýtandi fremr ýta
> auds sæfuna raudum
> thar er mætum gram mæti
> marblakks skipendr thakka.

The valuer of limb-skerries [gold] gives men depth-pyres [gold]. The gold-breaker [generous man] gladdens the court with extremely heavy gold ornaments. The wealth-thrower honours men with red sea-flame [gold] where the sea-steed's [ship's] crew thank the splendid prince for valuable objects.

Here there are the rhyme-syllables that we call *samhendur* [coincident rhymes] because they all have the same initial sounds and in the first and third lines they are in the positions of the half-rhymes in *dróttkvætt* form.

Now comes *idurmælt* [repeatedly said]:

> Seimthverrir gefr seima
> seimörr lidi beima.
> Hringmildan spyr ek hringum
> hringskemmi brott stinga.
> Baugstökkvir fremr baugum
> bauggrimmr hiarar drauga.

> Vidr gullbroti gulli
> gullhættr skada fullan.

The gold-generous gold-diminisher gives the troop of men gold. I hear the ring-liberal ring-spoiler throws away rings. The bracelet-hating bracelet-flinger honours sword-trunks [men] with bracelets. The gold-breaker, dangerous to gold, causes complete destruction to gold.

Here *samhending* [coincident rhyme] is used three times, twice in the first and third lines, while in the second and fourth it is kept as *afhending* [off-rhyme] as in *dunhent* [echoing rhyme] form.
This verse-form is called *klifat* [repeated]:

> Audkendar verr audi
> aud-Týr boga naudir.
> Thar er audvidum audit
> auds í gulli raudu.
> Heidmönnum býr heidis
> heidmildr iöfurr reidir.
> Venr heidfrömudr heidar
> heidgiöf vala leidar.

The wealth-Tyr [prince] covers the easily-picked out bow-forcers [men's arms] with wealth. There is granted wealth to wealth-trees [men] in red gold. The payment-generous prince adorns the soldiers' hawk-carts [arms]. The payment-performer accustoms the bright falcon-paths [arms] to payment-gifts.

Here the *samhendingar* [coincident rhymes] continue throughout the half-stanza and link with the second full rhyme in the second and fourth lines.
Now come the verse-forms that we call *stúfar* [docked, i.e. catalectic]:

> Hialdrremmir tekr Hildi—
> hringr brestr at giöf—festa.
> Hnígr und Högna meyiar
> hers valdandi tiald.
> Hedins mála býr hvílu
> hiálmlestanda flestum.

Mordaukinn thiggr mæki
mund Hiadninga sprund.

The battle-strengthener [ruler] engages himself to Hild [a
valkyrie], the ring is broken as a gift. The ruler of the host
moves under Hogni's daughter's [Hild's] tent [his shield]:
Hedin's beloved [Hild] prepares a bed [i.e. selects them for
death] for most helmet-harmers [warriors]. The lady of the
Hiadnings receives a wedding gift, a sword famous for
slaying.

Here the fourth line is docked and the syllable which in *dróttkvætt*
form has to follow the [second] rhyming syllable is omitted.
 This is the greater *stúfr:*

Yggs drósar rýfr eisa
öld módsefa tiöld.
Glód stökkr í hof Hlakkar
hugtúns firum brún.
Gedveggiar svífr glugga
glæs dynbrími hræs.
Hvattr er hyrr at slétta
hialdrs gnapturna aldrs.

The fire [sword] of Ygg's maid [valkyrie] tears the tent of
men's mood-thought [breast]. Hlokk's burnished ember
[sword] flies into men's mind-field temple [breast]. The
clashing corpse-flame [sword] glides through the window
of the transparent wall of thought [breast-wound]. The
battle fire is made keen to slice off the high towers of life
[heads].

Here the second and fourth lines are docked. Now comes the
greatest *stúfr.* Here all lines are docked:

Herstefnir lætr hrafn
hungrs fullsediask ungr.
Ilspornat getr örn
aldrlausastan haus.
Vilia borg en vargr
vígsára klífr grár.
Opt sólgit fær ylgr—
iöfurr gódr vill svá—blód.

The young battle-leader lets the raven fully sate its hunger.
The eagle is able to tread underfoot the completely dead
skull. But the grey wolf climbs the battle-wounded will-
stronghold [breast]. The she-wolf is often able to drink
blood, the good prince wishes it so.

These verse-forms that have just been exemplified are divided into
three types, because in the past poems have been composed so that
in the same stanza one half had one line docked and the other half
two lines, and that is a metrical inconsistency. The third type is
alstýfdr [all-docked], for here all lines are docked.

Now we shall give an example of the form that is called
skothendr [half-rhymed]:

> Sær skiöldungs nidr skúrum—
> sköpt—darradar—lyptask.
> Hrindr gunnfana grundar
> glygg of fræknum tiggia.
> Geisa vé fyrir vísa,
> vedr stöng at hlym Gungnis.
> Styrk eru mót und merkium
> málms of ítran hilmi.

The prince's spear-showers are strewn down, shafts are
lifted. Storm pushes the battle-flags around the valiant lord
of the land. The banners rush before the prince, the pole
advances to Gungnir's din [battle]. The powerful meetings
of metal [battles] take place under the standards around the
splendid prince.

Here there are half-rhymes in all lines, but it is otherwise like the
dróttkvætt form.

Now comes the verse-form that we call *lidhendur* (helping-
rhymes):

> Stióri vensk at stæra
> stór verk dunu geira.
> Halda kann med hildi
> hialdr-Týr und sik foldu.
> Harri slítr í hverri
> Hiarranda föt snerru.
> Falla thar til fyllar
> fiallvargs iöru thollar.

The spear-din-controller [ruler] becomes accustomed to carry out great deeds. The battle-Tyr [warrior] knows how to hold land under himself with warfare. The lord cuts Hiarrandi's clothing [coats of mail] in every fray. There fall there combat-firs [warriors] as food for the mountain-wolf.

In this verse-form there are *lidhendur* [help-rhymes, rhyme and alliteration falling on the same syllables] in two ways: on the one hand such that with the first rhyme-syllables in the first and third lines <there are full rhymes in the second and fourth, and on the other such that with the second rhyme-syllable there is half-rhyme in the second and fourth lines>.

Now shall be exemplified those variations of form which early poets have used in composition and which are now made into consistent verse-forms, though these poets have in some cases composed with metrical inconsistencies, and these variations in early poems are called *dróttkvætt*, and some of them are found in single-stanza poems, as when King Ragnar Lodbrok composed in this form:

> Skýtr at Sköglar vedri—
> en skialdagi haldask—
> Hildar hlemmidrífu
> of hvítum thröm rítar.
> En í sæfis sveita
> at sverdtogi ferdar
> rýdr aldar vinr odda—
> that er iarlmegin—snarla.

Hild's resounding storm [rain of weapons] is shot in Skogul's wind [battle] — but shields cannot be held — around the white targe's edge. But the friend of men reddens points energetically in the queller's [sword's] sweat [blood] at the troop's sword-drawing. Such is the earl's power.

Here form is lacking in the first and third lines, but in the second and fourth there are full-rhymes, while the chief stave, the one that determines the alliteration, is positioned in the second and fourth lines in such a way that it is preceded by one or two syllables, but in other respects it is like *dróttkvætt*.

Now shall be exemplified Torf-Einar's verse-form:

> Hverr séi iöfra ægi
> iarl fiölvitrum betra?
> Eda giarnara at gæda
> glym hradsveldan skialda?
> Stendr af stála skúrar
> styrr ólítill Gauti
> thá er fólks iadarr foldir
> ferr sig-Niördum varda.

Who could point to an earl better than this most wise
terrifier of kings? Or more eager to increase the quick-
swollen shield-din? No small tumult arises from the steel-
shower-Gaut [warrior] when the host's protection goes to
defend lands against battle-Niords [warriors].

Here form is lacking in the first and third lines, but in the second
and fourth it is half-rhymed and *ridhent* [rocking].
   Now comes Egil's verse-form:

> Hverr ali blódi byrsta
> bens raudsylgium ylgi
> nema svá at gramr of gildi
> grád dag margan vargi?
> Gefr oddviti undir
> egg nýbitnar vitni.
> Herr sér Fenris fitiar
> framkló lodnar rodna.

Who would nourish the bloody-bristled she-wolf with the
wound's red drink unless it were that the prince strengthens
the wolf's greed many a day? The leader provides the
watcher [wolf] with wounds newly pierced by edge. The
army sees the front claw of Fenrir's shaggy paw redden.

Here form is lacking in the first and third lines, but in the second
and fourth there are full rhymes and *ridhent* [rocking].
   Now comes Flein's verse-form:

> Hilmir hiálma skúrir
> herdir sverdi rodnu.
> Hrióta hvítir askar,
> hrynia bryniu spangir.

> Hnykkia Hlakkar eldar
> harda svardar landi,
> remma rimmu glódir
> randa grand of iarli.

The prince gives power to the helmets' showers with red-dened sword. White ash-spears fly, mail-coat plates ring. Hlokk's flames [swords] wrench off violently the hair's land [head], war-gleeds [swords] increase shields' damage around the earl.

Here the rhyme-syllables are arranged as in *dróttkvætt* form, but the rhymes are placed close together at the beginning of the line.
  Now comes Bragi's verse-form:

> Er til hiálma hyriar
> herium styriar væni
> thar svá at iarl til ógnar
> egnir tognu sverdi.
> Siá kná gard fyrir grundu
> grindar Thundar iadra
> er skatna vinr skialdar
> skyldisk galdr at fremia.

The armies can expect the helmet-fire's tumult [battle] so that there the earl can bait the drawn sword for battle. Thund's gate's [shield's] edges' fence [shield-wall] can be seen on the landscape when the friend of men pledges himself to perform the shield's chant.

Here in the first and third lines the last word is used as the rhyme word, but the earlier word that ought to form half-rhyme with it is lacking, but with this rhyme word there are rhymes in the second and fourth lines, and one of these rhymes is half-rhyme and *lidhending* [helping-rhyme, a rhyming and alliterating word] <and the other is full rhyme> with the first one, and these rhymes that come in the second and fourth lines are placed as in Flein's verse-form. It often happens in the work of early poets that there are several variations or metrical inconsistencies in a single stanza, and this ought not to be imitated though it is not considered a fault in early poems.

Now come those forms, divided into three types. which are
called *kimblabönd* [bundle-bonds]. This is one:

> Hiálmlestir skerr Hristar
> hreggöld Sigars veggi.
> Gramr lætr í byr brióta
> brands hnigthili randa stranda.
> Stálhrafna lætr stefnir
> styrvind of sik thyria.
> Thiggr at Göndlar glyggvi
> gagn oddviti bragna sagna.

The helmet-harmer [warrior] cuts Sigar's walls [shields] in
Hrist's storm-time [battle]. The prince makes the shields'
giving planks break in the brand-strands' [shields'] wind
[battle]. The stem-ravens' [ships'] steerer [seafarer] makes
the war-gale rage around himself. The troops of men's
leader gets victory in Gondul's tempest [battle].

Here in the fourth line in each half-stanza there is added a full
rhyme with two syllables at the end of the line, but in other
respects it is as *dróttkvætt*. Now comes the greater *kimblabönd*:

> Álmdrósar skylr ísa
> ár flest meginbára sára.
> Kænn lætr hvatt á hrönnum
> hiálmsvell iöfurr gella fella.
> Styriökla kná stiklir—
> stinn—mens legi venia benia,
> lætr stillir frár fylla
> fólk sund hiarar lunda unda.

The mighty wave of wounds [blood] washes nearly every
year the bow-woman's [valkyrie's] ice [sword]. The clever
prince lets the helmet-floe [sword] resound hard on the
fellers' [swords'] waves [blood]. The necklace-thrower
[generous prince] does accustom battle-glaciers [swords] to
the wound-sea, the swift ruler lets the sword-woods' [war-
riors'] wound-sound [blood] fill the stiff swords.

Here there are two *kimblabönd* in each half-stanza. This is the
greatest *kimblabönd*:

> Hrælióma fellr hrími (tími
> hár vex of gram sára ára)—
> frost nemr—of hlyn Hristar—Mistar
> herkaldan thröm skialdar aldar.
> Gullsendir brýtr grundar Hrundar
> gunnveggs stöfum leggi hreggi.
> Sóknvallar—spyr ek—svelli—elli—
> svá skotnar that—gotna throtna.

Corpse-light [sword] rime [battle] falls around Hrist's maple [the warrior], the noble wound-oar [sword] time [warfare] grows around the prince, Mist's frost [sword] strikes men's mighty cold shield-edge. The gold-giver breaks battle-wall-[shield-]staves' [men's] limbs in Hrund's ground's [shield's] tempest [battle]. I hear men are deprived of old age, thus this benefits the attack-field heaper [warrior].

Here there is a *kimblaband* with each line.

Now we shall exemplify the *hryniandi* [flowing] forms. This is the first:

> Tiggi snýr á ógnar áru
> (undgagl veit that) sóknar hagli.
> Yngvi drífr—at hreggi hlífa
> Hiör vélir fiör—bryniu éli.
> Vísi—heldr of fiörnis foldir—
> fólk—skiptir svá boga driptum—
> skúrum lýstr of hilmi hraustan—
> (hans fregnum styr) Mistar regni.

The chieftain makes it snow with battle-hail on the messengers of war. The wound-gosling [raven] knows this. The prince makes the mail-coat storm drive. The sword entraps life in the shield-tempest. Over the helmet-lands comes Mist's rain [battle]. Thus the leader organizes the bows' snowing [arrow-shots]. Sword-showers whip around the valiant ruler. We hear of his warfare.

Here the first and third lines have two extra syllables at the beginning which characterize the form, and if they are subtracted then what remains is as *dróttkvætt,* and from the second and fourth lines can be taken out a word containing two syllables, the fifth and sixth in the line. Then these lines also are *dróttkvætt*. In *hrynhent* [flowing rhyme] forms there are generally eight syllables to a line, but the rhymes and alliteration go as in *dróttkvætt* form. We call this the *dróttkvætt hryniandi*.

Now further arrangements of forms will be exemplified. This *hryniandi* is called troll's verse-form:

> Stála kendi steykvilundum
> styriar valdi raudu falda
> (rekkar stýrdu rétt til iardar
> rodnu bardi) austan fiardar.
> Oddum rendi eliunstrandir
> ýta ferdar hringa skerdir.
> Hilmir stærdi hvössu sverdi
> heila grundar meginundir.

The battle-ruler forced the steel-throwing trees [warriors] to put on red caps [gave them head-wounds] to the east of the fiord. Warriors steered straight to land their red-coloured prow. The damager of rings [generous lord] made points run on to the troops of men's valour-strands [breasts]. The prince increased mighty wounds with keen sword on brains' ground [heads].

Here there are eight syllables in each line. Here there are *hluthendur* [middle of the line rhymes] in all lines and three ordinary syllables follow each of these rhyme syllables, and half-rhymes and full rhymes and alliteration go as in *hrynhenda* [flowing rhyme].

This is one kind of *hrynhent* form:

> Vafdi lítt er virdum mætti
> vígrækiandi fram at sækia.
> Skerdir gekk í skúrum Hlakkar
> Sköglar serks fyrir rodnum merkium.
> Ruddisk land en ræsir Thrænda
> Ribbungum skóp bana thungan.
> Gunnarr skaut und Gera fótar
> grimmsetta il hiarna kletti.

The battle-cultivator hesitated little to advance when he met men. The harmer of Skogul's shirt [mail-coat] went before the reddened standards in Hlokk's showers [battle]. The land was cleared but the Thronds' chieftain gave the Ribbungs a heavy death. Gunnar put the brains' cliff [men's heads] beneath the grimly-equipped sole of Geri's [the wolf's] foot.

This is ordinary *hrynhenda*. The next is *draughent* [log- or ghost-rhyme]:

> Vápna hríd velta nádi
> vægdarlaus feigum hausi.
> Hilmir lét höggum mæta
> herda klett bana verdan.
> Fleina lands fylkir rendi
> fiörnis hlíd meginskídi
> (öflugt sverd eyddi fyrdum
> iöfri kent) holdi fenta.

The merciless weapon-storm managed to make the doomed skull roll. The ruler let the death-worthy shoulders-cliff [head] meet blows. The chieftain made the flesh-covered helmet-hill be run over by the spear-land's [shield's] mighty rod [spear]. The mighty sword belonging to the prince destroyed men.

In this form there are generally seven syllables in each line, but rhymes and alliteration as in *dróttkvætt* form, and here if there is subtracted one syllable – the one that stands next after the first – from the first or third lines, then all the sounds will fall out as in *dróttkvætt* form. Similarly the same syllable can be subtracted in the second and fourth lines and then they are *dróttkvætt*; and in some ways this is not all that smooth.

This form we call *munnvörp* [improvisation]:

> Eyddi úthlaups mönnum
> ítr hertogi spiótum.
> Sungu stál of stillis
> (stód ylgr í val) dólgum.

Hal margan lét höfdi
hoddgrimmr iöfurr skemra.
Svá kann rán at refsa
reidr oddviti thiódum.

The splendid duke destroyed highwaymen with spears.
Steel weapons sang around the ruler's enemies, the she-wolf
stood on the fallen. The prince, hater of hoards, made many
a hero shorter by a head. Thus does the angry leader know
how to punish people for plundering.

Here form is lacking in the first and third lines, but in the second
and fourth there are half-rhymes. Now comes the verse-form that
is called formless:

Ortak öld at minnum
thá er alframast vissak
of siklinga snialla
med sex tögum hátta.
Sízt hafa veg né vellum
er virdan mik létu
á aldinn mar orpit
(that er oss frami) iöfrar.

I have composed as a memorial for men about the valiant
princes whom I knew to be quite the most outstanding with
sixty verse-forms. In no way have the princes thrown to the
old waves [wasted] the honour and gold with which they
honoured me. This is a glory to us.

In this verse-form there are no rhymes, but the alliteration is as in
dróttkvætt form. Now there have been composed in two poems
examples of sixty verse-forms and, in addition, the eight sub-
divisions into which the *dróttkvætt* form was divided at the
beginning by means of the distinctions in content that go with the
form; and all these verse-forms are very suitable for composing
poems in if desired.

Now we shall begin the third poem, which is composed in the
lesser verse-forms, though there are many examples of these
forms being used in praise-poems in the past. Here begins *tog-
drápulag* [journey-poem metre]:

> Fremstr vard Skúli . . .
> Skala lof dvala;
> sem ek mildum gram
> mærd fiölsnærda.
> Meir skal ek stæri
> styrs hródr fyrir
> (kærr var ek harra)
> hers gnótt bera.

Skúli was most outstanding . . . [sentence completed in last line of next verse but one]. The eulogy shall not be delayed; I am putting together a many-stranded encomium for the generous prince. I shall continue to deliver glory to the battle's increaser before the multitude of troops. I was dear to the lord.

Here in the second and fourth lines there are four syllables and two full rhymes, and the chief alliterating stave positioned as in *dróttkvætt*, but in the first and third lines there are also four normal syllables and the fifth an enclitic syllable, i.e. *ek* or *af* or *en* or *er* [I, of, but, when] or the like. They also have half-rhymes and one word alliterating with the chief stave.

This is the second *toglag* [journey-metre]:

> Kunn bió ek kvædi
> konungs bródur thiód—
> thann veit ek thengil—
> threnn—fiölmennan.
> Fram skal in fiórda
> fólkglads vada
> lióss elds lagar
> lofun fridrofa.

I made the king's brother three poems, known to men. I know this prince has a large following. Forward shall step the fourth eulogy of the battle-eager destroyer of the peace of the bright sea-fire [distributor of gold].

The second and fourth lines here go as in the previous verse-form, but the first and third lines here are without rhyme, and there are two words alliterating with the chief stave as in *dróttkvætt*.

This is the third verse-form, which we call *hagmælt* [skilfully spoken]:

> Mitt er of mæti
> mart lag bragar
> ádr ókvedit
> oddbraks spakan.
> Hlýtr grams geta
> greppr óhneppra
> skýrr skrautfara.
> . . . skiöldunga ungr.

Many a poetic metre of mine has never before been composed in about a wise point-clash meeter [warrior]. The clear-minded poet gets to mention the ruler's successful splendid expeditions.
. . . of chieftains when young [continuation of first line of last verse but one].

In this verse-form there are half-rhymes in the first and third lines and alliteration as in *dróttkvætt* form, but otherwise it is like *togmælt* [journey-spoken]. In any variety of *toglag* it is not wrong if there are five syllables in the line when some of them are short and quick. For *togdrápa* form there must be a *stef* [refrain] for the first line and its sense is completed in the last line of the poem, and it is correct to construct the poem with as many *stef* sections as one likes, and it is usual to make them all the same length, and for each *stef* section the *stef* must form the opening and conclusion.

Now comes the Greenland verse-form:

> Slód kann sneidir
> seima geima
> hnigfák Haka
> hleypa greypa,
> hinn er af hlunni
> hesta festa
> lætr leyfdr skati
> langa ganga.

The gold-cutter [generous prince] knows how to make Haki's bucking horse [ship] gallop over the ocean's dangerous path, that praised lord who makes the painters' long horses go from the slipway.

Here the first and third lines are as *hagmælt,* but the second and fourth have full rhymes, and there are two syllables that rhyme and both end with the same sound. Now comes the short verse-form:

> Gull kná—greppar—
> glóa—róa,
> váss eru seggir
> samir framir.
> Eik má und iöfri
> una bruna.
> Thá nýtr vísi
> vidar skridar.

Gold can glow, men row, bold men are suited to hardship. The oak can be happy to press forward beneath the prince. Then the ruler enjoys the timber's movement.

Here the first and third lines are without rhyme, but the second and fourth are like the Greenland verse-form with shorter words. Now comes the new verse-form:

> Ræsir glæsir
> Rökkva dökkva
> hvítum rítum
> hreina reina.
> Skreytir hreytir
> skafna stafna
> hringa stinga
> hiörtum svörtum.

The king adorns the dark reindeer of Rokkvi's land [ships] with white shields. The thrower of rings decorates the smoothed stems of the black prow-harts [ships].

In this verse-form there are in each line four syllables and two full rhymes which both end in the same sound and there are no enclitics. This is *stúfhent* [stump-rhymed, having the rhyme docked]:

> Hafröst hristir
> hlunnvigg tiggia.

Bordgrund bendir
brimdýrs stýri.
Blá veit brióta
byrskíd vídi
bödhardr bördum
budlungr thungan.

Ocean-current shakes the prince's slipway-steed [ship].
Plank-ground [sea] bends sea-beast's steering oar. Battle-
hard ruler knows that the dark wind-spars [ships] break
heavy sea with prows.

In this verse-form there are four syllables in a line and rhymes and
alliteration as in *dróttkvætt* form except that all rhymes are
náhent [close-rhymed]. This is *náhent*:

Hrinda lætr hniggrund
hafbekks snekkiur,
thá er falla, fleinthollr
frár, mál, stálum.
Hlumi lítr hergramr
hirdmenn spenna—
en rædi raungód—
rógálfr—skiálfa.

The speedy spear-fir [warrior] makes warships push the
sea-bench's [ship's] tipping ground with prows when times
suit. The war-fierce hostility-elf [war-leader] sees courtiers
grasp oar-handles, and oars of tried quality shake.

In this verse-form there are four syllables in a line and it is not
wrong to have five in the first and third. In those lines there are
half-rhymes. In the second and fourth lines there are full rhymes,
both next to each other, and the first one is docked [i.e. mono-
syllabic], but the alliteration is as in *dróttkvætt*.
    This is *hnugghent* [deprived rhyme]:

Hrannir strýkva hladinn bekk,
haflaudr skeflir,
kasta náir kialar stíg
kalt hlýr söltum,

> svörtum hleypir svana fiöll
> sniallmæltr stillir
> hlunna of Haka veg
> hrídfeld skídum.

Waves stroke loaded planks, sea-foam is heaped up, cold bow gets to throw salty keel-path [sea], eloquent ruler makes gallop black slipway-boards over stormy swans' mountains along Haki's way [the sea].

Here in the first and third lines there are seven syllables and there is no rhyme but normal alliteration, while the second and fourth have four syllables and normal alliteration and half-rhyme and *oddhending* [rhyme on the first syllable] and the first rhyme docked [monosyllabic].

Now comes half-curtailed:

> Snydia lætr í sólrod
> snekkiur á Manar hlekk—
> árla sér—ungr iarl—
> allvaldr breka fall.
> Lyptask kná lýdr opt
> lauki of kialar raukn.
> Greida náir glygg vád,
> greipum mæta dragreip.

The young earl makes warships speed at dawn on the fetter of Man [sea], the power-wielder sees early the falling of breakers. The troop can often be lifted by the mast over the keel's ox [ship]. Wind gets to unfold the sail, halyards meet handgrips.

In this verse-form there are six syllables in a line, but it is not wrong to have five or seven. In the first and third lines there are half-rhymes, and full rhymes in the second and fourth; with, in both cases, the first rhyme just as in *dróttkvætt* but the second docked or curtailed, it is all the same thing.

This verse-form is all-curtailed:

> Hrönn skerr—hvatt ferr—
> húfr kaldr—allvaldr.
> Lá brýtr—lög skýtr—
> limgarmr—rangbarmr.

> Brátt skekr—byrr rekr—
> blán vegg—ráskegg.
> Iarl lætr almætr
> ósvipt húnskript.

Cold strake cuts wave, power-wielder goes fast. Branch-foe [wind] breaks sea, curved side pushes wave. Swiftly shakes dark sail, wind drives yard-beard [sail]. Outstanding earl lets the mast-head cloth be unreefed.

In this verse-form there are four syllables in a line and two full rhymes and they both end with the same sound and all rhymes are curtailed [monosyllabic]. This is Hod's metre:

> Læsir leyfdr vísi
> landa útstrandir
> blídr ok bláskídum
> barda randgardi.
> Ern kná iarl thyrna
> oddum falbrodda
> iörd med élsnærdum
> iadri hrænadra.

Honoured gracious ruler locks out-coasts of lands with shield wall and dark prow-skis [ships]. Socket-point-[spear-] keen earl can spike the earth with its storm-bound coast with corpse-adder tips [spear-points].

In this verse-form there are five syllables in a line and rhymes and alliteration as in *dróttkvætt* form.

Now come the forms that are called *runhendur* [end-rhymed]. These all share the same characteristic: every *runhent* form must have a pair of full rhymes with each rhyme-word in a separate line. This is normal *runhenda*:

> Lof er flutt fiörum
> fyrir gunnörum
> (né spurd spörum
> spiöll grams) snörum.
> Hefi ek hans förum
> hródrs örum
> ypt óvörum
> fyrir auds börum.

211

Praise is delivered before bold battle-keen men, nor do we hold back tidings we have heard of the prince. I have made known his glory-prodigal expeditions before unhesitant wealth-trees [men].

This verse-form maintains the same rhyme through every line; there is also the kind of *runhending* which separates the rhymes and changes the lines. It is for this reason it is called *runhent* [lit. series-rhymed]. This is the lesser *runhenda:*

> Fluttak frædi
> um frama grædi
> (tunga tædi)
> med tölu rædi.
> Stef skal stæra
> stilli Mæra
> (hródr dugir hræra)
> ok honum færa.

I have delivered news about the gainer of glory—tongue helped—with the oar of speech [tongue]. Refrain shall be extended for the ruler of Mærir—it is good to move praise—and presented to him.

Here the rhyme continues through half the stanza and there is another one in the second half-stanza.

This verse-form is docked or curtailed from the previous one; it is the least *runhenda:*

> Slíkt er svá,
> siklingr á
> (öld thess ann)
> ordróm thann.
> Iarla er,
> austan ver
> skatna skýrstr,
> Skúli dýrstr.

So it is, the prince has — men grant this — this glory. Most intelligent of lords east of the ocean, Skuli is most valued of earls.

In this verse-form there are three syllables in a line, and each pair of lines has a separate rhyme; the alliteration as in *dróttkvætt*. Moreover it is considered not wrong if the sound that determines the alliteration comes only once at the beginning of a word.

These are further *runhent* forms:

> Nadrs gnapa ógn alla,
> eydir baugvalla,
> hlunns of hástalla
> hestar svanfialla.
> Orms er glatt galla
> med gumna spialla,
> iarl fremr sveit snialla;
> slíkt má skörung kalla.

Swan-mountains' [sea's] horses [ships], O destroyer of circle-plains [shields], tower over high slipway-stands throughout the adder's terror [winter]. It is a joy to be in the company of the friend of men during the snake's harm [winter], the earl honours the bold troop; such a one can be called a paragon.

This verse-form is composed with full *runhending* and it generally has five syllables in a line, or six if they are quick. This is the second:

> Ord fekk gott gramr,
> hann er gunntamr.
> Miök er fullframr
> fylkir rausnsamr.
> Hinn er mál metr
> milding sízt getr
> thann er svá setr
> seggi hvern vetr.

The prince got good fame, he is accustomed to battle. The most bold leader lives in great splendour. One can scarcely find a prince that adjudges affairs who treats men thus each winter.

This is curtailed from the previous *runhending*.

> Mærd vilk auka
> Mistar lauka

góma sverdi
grundar skerdi.
Dýrd skal segia
(drott má thegia)
styriar glóda
stökkvi-Móda.

I will increase with gum-sword [tongue] praise for Mist's
leeks' [swords'] ground's [shield's] damager [warrior].
Glory shall be told — court must be silent — of the Modi
[warrior] who scatters the battle-glow [sword].

In this verse-form there are four syllables in each line and the chief
stave as in *dróttkvætt* form and with it there is one alliterating
word. This is the third *runhent* form:

Veit ek hrings hrada
í höll lada
(gott er hús Hlada)
hird ölsada.
Drekkr gramr glada—
en at giöf vada
vitar valstada—
vandbaugskada.

I know the ring-flinger invites into his hall – good is the
house of Hladir – the ale-sated court. The prince drinks the
harmers [warriors] of the circle-wand [sword] happy and
falcon-perch [arm] fires [gold] rush to be given [are quickly
distributed].

This is normal *runhending* and this verse-form is based on *toglag*.
Here there are four syllables in a line or five if they are quick. This
is the lesser *runhenda*:

Drífr handa hlekkr
thar er hilmir drekkr,
miök er brögnum bekkr
blídskálar thekkr.
Leikr hilmis her
hreingullit ker
(segi ek allt sem er)
vid orda sker.

The hand clasp [ring] is driven [given freely] where the lord drinks, very pleasant to men is the happy cup's stream [ale]. The pure gold goblet plays against the word-skerry [teeth] of the prince's army. I tell all as it is.

This is curtailed from the previous form. This is the least:

> En thá er hird til hallar
> hers oddviti kallar,
> opt tekr iarl at fagna
> vid ótali bragna.
> Búin er giöf til greizlu
> at gullbrota veizlu,
> thröngt sitr thiódar sinni,
> that er mestr frami inni.

And when the army's leader calls the court to the hall, the earl often begins to rejoice at innumerable men. Gift is ready for giving at the gold-breaker's feast, the company of people sits crowded, there is the greatest glory within.

This *runhenda* is based on *dróttkvætt* form and there are here the same number of syllables and also alliteration as in *dróttkvætt*. Now begins the fourth group of *runhendingar*:

> Hird gerir hilmis kátt,
> höll skipask thröngt at gátt,
> aud gefr thengill thrátt,
> that spyrr fram í átt.
> Slíkt tel ek hilmis hátt,
> hans er rausn of mátt,
> iarl brýtr sundr í smátt
> slungit gull vid thátt.

The prince's court becomes happy, the hall is filled tightly to the doors, the lord gives wealth constantly, this is heard from generation to generation. Such I declare is the ruler's way, his splendour is of mighty proportions, the earl breaks apart into small pieces gold twisted in strands.

This verse-form is curtailed from the previous one and is regular *runhent*. Now comes a lesser *runhenda*:

Mörg thiód ferr til siklings sala,
sæmd er thar til allra dvala.
Tiggi veitir seima svala,
satt er bezt of hann at tala.
Bresta spyrium bauga flata—
bragna vinr kann gulli hata—
(ædri veit ek at giöflund gata
grundar vördr) fyrir hringa skata.

Many people go to the ruler's halls, there is honour there in every one's stay. The lord gives cool gold, it is best to speak truth about him. We hear that flat rings are broken with the one generous with bracelets, the friend of men knows how to hate gold, I know that no land's guardian was gifted with greater liberality.

This *runhenda* is based on *hrynhent* form.

Thiggia kná med gulli glöd
gotna ferd at ræsi miöd.
Drekka lætr hann sveit at sín
silfri skenkt it fagra vín.
Greipum mætir gullin skál,
gumnum sendir Rínar bál—
eigi hittir ædra mann—
iarla beztr—en skiöldung thann.

The happy band of men was able to receive mead together with gold from the ruler. He lets the troop drink at his place the fair wine served in silver. Golden cup meets hands, the best of earls sends men Rhine-fire [gold]; a nobler man than this chieftain cannot be found.

This is curtailed from the previous *runhenda*. Here begins the fifth *runhent* group:

Getit var grams fara,
gert hefi ek mærd snara.
Thengil mun thess vara,
that nam ek lítt spara.
Finnrat fræknara
fædi gunnstara
mann né mildara
merkir blódsvara.

Mention was made of the prince's expeditions, I have made
a fine eulogy. The lord will expect this, I held back little in it.
The marker of blood-birds [reddener of eagles, warrior] will
not find a more valiant feeder of war-starlings [feeder of
eagles, war-leader] nor a more generous man.

This is also complete *runhenda*. The next is the lesser *runhenda*
and based on the half-curtailed form or *náhent* [close-rhymed]:

> Thengill lætr höpp hrest,
> honum fylgir dáð mest.
> Vísi gefr vel flest
> verbál ólest.
> Húfar brutu haf lióTT,
> heim lét ek iöfur sótt,
> yngva lofar öll drótt,
> iarls sá ek frama gnótt.

The prince makes happy events flourish, he possesses most
initiative. The ruler gives easily the most sea-fire [gold]
unblemished. Strakes broke ugly sea, I paid the lord a visit,
all the court praises the chieftain, I saw the extent of the
earl's glory.

This is docked or curtailed from an earlier verse-form:

> . . . gramr.
> Gulli söri Kraki framr.
> Efla frágum Haka hialdr.
> . . . aldr.
> Ormi veitti Sigurdr sár.
> Slíkt var allt fyr lidit ár.
> Ragnarr thótti skatna skýrstr.
> Skúli iarl er myklu dýrstr.

. . . prince. Noble Kraki sowed gold. We heard that Haki
waged war. . . . time. Sigurd gave the serpent wounds. All
this was in past times. Ragnar was considered the most
splendid of lords. Earl Skuli is by far the worthiest.

Málaháttr [speech-form]:

> Munda ek mildingi,
> thá er Mæra hilmi
> fluttak fiögur kvædi,
> fimtán stórgiafar.
> Hvar viti ádr orta
> med ædra hætti
> mærd of menglötud
> madr und himins skautum?

I bore in mind fifteen great gifts from the princely one when I delivered four poems to the ruler of the Mærir. Where does one know of praise previously composed with more splendid verse-forms about a necklace-destroyer [giver of jewels] beneath the sky's expanse?

Fornyrdislag [old story metre]:

> Ort er of ræsi
> thann er rýdr granar
> vargs ok ylgiar
> ok vápn litar.
> That mun æ lifa,
> nema öld farisk,
> bragninga lof,
> eda bili heimar.

Poetry has been composed about the ruler who reddens the lips of wolf and she-wolf [in waging war] and colours weapons [with blood]. This will last for ever unless mankind perishes or the world ends, the princes' praise.

Bálkarlag [Balk's metre]:

> Lypta ek liósu
> lofi thiódkonungs.
> Upp er fyrir ýta
> iarls mærd borin.
> Hverr muni heyra
> hródr giöflata
> seggr svá kvedinn
> seims ok hnossa?

I raised bright eulogy of the great king. Earl's laud is lifted up before men. What man is going to hear praise thus spoken of one slow to give gold and treasures?

This is the difference between these verse-forms that in *fornyrdislag* there is in the first and third lines only one prop, while in the second and fourth lines the chief stave stands in the middle of the line; but in Starkad's metre there are two props and the chief stave in the middle of the line, and in *Bálkarlag* the props and chief stave are placed as in *dróttkvætt*.

Starkad's metre:

> Veit ek verdari
> thá er vell gefa,
> bröndum beita
> ok búa snekkiur
> hæra hródrar
> en heimdrega—
> unga iöfra—
> en audspörud.

I know of young princes that brandish swords and set up warships who are worthier of higher praise than stay-at-homes, ones who give gold than one sparing of wealth.

> Their ró iöfrar
> alvitrastir,
> hringum hæztir,
> hugrakkastir,
> vellum verstir,
> vígdiarfastir,
> hird hollastir,
> happi næstir.

These princes are all-wisest, most dangerous to rings [generous], most bold in heart, most hateful to gold [generous], bravest in war, kindest to the court, closest to good fortune.

Liódaháttr [song-form]:

> Glöggva grein
> hef ek gert til bragar,
> svá er tírætt hundrad talit.

> Hródrs örverdr
> skala madr heitinn vera
> ef sá fær alla háttu ort.

Close account have I given of poetic form so that ten tens are told. A man must not be called unworthy of renown if he is able to compose in all verse-forms.

Galdralag [incantation metre]:

> Sóttak fremd,
> sótta ek fund konungs,
> sóttak ítran iarl,
> thá er ek reist—
> thá er ek renna gat—
> kaldan straum kili—
> kaldan siá kili.

I sought honour, I sought meeting with a king, I sought a splendid earl when I cut cold current with keel, when I was able to make keel run over the cold sea.

> Nióti aldrs
> ok audsala
> konungr ok iarl.
> That er kvædis lok.
> Falli fyrr
> fold í ægi
> steini studd
> en stillis lof.

May king and earl enjoy age and halls of wealth. This is the end of the poem. May earth, stone-supported, first sink into the sea before the ruler's praise [cease].

Annotated Index of Names

Figures in brackets indicate that the person or place is referred to but not named. A question mark means that the identification is uncertain.

232